Buy and Sell Domain Names for Profit

By

KRISS PETTERSEN

Cover graphic by the Digital Artist.

See more about Buy and Sell Domain Names for Profit at www.DomainNamesProfit.com.

ISBN-13: 978-1986030618
ISBN-10: 198603061X

Someday, the right buyer is going to buy that domain name ...

KRISS PETTERSEN

Table of Contents

Introduction

Buying and selling domain names can be a fun and rewarding side business or, if you find yourself becoming quite profitable, a full-time job. If you are new to buying and selling domain names online you will need to know the best places you can buy domains from, where to sell your domains, how to transfer a domain to a buyer, how much you should sell your domains for, and if there are any trademark issues when it comes to buying and selling domain names. And since there is low upfront investment required to get started, buying and selling domain names can be a great idea for you if you want to make good money online.

If you have already been buying and selling domain names, finding out more about what domain names are and some of the technical details about domains and Registries can only help. In addition, reviewing the buying and selling process, negotiation skills, monetizing domain names, and the legal and other risks involved with domain names will be a good refresher.

Although domain names (and the internet) have a relatively short history, many domain names have been shown to increase in value over time, especially if they have commercial value. Basically, you can buy a domain name at a low price, sit on it for a while (as an investment), and then sell it for a high price and make a profit.

How does it work? You identify domain names you think have market value to end users, or as an investment, and register or buy your desired domain names at the cheapest prices possible. And then, after you have identified potential buyers, sell them for a much higher price to make a profit. You can register brand new domains from a reputable domain Registrar. Domains are low cost, at about $6-$15 for one year for a .com or .net, from a domain Registrar.

There are also domain names that had previously been registered but expired or let to drop by their previous owner. Some of these domains may have built up a lot of traffic and quality backlinks. So, if you buy these domains at reasonable prices, they have the potential to earn money for you, both while you hold them and also when you sell them.

You can also buy domain names on the secondary market. Many domainers skip "hand regs" and instead look for value in domains put up for sale by others, whether through fixed price sales or through auctions. There are many over-priced domain names for sale through online marketplaces, so you first need to do your research before buying.

Most domain names become the identity for a business online, and having the right domain name could help bring high traffic to a website. Some people or companies may pay very high amounts of money for the right domain. For example, in 2007, VacationRentals.com was sold for $35 million!

This is a list of some of the highest prices paid for domain names. The list is limited to domains that sold for $3 million or more and have been publicly verified.

Domain	Price	Sale Date
Insurance.com	$35.6 million	2010
VacationRentals.com	$35 million	2007
PrivateJet.com	$30.18 million	2012
Internet.com	$18 million	2009
360.com	$17 million	2015
Insure.com	$16 million	2009
Fund.com	£9.99 million	2008
Sex.com	$13 million	2010 November
Hotels.com	$11 million	2001
Porn.com	$9.5 million	2007
Porno.com	$8,888,888	2015 February
Fb.com	$8.5 million	2010 November
Business.com	$7.5 million	1999 December
Diamond.com	$7.5 million	2006
Beer.com	$7 million	2004
Z.com	$6.8 million	2014 November

BUY AND SELL DOMAIN NAMES FOR PROFIT

Domain	Price	Sale Date
iCloud.com	$6 million	2011 March
Israel.com	$5.88 million	2008 May
Casino.com	$5.5 million	2003
Slots.com	$5.5 million	2010
Toys.com	$5.1 million	2009
AsSeenOnTv.com	$5.1 million	2000
Clothes.com	$4.9 million	2008
Medicare.com	$4.8 million	2014
IG.com	$4.6 million	2013 September
Marijuana.com	$4.2 million	2011
GiftCard.com	$4 million	2012 October
Yp.com	$3.8 million	2008 November
Mi.com	$3.6 million	2014 April
AltaVista.com	$3.3 million	1998 August
Whisky.com	$3.1 million	2014 January
Vodka.com	$3.0 million	2006
Candy.com	$3.0 million	2009 June
Loans.com	$3.0 million	2000 February

Of course, not all domains go for such lofty prices. If you take away the highest-priced deals, there are still thousands of domains that are bought and sold for profit every day. And this is where you can find your opportunity – profiting from flipping domains.

For years, domain names have been labeled as the "real estate of the Internet." Domain names represent the online presence or store for a business or organization. Just as real estate has developers that buy houses for a low price, fix them up, and then sell them for a higher price (house flipping), domain name flipping is similar.

Buying and selling domain names can be an exceptionally lucrative venture to get into. However, if you are starting off with very little cash to invest, it's advised to first purchase lower cost domains and generate small profits as you work your way up to higher-value domain names.

While the marketplaces where domain sales are most lucrative will change based on the types of domain names you are selling, your focus when starting should instead be on locating and purchasing low cost domains with high potential value and selling them for higher prices to end users – not on domain marketplaces where only other domainers will see them. This is the difference between selling domains for "end user" prices rather than "resale" prices.

One of the great aspects of domain flipping is that the up-front cost required is minimal – you really just need a computer with an internet connection and some money to start investing. The time you put into domain flipping is up to you. However, you will see that your time is necessary for your domain business to become successful and, if you follow the advice in this book, you will find how you manage your time could lead to greater results in a shorter period of time.

What if you were the lucky owner of the domain zelks.com and you decided to sell your prized possession because you need money for a new car? Or perhaps you want money to invest in more domain names? Here are a few questions to ask yourself:

What are you going to ask for your prized domain name?
After all, there are a lot of people wanting to make money, and this domain name is a short, "brandable" .com name with great potential value. You ought to be able to find someone wanting to develop a business around this name (business enterprise? information?, e-commerce? advertising?). So how much is the domain name worth? $1,000? $10,000? $50,000?

How are you going to sell this domain name?
Now that you want to sell, where do you find your buyer? Just putting the domain name on a web page and labeling it for sale is most likely not going to get you what you want, if anything at all.

But you've heard of other domainers making millions of dollars!
Yes, there are quite a few people in the domain name business that make a lot of money. But except for some luck, most of these domainers have been at it for a long time, have a lot of contacts, and treat domain names as investments.

So instead of worrying or complaining about why your domain name isn't selling, why don't you instead look at this scenario from the other side – that of an end user or buyer? Maybe there is someone out there who is indeed looking at creating an e-commerce company and they are looking for a fun and exciting name that no other company is associated with. They might even have already drafted a business plan and are now wondering what to call their venture. Their next step is to buy a domain name - and you want your domain to be able to be found.

However, as much as you think a domain name might be worth, the most important thing to remember, and a line that will be repeated multiple times in this book, is that a domain name is worth only what a buyer is willing to pay for it. You could have what you consider to be the most attractive domain in the world in your portfolio of names, yet if you don't succeed in tracking down a potential buyer, and you don't make a successful sale, then the domain name does not technically have any worth.

Buying and Selling Domain Names for Profit
This book is not a guaranteed path to overnight success in the domain market. There are no get-rich-quick tips or guarantees you will make a profit. Instead, the book is intended to either help the beginner who wants to become a serious domain name investor or someone who is already a "domainer" and looking to put more of their time and effort, and maybe a little more of their money into domains to be successful in the domain name business.

What this book will **not** do is make you an expert in domain names. That takes years and years of experience, and even then you may never be an expert. This book is written to give an overview of what domain names are and answer many questions domainers may ask. It is also intended to try and leave your mind open to new questions about buying and selling domains and then try and provide a path in order for you to succeed in the domain name business.

One of the most important things to remember, whether you are just entering the world of domain name investment or already own some domain names, is to keep your eyes open. If you blindly invest in domain names without a well-thought-out strategy, you may just be throwing your money away. But if you look at domain sales trends and research your market niches, you have a much better possibility on profiting from your domain name investments.

Overall, registering a few domain names isn't all that much of a risk. At about $10 for a one-year registration for a .com domain, you will then have the opportunity to not only gain some experience in the industry, but make a profit as well. However, if you jump in and take a big risk which you may not be prepared for, either financially or research-wise (like buying *hundreds* of domains that begin with the word 'top'), you stand the chance of losing a lot of money before you even get started.

What this book *will* do is give the domainer an understanding of what a domain name is, even diving into some of the technical aspects of domains. The details of registering domain names will also be covered. How to value domain names will be discussed, and an overview of buying domain names and a discussion about domain flipping. Selling domain names will also be covered, along with the risks and legal issues involved in the domain name business.

Finally, this book will outline ways you can make money buying and selling domain names. This approach will look at domaining as a business, and will also look at domain names through the eyes of a buyer or end user.

Appendices at the end of the book include domain name tips, domain name vocabulary terms, and a list of domain name extensions.

I hope you find this book helpful in making your domain name buying and selling adventures profitable!

Chapter 1 – Domain Names

What if everyone in the world were known by their telephone number instead of their name? That sounds like something you would never be able to remember, right? All of those numbers instead of people's names, you would be lucky just to know your own and a few of your family members' numbers and maybe that's about it. But we do have names, and it makes it a whole lot easier to not only remember who people are but to recognize them as well.

Domain names are a lot like people's names. Computers that are connected to the Internet are identified by a unique series of numbers called an IP address (for example, 46.182.18.40). IP stands for "Internet Protocol", and all of those numbers are not easy to remember.

Instead of a domain name, you could type an IP address into the URL bar of your browser and you would be connected to the computer it represents. But since IP addresses are so difficult to remember, the Domain Name System (DNS) was invented.

You could think of an IP address like your physical home address. Somebody wanted to use the postal mail and send you a letter, they would need to have your physical address. With computers, an IP address is the physical address of an online website. If somebody wants to connect to your website, their computer can find it by looking up the IP address associated with your domain name.

There are some larger websites that have dedicated IP addresses. This would be similar to having a single family home: one family with one home. But most websites share IP addresses with other websites, mostly because most websites are small and don't take up much space, sort of like apartments in an apartment building – they share a similar address but each has their own space.

And if the time comes when you move your website to a different hosting provider, your site will be assigned a new IP address, just like if you physically moved from one house or apartment to another. But your domain name would stay the same, so that's what you want people to remember. If you had to change IP addresses and that's all people knew to use to find your website, you would have a tough time getting users to find you.

So, in summary, domain names were invented to make it easier for users on the internet to find websites without having to remember IP addresses.

What Can a Domain Name Do For You?

Why would you, your company, or your organization want to register a domain name? Aside from domain investing or flipping, here are some reasons why you might want to register a domain name:

1. A domain name is your presence on the Internet
In today's world, to do any type of business online, you need a website. A large business that doesn't have a website will have a hard time surviving, unless it is a local business that only needs local customers. And other businesses that don't treat the online world as a major part of their marketing and/or sales will find it hard to survive in the competitive business world. That is why having a unique domain name is important. You want to stand out amongst the competition and, for as little as $10 per year, you can have your own domain name upon which to build your marketing brand for your business. And it doesn't matter how large or small your organization is (even if it is just you). Having a professional-looking website on a good domain name can put you on equal footing with the best businesses on the web.

2. Domain names can help your personal site
If you are simply setting up a web blog or other fun website, a domain name will help get you noticed. The free sites just won't bring much traffic through the search engines, so by having your own domain you can get visitors to your site you would not normally have without extra marketing and social media effort. If you are going to be spending your time creating content on the web, your goal should be to find an ever-increasing audience in order to be heard.

3. Domain names can help in promoting your website
A good domain name can greatly increase your chances of success, be it for a business or personal site. A domain name that is made up of common

10

keywords can also improve your site's ranking in search engines. So choosing a domain name related to what your content is (or is going to be) is important. In addition to improving your search rankings, a domain name will increase your visibility and branding when promoting or advertising your website. If a potential visitor sees a memorable domain name, they'll be more likely to visit your website than if they saw a long, non-memorable domain name.

4. Domain names can help your site be professional
For as little as $10 per year plus web hosting, you can have your own website under your own domain name. If you compare this to the available free sites, there is not a feeling of professionalism when seeing a site hosted on a free platform.

For one, almost all well-known websites have their own domain name. A site with a unique name, without being s subdomain to one of the free or ISP-hosted services, is both easier to remember as well as allowing for simple type-in traffic. This alone makes your business look more professional.

Which of the following domains is easier to remember?

DomainDS.com
or
DomainDS.blogspot.com

The free or ISP-hosted sites are typically used for non-professional blogs or hobby websites. Not only is the website's URL typically a subdomain of their own brand, but also usually forces their ad content onto your website or limits your website to a small number of templates where you don't have the ability to make your site stand out from others under the same host.

URLs versus Domain Names

Let's examine the different parts of a domain name, using our site as an example. Our website's domain name is DomainDS.com – if you type this into the location bar of your web browser you will then see the entire URL. Instead of just the domain name, instead you will see something like this: http://www.domainds.com/.

The "domainds.com" part of the URL is the actual domain name. If there is anything shown after that it is pointing to a page or post or other specific content within that same website. It works a lot like a filing cabinet. Content on a website is arranged according to hierarchy. In an office if you wanted someone to find a document that was filed, you would tell them (in English) to go to a certain room (the domain name) and then a specific filing cabinet, a folder within that cabinet, and finally the desired document. In this case you could have them find the English/Records Archive/Letters Received/2018 Folder/Letter4.

In this analogy, "English" is like the "http://" in a URL. "English" is the language used in the 'directions.' So with computers, the "http://" tells your web browser what language or 'protocol' to use when communicating with a website. Websites generally use 'http' which is the *hypertext transfer protocol*. The colon (:)separates the protocol from the rest of the address and the two slashes (//) means a connection is being attempted.

"Records Archive" is like the domain name, domainds.com, a specific website on the internet.

Each step after Records Archive indicates how the specific page is located. Everything after domainds.com points the browser to specific content or data in the website's files or folders to display.

Many times the URL will have a 'www' at the beginning. For example, the DomainDS URL could be http://www.domainds.com. The 'www' adds another level to the domain name -also known as a subdomain. "www" means World Wide Web, and at one point was necessary to load the web page. But now it is no longer necessary, and when creating a website you can choose whether you want your site to display the www or not.

If someone typed in http://domainds.com, they would still arrive at the same website as http://www.domainds.com. Aside from the www, there could also be other letters or numbers before the domain name that represent an actual subdomain, such as http://en.wikipedia.org, which is the English version of Wikipedia.

What is a Domain Name

When you examine the different parts of a domain name, its structure begins to make more sense.

For example, our site, http://www.domainds.com, has a basic structure. The first part (domainds) is the Second-Level Domain (SLD) and .com is the Top-Level Domain (TLD), also referred to as the "domain extension." When combined, the so-called hostname, together with the second-level domain (and sometimes a third level domain) make up the domain name.

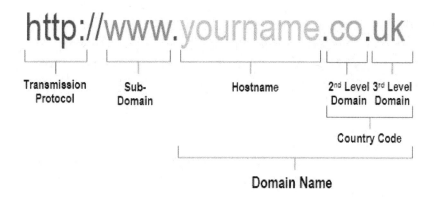

Top Level Domains (TLDs)

.com is the Top-Level Domain (TLD) or 'extension' for the domain name domainds.com. There are many different top-level domains available, from the most popular (.com) to specific applications (.mobi), to specific country top level domains such as France (.fr), Germany (.de – from Deutschland) and Colombia (.co). Every domain is categorized as a type of TLD:

- gTLD – generic Top-Level Domains are the most common and the most sought after names. These include .com, .net, .org, .biz, .info, and others.
- ccTLD – country code Top-Level Domains that were created specifically for a single country's use. That country can put any sort of restrictions on it that they choose. Some countries only allow citizens to register domains under their ccTLD. Other countries' TLDs have

become popular as domain hacks or other meanings. .ly, the official ccTLD for Libya, has become popular based on sites like bit.ly and heven.ly while .tv, the official ccTLD for Tuvalu, is used for many television domains.

- sTLD – sponsored Top-Level Domains are names that are controlled by specific agencies within an industry. For example, .museum is an sTLD regulated by the Museum Domain Management Association. They reserve the TLD for museum websites.

To see a list of most of the available TLD's, see Appendix C at the end of this book.

TLDs are more commonly referred to as domain extensions. If someone asked what domain extension you currently have or want to purchase, they are referring to your TLD. About two-thirds of all TLD domain names registered have a .com extension, followed by .cn (China), .tk (Tukelau), .de (Germany), and .net, each at just over seven percent.

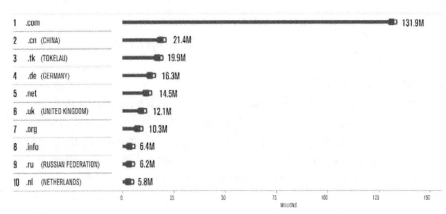

Top 10 Largest gTLDs and ccTLDs by Number, 2017   Source: Zooknic/Verisign

Of just the gTLDs, .com is by far the most popular, followed by .net, .org, .info, .xyz, and .top.

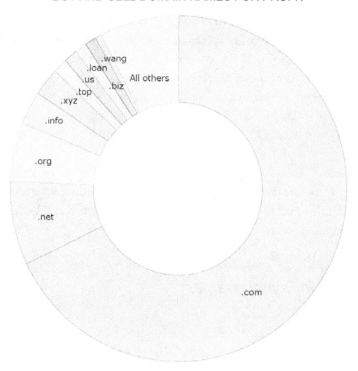

gTLD Domain Name Extensions Registered   Source: RegistrarStats

When pronouncing TLDs, the .com TLD is pronounced "dot-com." Other gTLDs, such as .net or .org, are pronounced "dot-net" and "dot-org" respectively. ccTLDs on the other hand tend to get spelled out. .fr is pronounced "dot-eff-arr" and .jp is pronounced "dot-jay-pee" for example. When it comes to domain names with both second and third level extensions (see below), they can use both methods, such as .co.uk which is pronounced "dot-co-dot-you-kay".

Second Level Domains
With the domain name domainds.com, "domainds" is the Second Level Domain (SLD). The SLD refers to the part directly in front of the last dot in a domain name. Second Level Domains can contain only English letters, numbers, and/or hyphens, except in the case of Internationalized Domain Names (IDNs) which will be discussed later in the book.

Most domain names have only the two parts, the SLD and the TLD. But some countries have split their ccTLDs into multiple parts, giving industry specific organizations their own ccSLDs (country code Second Level Domains). For example, in 1996 .uk ceased registrations directly under .uk and users were required to register a domain name under .co.uk (for general and commercial uses), .ltd.uk (for UK Limited companies), .me.uk (for personal websites), and so on. In 2013, the .uk TLD was re-introduced.

So with a name like domainds.co.uk, .uk would be the Top Level Domain (TLD), .co would be the Second Level Domain (SLD), and domainds would then be a Third-Level Domain (there is no acronym for this as TLD is already used for Top).

Limitations in Domain Names

When searching for domain names, a domain name can contain the numbers 0-9, the letters a-z and the dash or hyphen character ("-"). But although a domain name can contain a hyphen, it cannot begin or end with one. Also, domain names are not case sensitive, so you can change any letters to either lowercase or uppercase when writing out or typing a domain name. Our site, for instance, looks easier when typed as www.DomainDS.com. But it doesn't matter whether you type the domain name in upper or lower case letters – the browser will automatically convert to all lower case.

Even though the domain name can randomly contain both upper and lower case letters, the names of folders and files after the domain name are case-sensitive. In other words, http://www.domainds.com/about is different than http://www.domainds.com/About.

The maximum number of characters in a domain name is 67. This means you can have a domain name with 63 letters/number/hyphens followed by the "dot" and the TLD or extension, making for a long domain. The domain name 000000000000000000000000000000000000000000000000000000000000000.com is a real domain – 63 0's followed by the extension!

However, except for the rare 63 letter/number domain (which does have some value, but not huge numbers), the better value in domain name investing is in short names.

For most TLDs the minimum length of a domain name is 2 letters or numbers, although there are a few exceptions.

One-Letter Domain Names
As of the writing of this book, there are **only 3** one-letter .com domains names in use. December 2, 1993, at a time when the web was in its infancy, Dr. Jon Postel registered all still available 23 single-letter domains and assigned them to the Internet Assigned Numbers Authority (iana.org). It was Jon Postel's intention to avoid a single company commercially controlling a letter of the alphabet.

However, 3 domains were already registered:

q.com

q.com Logos   Source: Q.com, CenturyLink

q.com was owned by Qwest Communications, which was acquired by CenturyLink in 2010. As of this writing, q.com forwards to CenturyLink High-Speed Internet.

x.com

x.com Logos   **Source: x.com, PayPal**

x.com was owned by Weinstein & DePaolis and was the homepage of a
Netscape employee named Robert Walker. The domain was acquired in 1999
by the x.com financial services company owned by Elon Musk. X.com
eventually became PayPal and Musk was later forced out of the company.
However, the x.com domain name was reportedly purchased back by Elon
Musk in mid-2017, terms were not disclosed. The domain transferred out of
brand protection MarkMonitor to GoDaddy under privacy in July, 2017. Elon
Musk tweeted, *"Thanks PayPal for allowing me to buy back X.com! No plans right now,
but it has great sentimental value to me."* As of this writing, for a while, x.com
retrieved just the letter x, and then began to be forwarded to Elon Musk's
Boring Company's website.

z.com

z.com Logos   **Source: Nissan, Z.com**

z.com was owned by Nissan - now it is the GMO Internet Group, Japan's first
ICANN-accredited domain name Registrar in Asia (InterQ). The reported sale

was for $6.8M US in 2014. The first mention of z.com under the GMO Internet Group is from March, 2015.

All other one letter .com domains are unresolvable. However, trademark applications were filed to the USPTO in 2005, shortly after news got out that ICANN might distribute single letter .com domains which were previously restricted. But this hasn't happened and many of the trademark applications are now dead.

The availability of one character domain names in TLDs varies, but only six exist in legacy generic Top Level Domains (Q.com, X.com, and Z.com, I.net, Q.net, X.org).

Some other gTLD single-letter domain names are also in use, usually as shortcuts:

a.co: Amazon.com – Amazon's official URL shortcut. Generally used by Amazon in SMS messages for informing purchasers of activity on an order

a.org: AutismAwaremess.com – Awareness project coming soon by AutismAwareness.com

b.org: benevolent.net – Shortcut to benevolent.net

g.co: Google – Google's official URL shortcut

m.me: Facebook – Facebook Messenger's official URL shortcut

t.co: Twitter – Twitter's official URL shortcut

t.me: Telegram – Telegram's official URL shortcut

w.org: WordPress – Redirects to wordpress.org

Two Letter .com Domain Names
There are only 676 (26 x 26) .com domains that exist with only 2 letters, which also makes them rare. Because of their high value, these domains are primarily

owned by large corporations. Many of the owners of 2-letter .com domains use privacy protection, so not all of the owners of two-letter .com domain names are known.

Other Rules

Some top level domains from specific countries have additional limitations on length and on the number of characters in a domain. Some even specify a minimum length for a domain name of 3 characters or more. Be sure to check with your Registrar for the specific rules on your chosen TLD prior to registering a domain name with them.

The domain name system is a little more complicated when using Internationalized Domain Names (IDNs). Even though a domain name generally can only have letters, numbers and hyphens, IDNs are different. While the Registry databases will only accept letters, numbers and hyphens, the system had to adjust for countries that don't use the English alphabet, so a way to show other characters was needed.

Internationalized Domain Names (IDNs)

Earlier in this book, domain names were described as nothing more than a set of letters (with maybe numbers or hyphens) meant to represent an IP address somewhere on the internet. Domain names are used as an easier way to remember and type in web addresses than IP addresses. So when a computer wants to know where to find a site like DomainDS.com, it first looks at the Registry. The Registry tells the user's computer which nameserver to go to. So the user's computer goes to that specific nameserver, which then tells it exactly which IP address to go to. The user's computer goes to that IP address, and then the information from the associated website is displayed.

Domain names are stored in ASCII characters. ASCII stands for American Standard Code for Information Interchange, which represents the most basic English language characters (A-Z capital letters, a-z lower case letters, the numeric digits 0-9 and punctuation). ASCII is a standard that both computers and users can easily understand. For those in English-speaking countries, their keyboards typically are made up of these same ASCII characters. And since domain name Registries only recognize a portion of the ASCII characters, domain names are only allowed to contain English letters, numbers, and hyphens. This rule of only using English characters per the Registry restrictions is called the LDH (letter-digit-hyphen) restriction.

The Challenge with English-only Domain Names

Obviously, English is not the only language spoken (or written) in the world. So how would someone in Japan or China have a domain name in their native language for their online business? Because of the ASCII limitations, they would have to use English characters, even though the domain name wouldn't be recognized by their businesses' consumers.

Since the domain name structure was invented, this issue has been a concern for many years. After much debate, a system was devised where ASCII characters could be converted to non-ASCII, like Japanese or Cantonese characters. The non-ASCII keyboards are actually able to type in the characters in the native language and then are converted to ASCII format in a process called ToASCII. Domain names in this converted format are known as Internationalized Domain Names (IDNs).

Domain Name Structure of IDNs

In order for a non-English domainer to register a name in their own language, they would start at their Registrar's website. Let's say someone in Russia wants to register the Russian translation of DomainDS.com. So, they type in the name ДомаинДС.com in their Registrar's website domain registration window. The Registrar translates the letters into ASCII characters by first making sure all the letters are lowercase. This process is called the Nameprep algorithm. The "ДомаинДС.com" would become "домаиндс.com" (domainds.com). домаиндс.com is the U-label (the label in Unicode format). The name must now be converted, or translated, to an A-label (the label in ASCII format).

The domain name then goes through an algorithm called Punycode, in which the non-ASCII characters (or Unicode characters) are converted into a set of ASCII characters, preceded by the suffix xn--. The name that Punycode would come up with for ДомаинДС.com would be xn--80ahbpsid3a.com. Notice the xn--. These four characters precede all IDNs. The zn-- prefix is reserved for multi-lingual domain names.

In the case of someone in Russia wanting to register the equivalent of domainds.com, through translation the Registrar would then have the domain name in ASCII format and would check to see if xn--80ahbpsid3a.com had already been registered. If it had not, and the domain name was available, the Registrant would then complete the process of registering the domain name.

There are some Registrars that are able to register IDNs, but do not make the ToASCII translation as part of their service. For these Registrars, someone wanting to register the IDN домаиндс.com would first need to have it translated by an outside source and then register the A-label (the ASCII translation of the name). Such 'translators' are relatively common.

If someone in Russia wants to see домаиндс.com, they would type the name in their native language into their browser and they'll be taken to the domain name's Punycode registered in the example above. Many modern browsers will automatically translate the native domain name into the corresponding A-label. Most of them will display the A-label instead of the Russian characters if the computer is set up in English. This cuts down on potential IDN scams. And as the demand for more IDN domain names grows, there could be changes in the future.

With IDNs, any non-English letters are translated into a set of English letters, then preceded by an 'xn--'. So an IDN domain name spelled with Chinese characters would be translated to xn--longseriesofnumbers.com when stored in the Registry database. This has even been used to create emoji IDNs, such as ☮ which is xn--v4h.com.

Double Hyphen
Domain names can have two consecutive hyphens ("--") and this can be used for a website (although not recommended). But when the two hyphens follow 'xn', these are reserved for IDNs.

Sub Domains
When visiting some websites, you may notice a sort-of folder structure before the domain name in the URL address bar. This is because the website is set up using a sub domain structure. Although sub domains are not technically a part of the core domain name system, their increasing popularity deserves a mention in this chapter.

This folder-like structure adds a prefix to an existing domain name, separated by a period, and is known as a sub domain. An example of a sub domain is "support.office.com". In this example, the domain "office.com" is registered by Microsoft to sell their Microsoft Office Suite of software. On this domain, they use subdomains to help divide the sections of the website. Microsoft's training and help resources use support.office.com.

Sub domains are not technically handled in the same way as regular domains. But as far as the user is concerned, they work like a regular domain name structure. There are two main reasons sub domains are used: to manage large websites or to allow users to register otherwise unavailable domain names.

In the first instance, sub domains are used for organizational purposes. For an example you can look at how Microsoft organizes their website, this time with their main microsoft.com site. As with office.com, Microsoft has separated their various services into sub domains. If you go to support.microsoft.com, you arrive on their Microsoft Support site.

Using subdomains is particularly useful if you have a need to create a separate website for specific data or company departments, but need to keep it all connected within the main domain name.

In other cases, a sub domain can be created by an existing domain owner in order to allow others to use a new domain directly under their existing domain name, similar to how a regular Registry works. These sub domains can give a new website developer the opportunity to have a great sounding domain name that would otherwise be unavailable to register.

Although this is not the typical way websites are run, the use of sub domains that are rented or sold by domain name owners is acceptable. The entire URL including the subdomain is where the new website is located. And because the use of a recognized .com domain name is out of reach to most website developers, the opportunity to use a subdomain off of a great .com name is desired, and there is still a market for these if you search hard enough.

However, there have been reports that the Google search algorithm may penalize multiple subdomains. When searching in Google, instead of seeing each individual subdomain, the results instead may be limited to just the principal domain, leaving those trying to exist under a subdomain unable to be ranked high in search for their website.

Top Level Domain Names (TLDs)

A TLD (Top-Level Domain) is also referred to as a domain extension. The domain extension is the letters that appear at the end of a domain name. For example, in the domain name "www.domainds.com," .com would be the TLD.

Most people are familiar with .com as it has become the industry standard for domain name extensions. Although originally set up as the abbreviation for "commercial," today .com domain names can represent any type of website, whether for commercial purposes or not. But there are also many other types of TLDs assigned by the IANA (Internet Assigned Numbers Authority) that are commonly used, but many people are not familiar with their meaning or their usage.

Common TLDs
Aside from country-specific codes (which we will discuss later), there are about 20 different TLDs available that are commonly used. Many other TLDs are also available (like .aero as an example), but these are not widely used. Here is a list of some of the most popular TLDs and the use for which they were originally set up (and which many still follow):

• .com (commercial) – The most popular TLD, .com was meant to be used for commercial purposes, but is now used for virtually every cause imaginable.
• .net (network) – Intended for network web sites, this TLD is also commonly misused for a variety of purposes; many turn to .net of the .com is taken.
• .org (organization) – Another commonly misused TLD, .org was originally meant for sites that represent organizations and non-profits.
• .edu (education) – This is usually used by colleges and other educational institutions, and it is not typically available for public registration.
• .mil (military) – Restricted to military use only, .mil is not available for public registration.
• .gov (government) – Restricted to government use only, .gov is not available for public registration.
• .co (company) – A shorter TLD, .co is used by many companies that are not

able to register the .com and/or may use the .co in their brand or marketing.

• .biz (business) – This is another company-related TLD intended for business use, but it does not have anywhere near the popularity or value as .com.

• .info (informational) – This TLD had a speculative marketing push when it came out, and still ranks highly in the search engines when used for websites. But many domain investors got caught buying these names on the secondary market before the value of these domain names dropped. Today the registration for .info names only costs about a dollar.

• .me (personal) – The least common on this list, .me is often used for personal websites.

More about TLDs

Since .com, .org and .net have the most use and generally rank higher in search engine results, these extensions are the most popular TLDs. Besides .me and .info, most common TLDs contain three letters. There is another TLD that most don't know about, and that is .arpa. ARPA is the designation for Address and Routing Parameter Area. These domain names are used to maintain the integrity of the internet. Most .arpa names are for domain servers that run domain databases on the internet.

Country Code TLDs

After the top level domains, next to discuss are the county specific TLDs, of which there are about 200 different extensions available to register. It's important to note the .co extension mentioned earlier was originally intended to be a country code for Columbia. But because of its demand for global commercial use, the .co is also considered a common TLD and is even marketed as an alternative to .com by many Registrars.

When country code specific TLDs were first made, they were to contain two letters following a .co. For example, the country code TLD for the United Kingdom was .co.uk. That has changed so country codes are now similar to TLDs in that they do not need a Second Level Domain such as .co any more. Some country codes have become popular for various reasons. For instance, the .io domain extension (British Indian Ocean) is used by many startup companies. Other country code extensions are used to make words (known as "domain hacks"), such as bit.ly or heaven.ly using the .ly extension (Libya). You can find a list of country codes in Appendix C.

How A Business Might Choose a TLD for Their Domain

When someone starting or running a business goes to register a domain name, their company name in a .com may not be available, and so they may need to think about a different TLD (top-level domain) or extension for their website. This could end up being a difficult process, especially when the .com version of the domain name is not available. Since most internet users generally type in a .com when they don't know whether another extension is used by a company, the .com is usually the preferred extension. Many companies that use an extension other than .com run the risk of losing potential business due to not getting as much "type-in" traffic as they otherwise would.

But if a company is able to market its business using their website's TLD as part of their name, then the domain extension, when not a .com, can be easily memorized by users and is not a problem regarding traffic. And as more and more traffic is determined by search engine results and other links to websites, the type-in traffic loss is becoming less of a concern.

The Website's Purpose

When starting a new website, the owner usually already knows what they want to use the website for, or its desired purpose. If it is going to be a commercial site that sells products, then a .com (or .biz as an alternate) is best. But if the website is more for a non-profit organization or for a concept or idea that an owner wants to develop a site for, then the .org extension may be most acceptable. If you just want to set up a personal blog about yourself or your family life, then maybe a .me could work, especially if the .com is already taken with the website name you want to use. If your website is just going to be used to teach people about some topic or particular idea, then a .info extension can generally be used. For computer networking websites, the .net extension is still appropriate, although many companies and for-profit businesses also use the .net when the .com is not available, as the .net extension is typically the second choice.

Before selecting a domain name for a website, most owners should take their time and look at different names and extensions before making a decision. Since the one website is most likely the only location on the internet where the company or information will be located, it is worth looking at many name and extension options first before making a selection.

Local Options

Instead of choosing a generic TLD, website owners may only be interested in attracting local visitors that are geographically located in their part of the world. For instance, a restaurant in a small town is most likely not interested in having visitors to their website by people from other counties around the world. These website owners may then be interested in using a country code TLD, which could better target their potential customers.

With over 200 country code TLDs available, most countries are represented, like .us (United States), .co.uk (United Kingdom), and .com.au (Australia). There are even newer city TLDs, such as .boston for Boston, Massachusetts.

The biggest advantage of using a country code TLD for a website is to target traffic from that specific area of the world. Companies in the United States tend not to use the .us extension, preferring the more generic .com or .net extensions because of the exceptionally large number of users in the United States. But for other countries not targeting visitors from the Unite States, then a country code may be preferred. Also, when using a country code, your website's search engine ranking may very well end up higher than similar .com and other TLD extensions based on where the user is searching from. This is possible because search engines return different results depending on the location of the IP address of the person doing the searching. When the results are returned, there could be many local results shown on the first few pages.

As an example, if a person in India visits the Google web site, they will be brought to Google.co.in, which is the Indian version of Google. The person in India will have many more .co.in TLDs in their search results before sites with a a .co.uk TLD for example. But the common .com extensions will still be prominent in search results, regardless of the country in which the search is being executed.

If a website owner has a local business and only wants to target local traffic to the site, then having the appropriate country code TLD should work fine. Aside from using a country code TLD, the owner can also list their site in local online

27

business directories and market their website name using the country code TLD. As far as cost, country code TLDs generally have the same yearly registration fees as a .com name, so there isn't much difference for most country code TLDs..

Name Availability

Another advantage of using a country code TLD is that a business or website owner is much more likely to find a popular name available using the country code as opposed to a .com extension. Since there are so many more domain names already registered using the .com, .org and .net extensions, if a business name is already taken in these other common extensions, then using a foreign country code TLD with their business name is a good choice, as long as it is not in violation of any copyright laws.

For example, instead of trying to register zelks.com, which is currently not available, the business owner may instead register zelks.com.au (the Australian version, if available). Although this would mean the business owner is targeting the Australian market, they could also register the same domain names in other country code TLDs, such as zelks.co.uk. The alternative, if the business owner is adamant on registering their business name in the .com extension, would be to contact the present owner of the domain name in the .com extension and negotiate a price to purchase the name, which could end up getting quite costly if it is a popular or otherwise valuable name.

Search Engine Optimization (SEO) Differences

Business owners should always think about the Search Engine Optimization (SEO) aspects before selecting their TLD. Some domain name extensions are more likely to rank higher in the search engines than others, which is why most people select a .com domain.

Any TLD can rank number one with the right search engine optimization practices, and most people don't realize that the only reason why .com is ranked at the top most frequently is because it is the most popular domain TLD. But country code domain extensions can also rank as high, particularly for targeted local or country internet users. To see a listing of ccTLDs, see Appendix C at the end of this book.

Domain Name System (DNS)

Although you may not need to know a lot about Domain Name System (DNS) servers to become a successful domainer, there are times when knowing about DNS and name servers can come in handy. However, if you would rather move on to Chapter 2 and Registrars, you can always come back to learn more about DNS servers later.

A DNS (Domain Name System) server is a web server that interacts with the domain name system - the directory of IP addresses and their corresponding domain names. The domain name system is essentially all of the global domain name servers, which together make up the largest digital database around the world. DNS servers use distinct software that sends data to different web hosts when requested. Without the DNS servers and the Domain Name System, the internet as we know it would be unable to operate.

DNS Root Servers

The base of the domain name system uses DNS root servers, which communicate only with other root servers using private network encryption protocols. The root servers sit at the top of the internet hierarchy and store all information related to an IP address and its domain name.

Of the total of 13 root servers, one is located in Sweden, one in Japan, one if England and the other ten are in the United States. They are labeled by a single letter of the alphabet, A through M.

DNS Hierarchy

As the DNS root servers, which hold the entire database, are at the top of the DNS hierarchy, the rest of the DNS servers web hosts and websites, which are only parts of the overall database. Internet Service Providers (ISPs) of private businesses run these next level DNS servers.

When you are connected to the internet and open your web browser, you are linked to your ISP's DNS server which then retrieves data from other servers which host the domains you are accessing before displaying them on your computer. Many times all of the information you are accessing is on the same DNS server. But if you are accessing web pages hosted in other countries your

ISP's DNS server is acting as a DNS client in order to retrieve data from a different DNS server.

All computers that are connected to the internet are also connected to DNS servers. So when you first set up your internet service, be it through cable, DSL, T1 or fiber, you are identifying your computer with a DNS server, and are given an IP address that identifies your computer on the network.

DNS Records

Just like your computer has an IP address, so too does every web site on the internet, and this number locates the website in the database. The DNS record, or zone file, for each website tells the web server how to respond to your input.

What DNS Records Do

You can access your domain name's DNS records through your Registrar's website. The DNS records are files that tell the DNS server which IP address the domain is associated with, and how to handle requests sent to each domain. When someone visits a website, a request is sent to the DNS server and then forwarded to the web server provided by a web hosting company, which holds the data contained on the site.

DNS syntax are strings of letters that are commands for actions. These can also be called DNS records, and include A, AAAA, CNAME, MX, NAPRT, NS, PTR, SOA, SRV and TXT. Below are further explanations for some of these:

An "A" record means "address" and is the most basic type of syntax used in DNS records, indicating the actual IP address of the domain. The "AAAA" record is an IPV6 address record that maps a hostname to a 128-bit Ipv6 address. Regular DNS addresses are mapped for 32-bit IPv4 addresses.

The "CNAME" record means "canonical name" and serves to make one domain an alias of another domain. CNAME is often used to associate new subdomains with an existing domain's DNS records.

The "MX" record means "mail exchange" and can list mail exchange servers that are to be used for the domain.

The "NS" record means "name server" and indicates which Name Server is authoritative for the domain. Many Registrants "point" to a Name Server other than the Registrar for web hosting, parking or other uses.

The "PTR" record means "pointer record" and maps an Ipv4 address to the CNAME on the host.

An "SOA" record means "State of Authority" and is used to store information like when the domain was last updated or other important information to the Registrant.

An "SRV" record means "service" and defines a TCP service on which the domain operates.

A "TXT" record means "text" and lets the administrator insert any text they'd like into the DNS record, and it is often used for denoting facts about the domain. The TXT record is a way to prove to a domain marketplace, for instance, that you are the Registrant for the domain name.

DNS Records Summary
Many times a domain name owner will need to modify the DNS records for the domain, particularly if you are developing a website and your web host is different than your Registrar, or if you want to park your domain, or if you are going to place it for sale on certain marketplaces.

DNS Lookup

DNS servers are used to carry and transmit data from one computer to another. All of this data is stored on a network that is backed up by thousands of separate DNS servers and stored on one of the thirteen root DNS servers.

Sometimes internet users want to search or "look up" information stored on DNS servers. Here are some examples.

Whois Lookup
The database that stores all of the DNS records of the world is called the Whois (pronounced "who is") database. Whois searches can be done through many different websites. One is Network Solutions, who is not only a Registrar but

also has responsibility for maintaining DNS records. However, access to these records is slowly changing to better protect Registrants' privacy.

Since the Registrant information in the Whois database is entered by the Registrants themselves, there is no guarantee the information is correct. And many Registrants offer Whois privacy to default all Registrant information back to their Registrar by placing proxy information in the record.

Reverse Lookup

If you have a website that is getting frequent spam attacks, it is possible to find out the IP address of the computer where the spam is coming from. Through the use of a reverse DNS lookup tool, you can find out the registration information for an IP address. If that information is private, you would at least know who the Registrar, and maybe even the web host from where the spam is coming from. This tool is different than the Whois lookup as the reverse DNS lookup is searching for an IP address, not a domain name.

Even worse than spam is a DDoS (Distributed Denial of Service) attack, which can come from multiple IP addresses sending a large amount of fake traffic in a short amount of time in order to overload and crash your server. DDoS attacks can also be used to send multiple requests to a password protected site in order to figure out the correct password. If you suddenly notice an unusual amount of traffic you should do everything you can to try and figure out what is going on before your site crashes, which could include using a reverse DNS lookup.

Types of DNS Servers

A Domain Name System (DNS) server, also sometimes called just a name server, is a web server that connects to other web servers to pass information back and forth, while also connecting to root DNS servers that hold all of the information as well. The DNS server your domain name uses has records that include the name's Registrant, web host, nameservers and other information.

A domain name's DNS servers are listed in the domain name's control panel along with the Whois database, and appear as NS1.NAMESERVER.COM and NS2.NAMESERVER.COM.

There are primary and secondary name servers. These two types of DNS servers work together to provide better security while also making administration tasks easier for each domain name. Some Registrars actually divide a DNS server to hold different zones of information for the same domain.

DNS Servers - Primary

A primary or master DNS server reads data for the domain zone from a file located on the hosting account's web server. The primary server also sends information to the secondary server.

Information the server administrator specifies that tells servers how to act and communicate with other servers is called zone data. A zone transfer is when a primary server communicates with a secondary server as zone data is being transferred from one DNS to another.

DNS Servers - Secondary

A secondary DNS server, also called a slave server, automatically receives zone data from the primary server after starting, then holds it in a zone. The secondary server requests information from its "master" every time it functions. In some cases, the master server can also be a secondary server.

Secondary DNS servers provide security in the form of redundancy so they are just as important as primary servers. The secondary server can also take some of the load from the primary server and make sure a server is always delivering data. Website (and internet) security can be ensured because of the diversified administrative structure of the two domain name servers, which automatically share zone data.

Creating a Name Server

When setting up web hosting with a hosting company, the company will give you two name server addresses to put into your domain Registrar's DNS settings in order to point your domain name to the web hosting company's server. Then back in your web hosting account you will confirm you own the domain, which will then be associated with your web hosting account.

There are two name servers used, with names like NS1.NAMESERVER.COM and NS2.NAMESERVER.COM, and are generally found in the control of your web hosting account. Some Registrars input their default name servers automatically when you register a domain name with them. If you have a web hosting plan with the same Registrar then the name servers are generally also automatically set by the Registrar.

The name servers you input in your domain Registrar's DNS settings are able to be seen in the public Whois database, unless you have your domain name set to private. Some online businesses like to create their own name servers thinking it looks more professional and independent, whether they are or not. These names show up in a public Whois record.

Your Own Name Server
When creating your own name server, the first step is to install DNS software on your web server. When installing DNS software, you also need to have access to the server's root. Most basic hosting accounts do not allow you to install your own software, so if your goal is to have your own name servers, then you need to be sure you buy the appropriate hosting plan, be it dedicated hosting or VPS hosting.

Another reason to have something other than a basic hosting plan is that you will need access to at least two IP addresses within your hosting account.

Your name servers will also need to be associated with a domain name. You can use the same domain you're making a website for, or you can have a separate domain name for your name servers.

You then add the name servers to your web hosting control panel. This is usually done as a subdomain before the domain name of the name server, like dns1.nameserversite.com or ns1.nameserversite.com. The complete process can be different depending on the hosting provider and the type of DNS software you are using.

Chapter 2 –Domain Name Registration

Every domainer needs to deal with domain name registration. You would think this was easy - that all you would need to do is go to a domain registration website, find your available domain name, then buy or register it. However, this is only just the beginning.

As discussed in the last chapter, when you "buy" a domain name you are actually registering an exclusive right to use the name – all of your details as the Registrant are recorded in the Domain Name System, or DNS. The companies that let you register domain names are called Registrars. For most companies and website owners, this is about all they need to know about domain name registration.

But to better understand domain registration and its particular applications, it makes sense to dive a little deeper into its structure, rules and regulations.

To start with, here is the basic structure:

- ICANN (Internet Corporation of Assigned Names and Numbers) is the non-profit organization created to oversee global internet-related tasks that were previously managed by IANA, under a contract from the US Government. ICANN is primarily responsible for managing the Internet's top level domains (TLDs), overseeing the allocation of IP addresses and managing the root server system. Some specific examples of ICANN services include approval of new generic TLDs, approval of Registrars to sell domain names, and resolving domain name registration disputes under its Uniform Domain Name Dispute Resolution Policy, or UDRP.

- A Registry controls their specific TLDs. VeriSign is the Registry for all of the .com domain names (along with several other TLDs). The Registries delegate the ability to add and update information to Registrars.

- A Registrar is the company through which people and businesses (so-called end-users or Registrants) register domain names. If you want the domain zelks.com, you would go to a Registrar, see if the name is available and, if it is, register it. The Registrar then adds the domain name to DNS, stores your information and connects it to that domain name.

- A Reseller sells domains for Registrars. There are some Registrars that use resellers to sell domains for them instead of marketing their services directly to the public,. The resellers do not have direct access to the DNS, but instead use the Registrars as portals. Resellers are often hosting companies who find it easier to market their own services when they are able to register names for their clients themselves.

- A Registrant is the individual or organization to which a domain name is registered. Other terms used for Registrant are Licensee or Registered Name Holder. Although the administrative and technical contacts on a domain name record may have certain privileges, it is the Registrant who has the final decision on how to manage their domain name. If you are not listed as the Registrant on a domain record, you have no ownership rights to that domain name.

registrant
end customer who
registers domain names

registry operators
keep an authoritative master
database ("registry") of all
domain names registered for
each top-level domain

resellers
register on behalf of registrants but
have no contractual relationship
with ICANN, e.g. web hosting companies

registrars
ICANN accredited organizations
that process the registration
of domain names

ICANN
non-profit corporation for domain
name system management

ICANN

Domain Registry Process   Source: ICANN

Registrar Details

When domain name registration started, Network Solutions was the only company authorized to register domain names. In 1999, ICANN created the Shared Registry System and approved five additional companies as Registrars. Since then, the domain name market has become very competitive, with hundreds of companies now acting as ICANN-accredited Domain Name Registrars.

For each domain name they register, Domain Name Registrars must pay the Registries a fee, which is added on to the price a Registrant pays when registering a domain name by many Registrars. After that nominal fixed cost, each Registry calculates their own costs, determines their profit margin, then decides how much they want to charge for different TLDs. Before 1999, everyone paid $70 for a 2-year domain name registration. But now, with competition, Registrars offer different rates along with registration periods that can vary from 1 to 10 years.

To become a domain name Registrar, a company needs to apply to ICANN and pay an application fee of around $3,500. The company also needs to show proof of at least $70,000 USD capital. Once the company becomes an ICANN-accredited Registrar, there is a $4,000 USD annual fee plus a quarterly ICANN fee of around $800. Then, for each domain name registered, the Registrar pays ICANN a nominal domain fee of around $0.18 US along with the Registry fee, which varies according to the TLD (around $7.85 USD for a .com).

The Registrar also has costs for developing their website and software to process the domain name registrations. However, some companies may not have the technical infrastructure to adequately handle multiple registrations, or may not offer services like domain name transfers in order to cut their overhead to allow them to charge less than other companies for domain name registrations.

Registering Domain Names

After researching and finding a domain name you want to register, you must then choose a Registrar and go through the registration process. You can find many Registrars on the web – and you should do a bit of research into the different Registrars if this is your first time registering a domain name.

When you register a domain name, the Registrar will require the following:

- **Registrant** – This is the individual or company who "owns" the domain name.
- **Administrative Contact** – This is who is authorized to make changes to the domain name, such as approve a transfer of the name to a new Registrar or alter the Registrant name.
- **Technical Contact** – This is who is authorized to make certain changes to the domain name, such as changes to the DNS servers associated with that domain name.
- **Billing Contact** – This is who all bills and other correspondence will be sent to.
- **DNS Server Settings** – This is where you specify the primary and secondary name server you would like to associate with the domain name for your website or domain parking, typically provided to you by your hosting company (if you are developing a website) or parking company (if you are "parking" the domain name to earn revenue from just the name). Most Registrars assign default DNS settings to show a parked domain name page with their Registrar company information.

Most times the same person or company is listed for all contacts. Some Registrars even streamline the registration process by not allowing a different Billing Contact information, for instance. When registering, you will also be asked for payment information. Some accept online payment forms such as PayPal while others may only take credit card payments.

Before being able to register a domain name, you most likely will have already been asked to set up a user name and password with that Registrar. It is important to have an account with each Registrar where you have domain names registered so you can easily make any required changes to any of the domain name's settings. It is best to store the user names and passwords for each Registrar you use in a separate place, like a password app on your phone.

Whois Information

When you register a domain name, the contact information you provide for that domain name is not only stored with the Registrar, but is also recorded in a central database that is maintained by the Registry. The database information becomes searchable by the public, called a Whois (pronounced "who-is") search.

Here is what a Whois search of google.com looks like (Administrative, Technical and Billing information removed):

Domain Name: google.com
Registry Domain ID: 2138514_DOMAIN_COM-VRSN
Registrar WHOIS Server: whois.markmonitor.com
Registrar URL: http://www.markmonitor.com
Updated Date: 2018-01-30T10:51:07-0800
Creation Date: 1997-09-15T00:00:00-0700
Registrar Registration Expiration Date: 2020-09-13T21:00:00-0700
Registrar: MarkMonitor, Inc.
Registrar IANA ID: 292
Registrar Abuse Contact Email: abusecomplaints@markmonitor.com
Registrar Abuse Contact Phone: +1.2083895740
Domain Status: clientUpdateProhibited (https://www.icann.org/epp#clientUpdateProhibited)
Domain Status: clientTransferProhibited (https://www.icann.org/epp#clientTransferProhibited)
Domain Status: clientDeleteProhibited (https://www.icann.org/epp#clientDeleteProhibited)
Domain Status: serverUpdateProhibited (https://www.icann.org/epp#serverUpdateProhibited)
Domain Status: serverTransferProhibited(https://www.icann.org/epp#serverTransferProhibited)
Domain Status: serverDeleteProhibited (https://www.icann.org/epp#serverDeleteProhibited)
Registry Registrant ID:
Registrant Name: Domain Administrator
Registrant Organization: Google LLC
Registrant Street: 1600 Amphitheatre Parkway,
Registrant City: Mountain View
Registrant State/Province: CA
Registrant Postal Code: 94043
Registrant Country: US
Registrant Phone: +1.6502530000
Registrant Phone Ext:
Registrant Fax: +1.6502530001
Registrant Fax Ext:
Registrant Email: dns-admin@google.com
Registry Admin ID:
Name Server: ns1.google.com
Name Server: ns4.google.com

Name Server: ns2.google.com
Name Server: ns3.google.com
DNSSEC: unsigned
URL of the ICANN WHOIS Data Problem Reporting System: http://wdprs.internic.net/ .

This snippet just shows the Registrant information for google.com in a Whois search. There is also both Admin and Technical contact information, which is typically the same as the Registrant, but you have the opportunity to make these different if you want. All of this information is available to the public through a Whois search.

Unfortunately, there are also direct marketers who scrape this information, particularly from new domain name registrations, and send out mass emails to the domain name contacts or, worse yet, have people calling you on the phone.

In order to try and maintain your privacy and not be contacted by marketers trying to sell you services, you might think to put a false name and address as the contact information when registering a domain name. This is not a good idea. Not only might a prospective buyer for your domain name do a Whois search of your domain to try and contact the owner, but you also might not receive important emails about your domain name, including the warnings when your domain name is getting close to its expiration date.

If you want privacy, many Registrars offer privacy services either as part of their normal domain registration costs or for an additional cost. This is a much better option than giving a fake name and address.

Whois Privacy
It is a requirement that your contact details for your domain names be publicly available as per ICANN, the governing body for Internet domain names. So once you register a domain name, your contact information is stored on "Whois" servers where your information is available to anyone with an Internet connection.

By having your contact information available to the public, there is always the possibility that someone will try to steal your identity (and your domain names) or, more common, contact you to try and sell you services, whether through email spam, telephone sales calls and/or junk mail. These spammers set up automated robots that scrape Whois contact records, particularly targeting those that most recently registered domain names. They gather contact names and email addresses and phone numbers in order to sell you website design services or other products or services. These unsolicited sales calls can become rather annoying.

An option to consider during domain name registration is whether or not you would like the domain ownership details to be private. Some domain name Registrars offer a service known as Whois privacy, which will shield your personal information from the public Whois database. Think of it like getting an unlisted phone number to avoid telemarketers. The cost for this privacy service is usually less than the price of the registration itself.

What type of Whois privacy is available?
When using Whois privacy, your Registrant, Admin and Technical contact information will typically be in the name of your Registrar instead of displaying your personal information. Your name might instead be listed something like "Whois Privacy Service, Attn: YourDomain.com." There are different methods of Whois privacy services your Registrar may offer:

In this case, your entire contact record is replaced with the contact details of your Registrar. Users and potential buyers for your domain name have no way to contact you. This method is preferred by those who will never want to be reached through a Whois search as they become completely anonymous..

Email Forwarding
In this method, your name and address are anonymous (usually showing your Registrar's information instead) but an email address is shown which typically will forward to your personal email account, or you will be notified by your Registrar that someone is trying to contact you. Although this helps in reducing telemarketing phone calls and physical junk mail, you are depending on your Registrar and any spam-filtering techniques they may employ to limit junk emails that may get forwarded to your personal email.

Random Email
This method is similar to Email Forwarding in that you remain anonymous, only the email address shown in the Whois search is randomized, and could

look something like 6kl9f0sd@Registrar. The randomized email address usually changes on a regular basis, like once per day, to cut down on the spammers' emails getting to you. If there is a legitimate contact email, like someone wanting to buy your domain, these emails will typically not be stopped by spam filtering.

It is important to note that the Whois records are maintained by each Registrar for their clients. So if you buy Whois privacy from a Registrar then transfer your domain name to another Registrar, you will need to repurchase privacy with the new Registrar.

Another point to consider is how the Whois information is stored. Sometimes it takes a while (days, even weeks) to change contact information across all of the databases that store Whois records. So even though you may decide to change your contact information to be private, your public contact info could remain accessible on many Whois search platforms for a lot longer than you would like. If you are considering using Whois privacy, it is best to get it right when you first register the domain name.

Also, if it's not obvious enough, you should not do anything illegal with regard to domain names and try to hide behind Whois privacy. If you read the terms and conditions from your Registrar who provides the privacy, there are typically clauses where the Registrar will give your real name, address and phone number to law enforcement agencies if foul play has been committed.

How to Choose a Registrar

Many domain buyers simply go to one of the most popular domain name Registrars to register a domain name. For some, this may be good enough. But there is competition amongst Registrars and savvy domainers typically have domain registrations spread across multiple Registrars. Some Registrars may offer a cheaper price for domain registrations in certain extensions while others may bundle web hosting services with domain name registrations.

Price
If you can register a domain name in a certain extension at one Registrar for $12 and another Registrar for $10, why would you pay $2 more for that registration? The cheaper Registrar may not have good customer service, or its interface is

quirky and hard to navigate. Others may look at simply keeping all of their domains with one Registrar so may not mind paying a dollar or two more. But if you are registering a lot of domains, those one or two dollars add up, and you can always transfer your domains to another Registrar after 60 days, so why not save yourself the few bucks per domain and register with the least expensive?

Security

The safety and security of your domain names is important. Although every Registrar has user names and passwords for all its users, additional security measures to restrict access to your domain account should be considered. Some Registrars have timeouts after ten minutes or so of inactivity. This is good so that you don't inadvertently leave your computer to allow somebody else access to your account. Registrars should also use pin numbers or some other method for identifying those who call on the phone for support of their domain names. You would not want someone pretending to be you to have access to your domains over the phone. Also, many Registrars are on https or a more secure protocol which adds an additional layer of security. You should always research different Registrars to see what systems they have in place to keep your information secure.

Service

You should find out how different Registrars respond to their customers. One way is to research reviews of that company, keeping in mind that many reviews tend to lean toward the negative as it has been found that more people write reviews to complain than to praise. Some reviews may also be old and the Registrar may have changed their practices to solve whatever their customers were complaining about. It is also a good idea to simply call their customer service line to see how their personnel handle service calls, along with when their phone lines are "open" and what sort of wait times they may have before you actually get to speak to someone.

Convenience

How easy is it to access your domain name accounts? Does the Registrar have an easy-to-use control panel, or is it clunky and hard to find what you are looking for? You should be able to easily see everything about your domain names and make changes if needed without having to click through multiple pages or, even worse, not finding where some piece of information is located.

Some domain name owners are also web designers and many prefer that their web hosting is from the same company where their domains are registered. Although this can be convenient, others believe you should keep your web hosting separate from your domain name registration in order to not only find a better hosting deal, but also to give an extra layer of security between your domain name and web hosting.

Stability

How long (and successful) your Registrar has been in business is important. New Registrars may not be so stable and the last thing you want is to lose any of your domain names because your Registrar went bankrupt or just simply shut down its website.

Domain Name Registration

In order to connect a domain name with an IP address or website, you need to first register the domain by "purchasing" it from a Registrar. Registering a domain name is an easy task – most Registrars make it easy because that is how they make most of their money.

When you register a domain you are not actually buying it. Instead, you are registering the right to use that domain name, and you are called the Registrant. You can first register the name for one year or for up to ten years. But even if you only register the name for one year, you will get plenty of warnings from your Registrar that the domain name renewal is coming up, where you will have the opportunity to renew the registration, again for anywhere from one to ten years typically.

At some Registrars, renewal fees cost more than the initial registration fee, so if you plan on using the domain name for a website (and for a long period of time), it is usually best to register the name for many years. If the Registrant does not renew the domain name and it expires, the domain name is open for new registration by another individual or business (after going through the expiration process, explained later in this chapter). It is important to note that intellectual property rights do apply to domain names so you are not legally allowed to register a domain name that contains a term or phrase that is trademarked or copyrighted – see Chapter 8 for more on trademarks.

Connecting Domain Names to IP Addresses

When somebody types in a domain name in the address bar of a browser, they are actually connecting to a specific IP address. There is a domain name that is directly associated with that IP address when a website is created, and the connection of domain names to IP addresses is managed and regulated by ICANN (Internet Corporation for Assigned Names and Numbers).

If you know the IP address of a website, it is possible to go there by simply typing in the numbers of the address. But memorizing series of numbers isn't very user friendly, so the domain name does the same thing.

Domain Name Registration Basics

Domain names are simply words that are combined with a domain TLD to access a website through a browser. So the website's name is the domain name, even though it's possible to have many domain names pointing to the same website using URL forwarding.

Because domain names have value beyond just websites, there are many domain names that are registered that aren't connected to an IP address. Many of these are held by companies because they are similar names or names in other TLDs that the company does not want other people registering. Or perhaps the company has plans for new products and so registers domain names using these product names before the product is developed. Domain names that are not associated with a website are called "parked" domains.

Other names are held by domainers for resale, as an investment. Many domainers point the nameservers to parking companies that offer advertising revenue from the domain name.

Where to Register Domain Names

Domain names can be registered through domain Registrars that have access to the DNS database. Many web hosting companies are also domain name Registrars, and some even offer package deals that include discounts for hosting plans and domain names bundled together. In fact, some web hosts offer free domain names with certain hosting plans. Many times you can receive a discount when purchasing multiple domain extensions simultaneously. During the domain name registration process, there are a variety of options to choose from, some of which can be confusing to someone new to the domain name business.

It is also possible to purchase aged domains, or domain names that have already been registered for some time, from domain auction sites, domain marketplaces, or other individuals. Usually when you purchase a domain name from the secondary market, the registration is transferred to you. At some marketplaces, you may also have to add another year's time to the registration.

Pointing a Domain Name

Many Registrars automatically point a newly-registered name to their own "parking" page where the Registrar can advertise their own services. But you can change the nameservers yourself within the control panel of the domain Registrar's web site to a different parking page (there are companies that offer these services). Or, if you are developing a website, your web hosting company will instruct you as to what nameservers to use. You simply change the name servers of your domain in the Registrar's control panel, then the domain name will be pointed towards your new website or parking page. It is also possible to forward the domain name to another website through URL forwarding.

When first pointing a domain name to a website, it is important to remember that it can take anywhere from a couple of minutes to several days for a domain to become active on the internet after the official completion of registration and nameserver adjustments.

The Domain Name Life Cycle

In the early internet days, domain names could only be registered for a fixed period of 2 years. Registrars now allow for the registering of a domain name from anywhere between one and ten years. Sometime they will even offer discounts for multi-year registrations. The registration of a domain name begins its "life cycle" and is said to be "active."

When a domain name is approaching its renewal date, it is also said to be "expiring soon." The domain owner is given multiple warnings to renew the domain. If the Registrant renews, then the domain name remains in its active state.

When a domain name passes its renewal date (also known as its "expiry date") without the renewal fee being paid, the domain name is said to have "expired." The domain expiration path (the process by which the domain name expires, and then is made available for re-registration) differs from Registrar to Registrar, but is generally around 77 days.

The Life-Cycle of a Domain Name

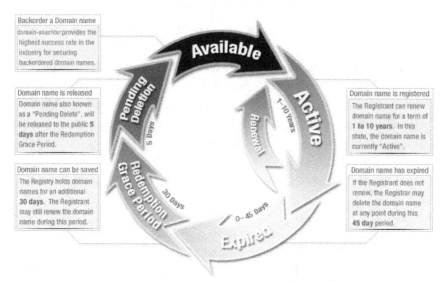

Backorder a Domain name
domain-snachter provides the highest success rate in the industry for securing backordered domain names.

Domain name is released
Domain name also known as a "Pending Delete", will be released to the public **5 days** after the Redemption Grace Period.

Domain name can be saved
The Registry holds domain names for an additional **30 days**. The Registrant may still renew the domain name during this period.

Domain name is registered
The Registrant can renew domain name for a term of **1 to 10 years**. In this state, the domain name is currently "Active".

Domain name has expired
If the Registrant does not renew, the Registrar may delete the domain name at any point during this **45 day** period.

Source: Fastcomet

Here are the typical stages a domain name will go through during its life-cycle, before the ~77 day expiration path is complete:

1. A domain name is registered for a period of 1-10 years
2. The user pays the Registrar for the usage of the domain for that time and the domain name becomes active.
3. The Registrar pays the Registry a small amount and your name is entered as the Registrant.
4. As the end-of-registration date approaches, the Registrar sends the Registrant reminders to pay the domain name renewal fee.
5. If the Registrant renews the name, then the domain name remains in its active status.

6. At the renewal date, if the renewal has not been paid, the registration expires.

7. The Registry then charges the Registrar a small amount to keep the domain for a short period of time.

8. The Registrar puts the domain on hold, sometimes deleting the domain's old nameserver information or modifying it. If the Registrar modifies the domain's nameservers, the new information usually points browsers to either the Registrar's website or to a page explaining that the domain is expired.

9. The user (as a result of being put on hold) loses the ability to transfer the domain name to another Registrar.

10. The domain name then enters a grace period as determined by the Registrar. During the grace period, the original Registrant can sometimes pay to renew the domain name, usually paying an additional fee to retain the domain. This would remove the name from its expired status and it would then be reactivated.

11. If the Registrar's grace period expires and the domain name was not renewed, the domain enters the redemption period. The Registrant still has an opportunity to renew the domain and have it returned to active status, but at a much higher cost.

12. Once the Registrar's redemption period ends, the existing Registrant loses control of the domain name and can no longer renew its registration. The domain then enters the pending delete period for five days and is about to return to the domain market. If the domain name is considered valuable, there may be many who either backorder the domain or who put in a bid to try and "catch" the domain when it drops with one of the domain name drop-catching companies.

13. As a final step, once the domain name has returned to the market, the Registry refunds the holding fee they had previously charged to the Registrar at no additional cost to the Registrant or new domain owner, if there is one.

Thousands of domain names end up becoming expired every day. Whether this is because the Registrant was lazy and didn't renew the domain (despite repeated reminders from the Registrar), or decided the name wasn't worth renewing, the expired domain lists contain names with varying values. The expiring domain lists can be an opportunity for a domainer to find good domain names for investment.

Domain Misconceptions

In review, it might be good to look at some things that some people may believe to be true (but aren't) about domain names.

1. You have to be a US resident or company to register a domain name
Anybody can register domain names in most TLDs, no matter where they live, so there is no restriction regarding US residency or being a US company. There are, however, some countries that have certain requirements under their ccTLD, such as only allowing residents of that country to be able to register a domain name in that country's extension.

2. You own the domain name when you register it
When you register a domain name, you are paying for the right to use that domain name for a defined period of time when you register it, you don't "own" it. Depending on the period of time you have it registered (usually one to ten years), as your registration end is approaching, you will need to pay a renewal fee to continue to keep the right to use the domain name. If you do not pay the renewal fee, the domain name expires and, if not picked up by someone else through backorder or auction, it is deleted and is then able to be registered by anybody else. But as long as you pay the renewal fees and the name does not infringe on a trademark, it is yours to use until you decide that you no longer want it.

3. You need a website to own a domain name
No, you can simply register a domain name and never attach a website to it. You may be planning to eventually develop a website or you are simply holding the domain name for resale. Many domainers register domains and park them with a parking service, then make money off the ad revenue. If you have a domain name with a parking company and later decide that you'd like to develop a website for it, you simply point the name to your new website.

4. You get a website when you register a domain name
No, since you do not need a website to own a domain name, you do not automatically get a website when you register a domain name. A website

requires a web host, which is a company that will store your website files on their servers and make the site accessible to the internet. Many domain Registrars offer web hosting as an optional, extra service when you register your domain, but you don't need to host with your Registrar. There are other companies that specialize in web hosting that may be a better option for you. And if you are simply registering domain names to re-sell or flip, you may not be interested in having a website for the domain name.

Also worth noting is that many web hosting companies are also domain resellers. Some of them will offer a domain name registration for free when a customer signs up for one of their web hosting plans. If you're thinking about using your new domain name for a website, you may want to look into your hosting options first, before you register your domain name. You might be able to get the domain registration for free.

5. You can get rich quick by flipping domain names

Although it is true you can make money by purchasing and reselling domain names, the chances of become rich as a domain flipper are very slim. There are stories of domainers selling names for over $1 million, but these types of domain names are not available to the new domainer. And when just starting in the business of domains, you generally will be looking for small to medium gains on your hand-registered names before moving up to more expensive domain names.

The truth is that unless a domain name is desirable because of current events or its scarcity, it may never sell in the aftermarket. In fact, somewhere around 90% of all domain names registered are unused and most of these are never re-sold for a profit. You might see other domainers post their names in marketplaces for very high and somewhat unrealistic prices, thinking that all domain names are valuable. Although some of these over-priced names may eventually sell, a majority of them will remain unsold and the owner will be faced with their renewal fees, trying to sell them for cheap, or letting them expire.

You *can* make money in domaining, and many people do. The key is to study the industry and invest wisely. As with any business or investment, it requires a lot of research and work to be successful.

Chapter 3 – Value of Domain Names

Domain names are an integral part of the way the internet functions, as they represent the names of a websites. Without domain names, users would need to type in IP addresses in the URL bar of their browsers, which is basically a string of numbers separated by dots. Obviously, these segmented number sequences are much more difficult to remember than the standard website name, which is why domain names were invented.

It isn't difficult to learn the basics of domain names, especially for those who already know how the internet works. However, trying to determine how much a domain name is worth is much more difficult. There are online websites that can estimate the value of a domain name based on recent sales and other domain name factors, but these can easily over- or under-estimate any particular domain name due to market trends and other influences. There are also companies and individuals known as domain appraisers that specialize in judging the value of domain names.

But, keep in mind, a domain name is only worth what a buyer is willing to pay for it. Although there may be some merit in looking at recent sales, each domain name is unique and its value can never exactly be determined.

With that said, domain names can have value without yet being sold. There are four basic factors that directly contribute to the value of a domain name: length, memorability, keyword/SEO optimization potential, and the value of the attached website, if it has one.

Domain Name Length

In the domain name secondary resale market, short names have generally sold for higher profits than longer names. This is because shorter domain names are usually more memorable and therefore, they become popular more easily than longer domain names. The length of the domain name is the most important factor that affects the memorability of an attached website. In addition, with a shorter domain name, there is a lessened likelihood of typos.

In today's domain name industry, it is impossible to register a new domain name, all letters (no numbers or hyphens), in the .com extension that is shorter than five letters – they are all already taken. And most short common English word names in the .com extension are also already registered. Many companies have made-up names, and usually the shorter the better for memorability. Names like eBay, Quora, Yahoo, and Bing are all good examples of popular websites with domain names that are under six letters.

Registering a .com domain name that is less than five letters or a common English word usually requires you to bid on the name at an auction site or purchase the domain directly from the owner. Either way, these domains are never cheap. And for short English words, the domain names are usually valued at more than $10,000 while two- or three- letter domain names with a .com extension are upwards of $100,000 or more.

Memorability

Domain names that are simple words or have catchy names will be much easier for users to remember than random words, letters or numbers. For instance, chewy.com was a company created to sell pet supplies solely on the domain name that was purchased. It is a memorable name, as well as being short, so is easy for people to type into a browser. Chewy.com has over 50% of the online pet supplies market. On the other hand, petflow.com, another online pet supplies retailer, has less than 2% of the market. The name Petflow just doesn't have the same catchy, memorable title as Chewy.com.

Keyword/SEO Optimization

Another important factor to consider when judging the value of a domain name is whether or not the name contains any frequently searched-for keywords. For example, although the word "insurance" is more than six letters, it is a very common term that would most likely receive a lot of web traffic through search engines.

When people purchase domain names, ideally they'd like to put forth minimal effort to begin seeing progress. For this reason, many domain speculators and webmasters only buy domain names that already have a significant keyword value. Thus, it is important to consider the predefined popularity of a name before judging its value. For example, while the domain name "amerona.com" may sound appealing to some people, it has no keyword value because nobody is searching for that term. When registering domain names, it is best to ensure that your desired name has some inherent keyword value.

Also, it is best if your keyword is competitive. If your keyword is a word that has many applications, like the word "chocolate," having chocolate in your domain name may not help your website in getting ranked by search engines. You would need to add another keyword to the domain name to make it unique. What word along with chocolate might people search for? If you owned hotchocolate.com then, with a good website, you could rank very high in the search engines for anybody who searched for "hot chocolate."

Website

Statistically, domain names that are shorter have been sold for higher profits. This is because shorter domain names are generally more memorable, and therefore, they become popular more easily than longer domain names. It takes a lot of work to get any website, regardless of keywords, to the top of the SERPs (Search Engine Results Pages) for competitive, highly searched-for keyword phrases.

But a low- to mid-quality domain name (by itself) could have a higher value if it is pointing to a successful website. A website with good content and SEO that ranks high in searches, and has a lot of traffic and backlinks, can easily raise the value of any domain name, whether it is an English word or not.

Other factors:

There are many other factors that go into assessing the value of a domain name:

Commerciality - Although the term "commerciality" is not technically a word in the dictionary, it is commonly used in the internet industry to describe something with commercial value. If the domain name pertains to something that can be sold or marketed, then there is a very high chance that it will sell for a greater price. A domain name that is related to a popular product would be much more valuable than a domain name that is simply related to a funny phrase or a personal opinion, even if the "non-commercial" domain is shorter. The more of an opportunity there is to make a profit with the domain, the more likely someone will make a substantial investment to acquire the domain.

Hyphens and Numbers - Even though domains that contain hyphens and numbers may be appealing, these domain names generally rank lower in the search engines. Most people do not include numbers or hyphens when they submit a search engine query. Thus, most domain speculators recommend purchasing a domain name that does not contain any hyphens (-) or numbers.

Many newbie domainers make the mistake of purchasing a domain name like "products4skincare.com" because the alternative "productsforskincare.com" is not available. If you run into a roadblock like this, it may be best to move on to a new idea rather than registering a domain name with hyphens and/or numbers. Choosing a domain name that is memorable, contains no symbols or numbers, and includes popular keyword phrases is the best way to ensure that your domain name investment can be profitable.

End User Domain Name Value

What makes a particular domain name valuable? If we look at it from the point of view of an end user, or someone who is looking for a domain name for their business, then value can be seen in different terms. For end users, the value of a domain name can be viewed from two sides: one side is based in fact or logic, the other side is based on emotion or attachment.

Domain Value - Fact

Domain names are valuable because they are a powerful marketing tool for businesses and organizations, so they have real world value. If you own a shoe store, would you rather have shoes.com or LarrysShoeStore.com? Shoes.com, of course!

Here's why:

1. It's easy to remember
2. You don't have to spend money branding it (it already is what it is)

In other words, shoes.com saves and makes you money; hence the value and marketplace worth.

When you spend money advertising shoes.com, it goes farther because people will remember it. No one is going to remember LarrysShoeStore.com unless you throw a lot of marketing money at it. You've got to get a jingle and play commercials over and over. It's a whole production. But with a simple generic domain name, everything's self-explanatory. There's no better domain name for a business than exactly what it is.

Also, the search engines almost always rank exact match domains (EMD's) higher. This means if you show yourself to be legitimate and optimize your site, you're going to get search engine rewards (and possibly first page rankings) for branding yourself as a keyword search term.

Of course, generic domains aren't the only valuable domains. Brandable/made-up domains or just catchy phrases can be extremely valuable as well. Who heard of Yahoo or Google before they became major online businesses?

Overall, domains have logical value because the right ones are worth marketing dollars. It might help you to think of a good domain name as a simple but very important part of the marketing process. Smart business people know how important a great domain name is. However, there will always be some business people who don't, and thus they won't value domains very highly.

Let's pretend you're about to launch a product. Say you're selling a new line of car decals so that parents can let everyone driving behind them know what sports their kids are in. Your marketing plan includes the following:

- Advertising (radio, print, online)
- Social media promotion (Facebook, Twitter)
- Referral program (pay people who send you referrals)
- Event booths (go to fairs, events, etc. and promote to passers-by)

Underlying each of these methods of promotion is your domain name and website. Your marketing dollars will go further if you have a great domain name that represents your product well. Credibility could also be a part of this marketing scheme. If you have a great domain name, it makes you look more legitimate. For example, if you were to start an online casino site (where your credibility is a major factor in people playing), it helps a lot if you buy a strong domain as it shows you've at least invested that much money into the site.

Domain Value - Emotion

There are two types of emotional responses that could add value to a domain name.

First, a domain name can be marketed to play on another's feelings. This can be based on a perceived emotion, like the way a name sounds. It could also be how the name is marketed. As in advertising, how you sell a product can tap into an emotional response. Sometimes if a name sounds appealing, it can be worth more.

Let's look at bing.com for example. Yes, the domain name has value on its own because it is a short English word in a .com extension. When Microsoft was creating its own search engine, it could have named it MicosoftSearch.com or something like that. But Microsoft also capitalized on this name because its use as a search engine can evoke an emotional response, like Bing! - the sound of a great idea coming to mind, or the sound of winning a prize.

Second, a domain name can be marketed for sale using an emotional strategy. It's fairly common to see domain name sales that are emotionally or situationally charged (from both buyers and sellers). Many times, these sales can end with a very high price, and you might wonder how such a name was able to sell for such a high price.

Experienced domainers and domain brokers often market domains for sale using emotional connections to potential buyers. Many domainers come up with a graphic image of what they think their domain name can mean and display the graphic image with the name of the domain on a website where they are listing the domain name for sale. The name by itself might not mean anything, but tied to an image of something may spark interest in a buyer.

Another way to play on emotion could be in an auction setting where more than one potential buyer is bidding on a domain name. The auctioneer or domain name owner can further promote the name for sale and cause a bidding war, possibly ending up with a sale for much more than the domain name was initially valued.

What Makes a Domain Name Premium?

Premium domain names are short, memorable, easy-to-spell names that end in a popular extension like .com. These domains tend to cost a lot more than normal domains because they are more likely to be easier to remember.

Exact Match Business or Geographic Names

A domain name that is one- or two-words and is a business category or geographic location can be a premium name. Some examples of this include: Insurance.com, Boston.com, Beer.com, GiftCard.com, Tickets.com etc. Names like this are very high in value and when auctioned, generate a lot of interest. These names are attractive to both business owners and investors.

Acronyms and Short Names

Acronyms are always in demand because they are easy to type and easy to remember. Two-letter .com domains like BC.com have significantly high value, and other short .com names like TBD.com are worth a large sum as well. Because of scarcity, any two- or three-letter .com, if not purchased over its value, will be a good investment, albeit with a investment cost.

The next tier of short names that have become popular are NNNNN or 5N.com and LLLL or 4L.com. The 4L.coms are domain names made up of 4 letters of the alphabet in the .com extension and not an English word or well-known acronym. As seen on the chart, there was a huge spike in the sales price of these domains in 2015. Chinese investors bought out all of the remaining domains in the LLLL.com market, with particular emphasis on domain names without vowels or the letter V – so-called "Chinese Premium" domains. The market soon settled lower the following year, and has decreased somewhat since then. Who knows when the next surge will come, but for now there is a lot of evidence as to the current value of these types of domain names.

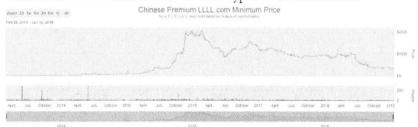

Source: shortnames.com

English Generic Words

Domain names like Yahoo.com or Bing.com have become highly valued as a brand name for a corporation or business, even though they don't name an exact service or product. By themselves, they may have potential worth, but once a company brands the word and people think of the company based on the word before anything else, the domain name's value increases exponentially. Many companies seek out words that have not yet been branded.

Advertiser Competition Names

If you type in a product or service in a search engine and see many high level advertisers in the results, that means that product's or service's name has value. As an example, if you type in "car insurance" and you see many large companies competing for traffic, then you can assume that carinsurance.com has a high value.

High Search Volume Domains

Most premium domain names are a word or term that is often typed into search engines. You can find different tools to see how often different words are searched. If a word or phrase has a high search volume, advertisers will pay more for placement in response to these words. The domain names that are exact matches for highly searched words (or keywords) or phrases will have high value.

Names With High Traffic

If a domain name has already (or previously) been developed as a website and still receives a lot of traffic, the name can have increased value based on volume and back links (or links to this domain name from other websites). Based on the quality of the volume, such as the predominant countries the traffic comes from, domain names that have a lot of traffic can be premium not only by their name but also the volume of people that access their websites.

Aged Domains

Domains that have been registered for over a year and never dropped are called "aged domains." These domain names typically sell for more than a new one does because it has been around for a while. Many buyers look specifically for aged domains of over five years as it can help them develop an existence online, a history, or credibility in their niche markets simply because if the domain has been around for years it may appear that they have been as well.

Aged domains can be found for sale on forums, auctions and other marketplaces for sale. If you type in the keywords "aged domains" in the search bar you should be able to easily locate older domains for sale.

.com TLD

While there are a few exceptions to this rule (twitch.tv for example), in order for a domain to be premium, it should have the .com extension. As previously described in this book, the domain name in .com is worth more than .net, .org, etc. As more gTLDs, or General Top Level Domain extensions are added, such as .club and .boston, there is even more competition for keyword domains. However, for the most part, most people using the internet first assume a domain name ends in .com, so .com is still the "king."

Common Sense

There are all sorts of tools available on the internet to analyze domain names. But many times you have to objectively look at the names based on your experience and ask yourself if the domain sounds like a premium name. If you have a "brandable" name that is not an English word, or a name that has keywords in markets that have "potential," these names are <u>not</u> premium. And unless a name is already developed in an extension other than .com, it is not premium unless it is in the .com extension.

Finding the Value of Your Domain Name

Of the over 300 million domain names that have been registered, probably 90% of those domain names cannot be sold for more than their registration fee, even though appraisers and appraisal services may say they are worth more.

As mentioned before, a domain name is only worth what a buyer is willing to pay for it, no more and no less. But as you sit there looking at your list of domain names you've already registered, no matter how long the list, there is a desire to assess what the overall value of your portfolio may be. Just be prepared to accept that most, if not all, of your domains may only be "ref fee" domains.

But if you have what you think is a top or premium domain name that you think could be worth a lot of money, then using a domain name appraiser could be to your benefit. For most domainers, paying for domain name appraisals does not make much sense as you will be spending additional money unnecessarily, as most domainers don't have any of these high-priced domain names. Therefore, it is best to run each of your domain names through one of the free online appraisers, just as a point of reference knowing that no online valuation tool is going to tell you what your domain names are really worth.

As an example, the domain name Shoes.com has a very high value, well into six figures and probably seven, and may be worth using a professional appraiser to help determine its potential value. RunningShoes.com also has very good value and, for the right buyer or seller, getting an appraisal makes sense. However, TopSellingShoes.com may have more value than its registration fee, but paying additional money for a professional appraiser probably isn't worth it. And lastly, BuyYourFavoriteShoesHere.com is not really worth anything at all, even though automated appraisers may give it a value in the hundreds of dollars.

This is what no appraisal system will tell you – that your domain name(s) may be worth less than even its registration fee. You can see this for yourself on some of the domain name auction sites as domainers try to get whatever money they can from domain names that are getting close to their end of registration dates. Many times, after a year of owning a domain name, the owner now realizes the name is not even worth re-registering so tries to get anything they can out of it before it expires, as they don't plan on spending money to renew it.

Even with bad domain names, you have the option to generate value by creating a website on the domain and developing it into a viable site, complete with traffic and links. Once a domain name has an established website, sometimes, no matter how bad the domain name is by itself, it will be more valuable.

Domain Appraisers

If you want to get an independent, third party opinion of the potential worth of one or more of you domain names, there are domain appraisal services that will identify a domain's value for you. They advertise using their "years of experience," and the "world's largest database" of domain sales to help determine your domain's "precise" market value. However, it is important to know these appraisers are most likely looking at the same data that you could find on your own with a little effort, and there is no such thing as a precise value of a domain name.

About Appraisers

Appraisers have their place in the domain name business. They can assist you whether you are a buyer or a seller. Based on their experience, an appraiser could save you a lot of money as a buyer if you are looking to invest in higher priced domain names. And when considering putting a domain up for sale, an appraiser can not only give you a range with confidence where they think a domain name will sell, but also assist you in finding the right marketplace or even end user who may have interest in your domain name. However, you still need to remember – no matter what an appraiser says, a domain name is only worth what someone is willing, ready and able to pay for it.

Selecting an Appraiser

What you want from an appraiser is someone who is very knowledgeable about the domain name industry. They should have completed many sales and show you examples of domains they appraised for other clients and what the final sales price was for each of those domain names. You don't want to trust someone who is just going to give you inflated prices and then blame the marketplace if it doesn't sell for anywhere near that price (if at all). Also when selecting an appraiser, you should choose someone who is just offering appraisal services, not trying to sell you on other services like domain brokerage or escrow.

It is very easy for an appraiser to give a potential buyer a higher price than a domain name is actually worth. While there are a number of variables that consistently help predict the value of a domain name, there are just as many unpredictable factors, and therefore it's virtually impossible to come up with an accurate price.

Using our previous example, let's say the owner of the domain name runningshoes.com has the site listed on a domain marketplace for $20,000 and you want to know if the domain could be worth much more before investing the money. That same marketplace may give a "valuation" of the domain name, but that value should not be trusted as the marketplace is getting a commission on the sale, so the higher the sale price, the more money they stand to make.

How Appraisals Can Be a Hindrance

Even though it seems like appraisers can help by giving you a realistic value of an overpriced domain you want to buy, or giving you examples of similar high priced domains as yours that you want to sell, appraisers can also get in the way of a good sale. For instance, a seller who has an overpriced domain that you want, and also has an appraiser convincing them that the high price is what it is worth, will probably never negotiate down what you think the domain is actually worth. Also, there are many new domainers in the market who are registering domains that really have little to no value. But these domainers seek out appraisers, many of whom give them higher values to keep them paying for more appraisals for more of their bad domains.

There are also automated appraisal websites, like Estibot and GoDaddy. These sites use algorithms looking at things like website traffic or recent similar sales. More times than not, these sites tend to overvalue domains that aren't really worth very much, but undervalue premium and top domains. When sellers quote these automated appraisal numbers in their domain listings, they are usually finding the highest similar sales they can find to either make their initial Buy It Now or BIN high price seem more legitimate, or to get bidders to bid higher if in an auction setting. And a great domain name that does not have an active website will not have the traffic which could lead to a high valuation, so any automated tool looking at traffic should be ignored for top domain names.

When seeing appraisal values in any domain name listings, you should always do your own research to either confirm this is a reasonable price for the domain or else find other evidence that shows a domain is worth less that you can use in your negotiating to buy the domain.

There are also domain name appraisal scams. Many domainers receive emails from potential buyers offering to buy their domain names. However, before agreeing to a price, they will demand you go through a certain appraisal service first – and they give you a link directly to that service. However, they are really just making an affiliate commission on getting you to do that appraisal and have no intention of buying your domain name.

Other Questions to Ask Yourself

Even after all of these considerations, you still want to know whether your domain names have value. Here are a few questions to ask yourself about the potential value of your domain names:

Does the domain name have a ".com" extension?

This is the number one question as .com is the "king" of all TLDs. A .com domain name could have ten times or more the value of the same name with any other extension. Shoes.com may be worth a million dollars, but Shoes.net probably couldn't even sell for twenty thousand dollars. With .com domains, there are many recent sales that can help you determine an approximate value. With other extensions, not so much – particularly for the new TLDs. For instance, Shoes.com can more easily be measured based on sales of other similar, popular, short one word domain names in the e-commerce industry. But how much might shoes.online be worth? Or shoes.io? There just aren't good reference points for the non- .com domain names to help you judge each domain's potential value in another extension.

How long is the domain name?

With most domains, short names are worth much more than longer names, the main exception being a longer name with a great keyword is better than a shorter name that isn't even a word (except for two- or three- letter .coms). ReachForIt.com is a good domain name. But Reach4It.com is not worth very much as users will most likely type in "for" before "4" in their browser.

Is the domain name hyphenated?

There are many websites on domains that have hyphens, but more often than not this is because the same name without the hyphen was already taken. Domain names with hyphens, like Best-Shoes.com, will typically sell for much less than BestShoes.com.

Is the domain name spelled correctly?

Actual word domain names, spelled correctly, can be worth a lot. For instance, BestShoes.com is a good domain name. However, BastShoes.com isn't worth much. And misspellings of trademarked names, like Gogle instead of Google, could land you in legal trouble.

Do you receive unsolicited offers on your domain name?
If you don't have your domain name listed for sale anywhere but you get emails with offers to buy your name, then you know if has value. The interested buyers are most likely taking the time to find your name through a Whois search – and they wouldn't use their time doing that if your name wasn't worth much.

Is the domain name a singular or plural word?
In most cases, putting an "s" after a popular word, although still an English word, is not as valuable as that singular word. Think start.com versus starts.com. But there are some cases where the plural word can be worth more: Shoe.com is most likely worth less than Shoes.com - who is only going to buy one shoe?

Does the domain name use a prefix or suffix?
A prefix or suffix in a domain name generally hurts the name's value. For example, if you put the words "best" or "my" in front of the word, or possibly "site" behind it, you have a name that is not worth anything close to the domain name of just that word. Even single letters, such as "e" or "i" make the name worth less than without that letter. There may be exceptions to this, typically if a major brand, such as eBay.com, is created using a prefix or suffix.

Is the domain name a single word? Multiple words? How common are these words?
For the most part, a single word domain name is worth more than a name with two or more words. But a common two-word name (or possibly three-word, if the words are good enough) is most likely worth more than a rare one-word domain name. For example: RunningShoes.com is worth more than Cajolers.com. FreeEmailAddress.com is worth more than Unconvince.com.

When looking at domain names with the same number of words, you should think of a business where that domain name might be applicable. For example: Shoes.com is obviously a very good commercial one-word domain name. Cajolers.com, while having value because it is a single word in a .com extension, does not have a very clearly defined audience or potential use, and is much less commercial. Shoes.com is probably worth more than a thousand times the value of Cajolers.com, yet they're both one-word domain names.

You might think since a domain name is a single English dictionary word in a .com extension it is valuable. But if the domain name has no identifiable commercial use, then it probably has little or no value as a domain name. For example: "unconvince" is in the dictionary, but unconvince.com has nowhere near the value of whiskey.com, even though both are single English words.

After thinking about the answers to the above questions, you might start to get some idea of the value of your domain names. If you have a one English word (correctly spelled) in a .com extension that could be used by a business, then you definitely have something valuable, especially if you are receiving offers for the name without having it listed on a marketplace. But if you have a three or four-word name, one word which is misspelled, then you probably have a name that has no value. Same goes for a name in a different extension besides .com. The .net, .io, .ca or any other extensions will not only have less value than the same name in .com, but will also be more difficult to sell.

You might be asking yourself why there isn't any one evaluation method to determine how much your domain name may be worth. As for evaluating a name, in the end, it is up to you, the owner (and seller) of a domain name to find out as much information as you can about the name, and come up with your own opinion of what the domain name's value may be. It is worth this continued evaluation effort and experience because without any idea of value, you're going to find it much harder to negotiate and close a deal on your domain names.

Online Resources

Once you have considered what you think may be your domain name's value, if you haven't already done so, it is time to turn to some online resources as a sort-of "check" as to what the name may be worth.

Caution should be used when using some of these online tools because they may not be able to consider any special considerations for certain properties of a name, and some are limited in the data that is used. It is only with use and experience when you can best learn how to effectively use these resources.

Recent Sales

A website like namebio.com is a great resource.

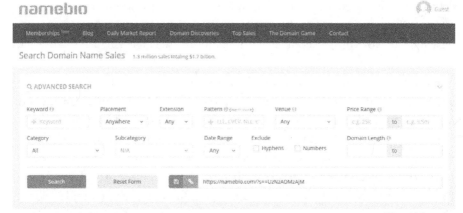

Namebio.com

Looking at past domain name sales could be a good indicator as to your domain name's value. You can search under keywords and/or domain name length, as well as filtering by extensions. Tracking sales history of similar names will allow you to be able to reference other similar names and their sales amounts if you get into negotiations for the sale of your domain name.

Automated Evaluators

As a final check, you can run your domain name through a few free automated domain name valuation tools. Estibot and GoDaddy are two of the most popular.

Estibot.com

Domain Name Value & Appraisal

How much is your domain worth?

It might be more valuable than you think.

Enter a domain name | GoValue™

Godaddy.com

As mentioned earlier, some evaluators like Estibot will consider whether a website is attached to the name and looks at the traffic. Others, like GoDaddy's Valuation Tool, only consider the domain name itself and compares the name to recent sales of similar names on the GoDaddy platform. However, you should be cautioned about the lowest-valued names. Sites like GoDaddy tend to only find similar names that sold and does not consider all of the other similar names that never sell, and so may over-value what you should actually think is a reasonable target for your domain name. It also is not able to accurately judge any current or emerging trends, as evidenced by the quick rise in popularity of crypto currency domains. Domain names containing the words "crypto" and "bitcoin" had a huge rise in valuation throughout 2017, but domain name evaluation tools were not able to keep up with the sudden increase in demand.

The automated evaluations can sometimes be used when you are selling a name that you don't think is as valuable as the recent sales of similar names. In this case, the Estibot or GoDaddy evaluators may give you a value that you can quote in your write-up for a name you are selling on an auction platform, or in email correspondence with a potential buyer while you are negotiating a final sales price. Even though more savvy domainers discount these automated evaluators, there may be end users/buyers who aren't as familiar with these tools and may be able to be influenced to pay you the evaluation amount for your domain name as an "independent" estimate of a domain's value.

But remember, these online resources may give you wide swings in estimating a domain name's value and you should only use these tools as a final resource.

Final Thought

If you have domain names that, after owning them for six or eight months, have not been getting any response to outbound emails or domain name listings on the secondary market, you may need to rethink the value of these domain names. If, after taking a more realistic look at your domain names that aren't getting any traction, you may come to realize that they are not really worth much of anything. At that point, you can either:

A) Develop a website using the domain name (this adds value to it) ... or

B) Try to get whatever you can for the domain name by trying to sell it cheap on a domain name forum . . . or

C) Take a deep breath, accept the fact that the domain name is not worth renewing, and let it expire and move on.

Chapter 4 – Buying Domain Names

When you buy a domain name, you are actually registering the rights to a domain in your name for a period of one, two, or up to ten years. You can register domain names from domain Registrars or through Resellers. You will type in your chosen domain name in the search box at a Registrar and, if it's available, you can "purchase" it for about ten dollars per year.

If you would like to own a domain name that is already registered by someone else, you can find the owner and see if they want to sell it. There are online marketplaces that have auction and/or fixed price sales websites where owners can list their domain names for sale. Many domain names expire if the owners overlook or forget to renew them or if they no longer want them. You can register these domain names when they become available to buy if you think you can sell them for more in the future, or use them to develop a website.

Again, you don't actually "own" the domain name. You instead have an exclusive right to use that particular name. Remember you will also have to pay yearly renewal fees to keep the domain name in your Registrar's account. Since the domain name isn't technically yours, there are circumstances where the domain name can be taken from you, either by a committee with authority over the Registry database or even a court of law.

Here are two simple rules where you shouldn't register just any domain name:
- Trademarked by a company or person.
- Are a company or person's name.

Trademarks and domain name risks will be covered in Chapter 8. But before registering any domain name, you should do your research and find out all you can about the name before registering. Domain name buying and selling is a business. And like any business, you should know what you are doing. If you just simply start registering names without understanding the domain name business and the risks involved, you could end up not only losing money by registering names that have no market value, but could lose more by having names that are trademarked where you might find yourself in legal trouble.

Think of buying domain names as an investment.
Before registering domain names for investment (whether through new registrations, expired names, or names bought on the secondary market), you should already have developed a strategy as to how you are going to be profitable. If you don't have a clear vision as to how you are going to make money with your domain investments, you should probably either wait and do more research or stay out of the domain name investment business altogether. Otherwise you may just be throwing money away.

Domain name investing not only includes finding marketable domain names, but also making some money for your business while you are holding the domain. A domain name that is just sitting in your Registrar's account that is not on a lander or marketplace getting sales inquiries, or not parked somewhere generating traffic and/or ad revenue, is actually going to cost you money. Not only have you invested the registration fee, but if you don't do anything with the domain name, you will also be faced with renewal fees to maintain the registration.

Domain investing is to try and generate as much revenue as you can, both while you are holding the domain and then the greater value for a final sale. If you can use good strategies to earn money through parking ad revenue or leasing, you can essentially pay for the domain name's renewal fees year after year while it increases in value over time. Generating revenue from a domain name will be covered in Chapter 6.

Domain Name Investment Rules

The main goal in domain investing is to find marketable domains and sell them (eventually) for a profit. However, with domain names being registered at an alarming rate with heavy competition for the best names, it can be difficult to come up with good domain names that have not already been taken by somebody else. The domain rules below are meant to be a quick guideline - more to keep you from registering bad names than finding profitable domain names. You will soon learn that finding domain names that will eventually sell for a profit requires a lot of thought and effort, as well as experience.

Rule #1: Avoid Clever Domain Names

The most profitable domain names do not use clever tag lines. If a domain name makes you chuckle or is the slightest bit embarrassing (or has a sexual connotation), that does not make it marketable Instead, domain name investments should always look at how a business or company would use that name for their online presence. If you think a name that is funny, like it was based on a joke, can be resold for a big profit, you should think again.

For the most part, you should also avoid abbreviations and minimalist spellings. If you register the domain name "4tune.com" you will be sending free traffic to "fortune.com" every time you mention the domain name in conversation. The same goes for the use of "2" for "to", "u" for "you" and other similar substitutions. And although short acronyms can be a great investment, longer acronyms (like 6 letters long) are a tough bet

Other domainers and webmasters have known this for a long time and they're not going to buy up your collection of substitution domain names. As a matter of fact, many such names have already been registered and then dropped because of their lack of resale value.

You should also avoid "domain hacks" such as heaven.ly or buy.it. Although there have been a small number of reported big sales with these, they are long-shot investments at best. These clever, joke and domain hacks will more often than not only end up with you trying to sell these names to other domainers, lucky to make any profit at all. Most likely you will end up dropping them because they don't have any resale value at all.

Rule #2: Use Good Investment Strategies

To be a good investment, a domain name for a business must be able to distinguish itself from that business' competition. Even if you are simply wanting to flip the domain name for profit, you should still think like you are setting up a business while researching good domain names. There are several things to focus on in your research:

What is your target market ...

First think of business markets that you may already know something about or have a keen interest in. Try to research domain names about this market, but not too specific of a niche at the start. Use search tools, such as Google's Keyword Tool, and other resources to identify keywords related to business categories in this market. With these keywords, search for available domain names that might appeal to a business owner in this market.

While most of the highest value generic domain names have already been registered, keyword searches may uncover niches in business market categories that may be untapped. And with shorter generic names unavailable to most investors, domainers are looking more at how the popular search engines are considering rankings. One newer trend is "long tail" keywords. These are domain names with three or more keywords related to specific businesses where if someone searches these keywords, a website built on a longer domain may rank higher, making it more valuable. An example of a long tail keyword domain name is: SacramentoHealthCareProviders.com

What is trending ...

Investing in domain names can be a lot like investing in the stock market. For those that took a chance on Amazon or Apple stock back when those companies started, if they held on to that stock for a long time they made huge profits on their investment. Good domain name investors follow the latest news and trends, particularly those regarding new cutting edge products in technology. Some trends, like crypto currencies, seemed to come out of nowhere. But there were many investors back before 2016 that had already registered great crypto and bitcoin domain names at a time when hardly anyone knew what these were. Good artificial intelligence (AI) domain names are mostly in the hands of investors, as well as cannabis/marijuana domain names as this product is becoming legalized in many states in the US.

Other trends turned out to backfire. As hoverboards quickly increased in popularity, domain name investing skyrocketed. However, once they started having fire problems with their batteries, the demand for this product dramatically dropped and nobody was interested in hoverboard domain names any more.

Longer term trends include nanotech, virtual and augmented reality, driverless vehicles, blockchain, etc. None of these is likely to disappear in the coming years, although the popularity of each may fluctuate. And this is just in the technology field, one of many different fields of interest.

What is your own idea ...

Sometimes you have to take a few risks in investments and, with a little experience in domains, you might have your own ideas about what might be profitable. Just because you are the first in a potential market does not mean it won't payoff in the end.

But you should still first do as much research as you can so you aren't blindly buying names. And don't get carried away and invest hundreds, or even thousands of dollars on your idea. If you keep these kinds of investments as a smaller part of your overall portfolio, they may pay out in the long run with less risk.

Rule #3: Consider Buying Domain Name Alternatives

If you find a good .com domain name in a market you think is valuable, you may want to consider spending a little extra on registering some of the other top extensions with the same name. With a number of extensions in the name secured, the package of names could be marketed to a potential business. But remember, there's no need to go crazy on alternative extensions (unless you want to), as long as you make sure you at least buy the .com, .net and .org versions of the domain.

You can also consider registering the singular and plural forms of a domain name, along with any good hyphenated versions as well. For instance, "GreatCar.com" and "GreatCars.com" but also "Great-Car.com" and "Great-Cars.com." But this type of investment should only be done if you have a very specific plan on marketing these names to an end user.

As a domain investor, you should avoid domain names that are misspellings of popular online businesses. This is called typo-squatting and is covered in Chapter 8 in more detail. There are businesses that sometimes register these so if a user is typing their main website name in a browser but misspells the name by one letter, that misspelled name could forward to the correct site. But domain name investors should stay away from these.

You also shouldn't register hyphenated names of already-popular websites as this is a variation of typo-squatting. And avoiding trademarks is a must. As stated several times through this book, you should never tailgate on a registered trademark. The Dell Computer Company was notorious for filing lawsuits against domainers that had registered names with the word "Dell" in them. This was true even for sites such as DellSolutions.com and DellBackup.com, which were in essence helping the company. If you register domain names with trademarked terms, you could find yourself facing legal challenges from a major corporation.

Rule #4: .com is King

The .com extension of a domain name is always worth more than any other TLD for the same name. However, the smaller price tags on alternative TLDs of short English words could make them ideal for someone starting on a low budget, but they are much harder to market for resale.

As an investment strategy, you should not be putting loads of money into second-choice names with alternative TLDs. A name like computer.com is great, although unreachable for most investors. A name like computer.net is good, but not nearly as good as computer.com, and better marketed as an online networking site than computer sales. But a longer name with a new TLD extension like thebestcomputers.online is practically worthless in terms of resale value, unless a good website is built and marketed to get traffic for the site. If the .com is not available, it is best to turn your attention elsewhere.

Buying Tips for Newbies

Since every domain name investment is unique, it's difficult to give advice that will be beneficial to a specific opportunity. And for someone with little-to-no domain buying experience, much of what you read may not make sense without having that actual experience. So if you want to start registering names, and after following the general investment rules above, here are some general tips for novice domainers in terms of domain name investing to help get you started.

#1 Put Your Name Out There

When you register a domain name with the intent to resell it later, it's important to make it as easy as possible for potential buyers to get in touch with you. Of primary importance is for the information you enter in the domain's Whois record to be correct. If you have an incorrect telephone number or an email address that you never check, you may never know if a potential buyer is trying to contact you.

The next most important thing to do is get your domain name on a landing page somewhere. Even if you are not yet ready to set up your own website, there are many sites that will allow you to place and market your domain names for sale.

#2 Don't Settle for Just a Small Profit

If you register a domain name for $10, you should not be looking to sell it for $20. Even though this is double the money, the small amount in dollars you earn is not worth your trouble.

When buying domains on the secondary market, be very careful about overpaying for domains. If you see a domain on the market for $500 that you feel confident you can resell for $750, you should probably just walk away from that domain. That difference can easily be used up, not only in your invested time, but also in any fees associated with selling the domain name.

Domains are usually so hard to sell that there has to be a clear profit margin of many multiples of your original investment. If you're registering new domains, you've only lost the small registration fee on a bad domain if it doesn't sell. But for domains purchased on the secondary market you have more investment dollars at risk. A domain purchased for $200 is a much larger loss than a $10 domain if it doesn't pay off. This is why it's necessary to do your research and try to find better value: the $200 name that should fetch $1,000 or more, or the $500 name that should fetch $5,000 or more. The more you spend the higher your risk may be, but you may also realize a much larger profit to make up for other domains in your portfolio that don't sell..

If, for instance, the best you can do is double your money on a domain name sale, you would have to sell half of your entire portfolio for double your investment just to break even overall. And some of your domain names just won't sell – all domainers go through this. It just happens. Even the best domainers with large portfolios may be lucky to sell 5% of their inventory in any given year. What you think might be a great name can instead wind up sitting in your portfolio for years. And near the end of each year when you are faced with the decision to renew the registration or not, you may be asking yourself, "Now why did I think that domain name was worth anything?"

#3 Try Diversifying

There are some investors that wait to register the perfect domain name. Although this is a safe way to invest (and requires a lot of patience), relatively few domainers can actually practice this. Others end up registering names right and left, hoping to play the percentage game by making enough money off of the small number of their domains that will actually sell to offset the registration costs of the other names still in their portfolio.

When starting, it is probably best to be somewhere in the middle. You need experience buying and selling domains to better understand the market. But you don't want to over-invest in worthless domains. A diversified approach, using keyword domains as well as trending markets may be best, concentrating on the .com extension. Having a diverse portfolio will allow you to have more chances in different markets to increase your chances of making a profit.

#4 Don't Bet Money on Credit

There is risk in domain name investing and it takes upfront money to get started. And once you become somewhat knowledgeable in the domain name business, you may think you have certain angles or methods that require you to invest more money than you have.

The worst thing you can do is start betting that the next domain name will make you the profits needed to pay off your previous domain name registrations or, worse yet, losses on domains that didn't sell. There are many stories of domainers who got trapped in a cycle of registrations and renewals using credit cards to invest in the next big thing, only to sink further into debt.

Remember you should only invest money that you can afford to lose. Yes, there are success stories of people who started small in this business and ended up hitting it big. However, most domainers are barely breaking even and there are many who have lost money, sometimes significant amounts, betting on domain names.

#5 Don't Think a Domain Name Will Sell Itself

Domain investing takes time and effort, not only to research good domain names, but to also sell them. Just because you think you have made a great domain name purchase, that does not mean you can just sit back and wait for the offers to come.

To get the most profit out of your investment, you need to properly market your domain names. That means not only setting up landing pages for your domains to capture any "type-in" buyers, and it is best if each domain name has its own lander – with the domain name forwarded to that landing page. Your best potential profit will come from prospective business owners, who you will need to seek out through good research, and then contact through proper outbound emails.

Finding Available Domain Names

When looking for domain names to register, you want to take your time and do your research. Understanding the availability of domain names also helps. To get a feel for different types of domain names, it is a good idea to follow online domain auctions and make-offer/buy it now classified listings. It is also a good idea to stay on top of recent domain name sales. Through all of this knowledge you will have a much better understanding of what other domain names are selling for as well as domain name availability on the secondary market.

Through this research, you may see some trends in certain keywords for new names to register, or you may find some names you might want to buy. If you are registering a new domain, you will simply go to your prefered Registrar and type in the name and buy it. However, for secondary market purchases, other factors should be taken into consideration before making your purchase, including:

- Is the domain name in an extension (like .com) where you will have a much easier market in which to resell it?
- How important is it for you to secure this specific domain name?
- What kind of budget do you have available for purchasing the domain name?

When looking for names to buy, you should have an idea if you are looking to try and sell it quickly, use it as an investment and be ready to sit on it for a number of years, or develop it into a website. There could be different approaches to choosing names depending on how you are going to use the domain name.

As an example, if your goal is to build a website, then you will want to find names that are related to profitable websites, like travel or technology. These niches tend to have the best affiliate programs and you may find it easier to generate traffic to these types of websites. You could also look at e-commerce names in order to set up an Amazon FBA or affiliate site. Again, targeting a good name in a particular niche (and with a .com extension) can be profitable with a little effort.

If your intention is to buy a name and hold on to it for a while for a longer term (and potentially greater profit), then short names in the .com extension are a good bet. Since nobody can hand register a short name (such as LLL, LLLL, NNNN, NNNNN – see Appendix B under "Domain Types" if you don't know what these letters mean) as they are all "taken," if you do some research in these markets then you may be able to find one that is undervalued and stash it. These names will most likely only go up over time, although some markets, like the LLLL.com (or 4L.com) market had some tough fluctuations which led short-term investors to lose money.

Other domain names to buy as an investment are good keyword domains. These can be found after doing a bit of research. A good place to start is the Google Keyword Planner. You first should have an idea of a market or niche you are interested in. Once you type in keywords associated with that market, you will see a list of words, some better and some worse, and how popular they are. It is best to stay away from trends when looking to buy a domain name for a longer term investment.

But if you are looking at turning over domains in a shorter time span, then searching for names with trending keywords is usually the best way to go. Many domainers set up their business strategy based on shorter-term volume sales.

Types of domain names to consider:

- **Timely Names**

  This works best when you can equate a time-frame to a specific event during that time. An example here could be WorldCup2022.com, which was first registered back in 2003. But as you can see, you will need to buy these well in advance so someone can see the value of buying the name well before the event happens. Once the event is over, the name becomes virtually worthless.

- **Business Names**

  Here the focus is to try and find generic business names. If you have an opportunity to buy names, such as doctor or dentist, then it will be great. You can give your investment a further boost if you are able to get both generic business names and geographic names.

- **Geographical Names**

  These refer to names of countries or cities. New and emerging places can potentially land you a nice profit on your investment. Your potential targets could be some that developers may wish to build some community-based portals, or design brand new services to cater to those particular communities.

- **Generic Names**

  These refer to simply a service or product. If you move fast enough for a new and emerging product, then the upside can be profitable. It's best to stay generic, such as with virtualreality.com and not oculusrift.com - you don't want to get caught with trademark or copyright issues.

It is a good idea to keep lists of keywords and domain name ideas. With these lists, you will be taking a more calculated approach to buying domains. Too many domainers make the mistake of registering arbitrary names, or finding names on an auction site or forum and bidding on them or buying them because they sound good, without actually doing research into available markets and opportunities for each name.

There are also online websites that can "help" you find available domain names to register. These sites are typically based on keywords – you type in a word and the site will return lists of available names to register with that word as part of the name. You can usually filter by extension, domain length, etc. Although these sites can be helpful, more times than not they will tempt you to register more names than you should in a particular market or niche. These types of sites are actually geared more towards end users than domain investors.

Where to Buy Good Domains

There are a lot of places (and ways) to buy domain names – direct buys, auctions, expired domains, registering new domains, backordering domains, etc.

Here are some of the options you have:

1. Buy Domains from Registrars

When it comes to registering domain names, you can use any domain Registrar. There are many Registrars to choose from so it is recommended to use a Registrar you can trust, which we will cover more in Chapter 8 – Domain Risks.

Typically, a domain will cost you anywhere from $7 to $12 or so for a .com extension for one year of registration. Some extensions cost a little more and some are less. But you should always be looking for where you can register your names for less, unless you value a trusted Registrar more. Be sure to always look for coupons and promo codes before registering any domain. Most Registrars offer deals from time to time.

Some Registrars, for example, offer 99 cent domain specials, or a free domain name when you sign up for web hosting. It is recommended to use coupon sites like RetailMeNot.com to check for coupons codes, and you should look to use a code with every domain name registration – you should not pay a Registrar's full domain registration price if possible, even if it only saves you a few dollars – those few dollars add up when registering multiple domain names.

And even if you find a good deal at a Registrar where you may not want to keep the domain, look at their policies regarding domain name transfers. After a period of time, usually 60 days, you can transfer your domain name from one Registrar to another. You might want to transfer because you want to keep all of your domain names in one place to better manage them. Or, perhaps you find out the Registrar where you have the domain is not trustworthy. You may also want to transfer to a Registrar that has lower re-registration fees, especially if your domain name is about two months from its end-of-registration date and you are thinking of keeping it for a longer period of time.

2. Buy Domains at Online Marketplaces

There are many online platforms where you can buy domain names. Some are auction style (see below), some are "fixed price" or "make offer," and some are a combination of each. If you find a domain name you are interested in that is listed as "Make Offer," it never hurts to send a query with the possibility to begin a negotiation. Many times, however, the seller has a very high price in mind and won't even respond to what they consider "lowball" offers, so you may not even get a response.

There are many fixed price or "Buy It Now" domains on many marketplaces. These are easiest because the seller has already selected the price they want to sell the domain name for and, if you think it is a good price, you simply select the name to purchase and the deal goes through, no negotiation required. But that shouldn't stop you from still trying to negotiate. If the domain name is something you have a great interest in and you see it listed for sale at what you think is too high of a price, you can always check to see who the owner is through a Whois search and then try to contact them directly to see if you can negotiate a lower price.

3. Buy Domains at Online Auctions

Buying domain names on an auction website can be thrilling. Excitement can build when you place a bid and wait to see if anybody else bids higher or you win the auction. But you should use the same type of research for bidding on a domain at auction as you would when registering a domain name as you don't want to waste money on something that you can't sell.

Somebody is selling a domain name in auction that you think may have some value. The listing says the domain name is parked and is getting a lot of traffic. But auctions are sometimes slow and there is only one low bid so far. Do you go ahead and place a bid? You shouldn't until after you first do some research.

It is a good idea to watch a number of auctions on a number of different auction sites to see how they work. You can also post in domain name forums to learn more about any specific rules or what type of domains sell best. particular auction site.

For each auction site, it is important to understand their rules regarding starting prices, reserve prices, the BIN (Buy It Now) price, bid increments and any other particular guidelines for the buying and selling of domain names on their platform. For instance, some sites might extend the auction end time if someone places a bid in the last hour or X number of minutes, while others have a set end time and potential buyers can wait to place their bids at the last second and try to "snipe" the auction.

When buying at auction, it is important to remember that once you place a bid it is binding and cannot be retracted. Your bid only becomes void if someone else places a higher bid. But if your bid has not met the seller's reserve price (if one is set), then you won't win the auction, even if your bid was highest.

Many auctions may start at a low price to encourage bidding, so you should understand what your highest price point may be for a particular domain and stick to it. If you get caught up in the excitement of an auction you could end up over-paying for a name. Some auction sites allow you to bid a "Max Price" – it will only show the lowest bid, but will automatically increase your bid when others place a bid that is not equal to or more than your Max Price bid.

Some domain name sellers use auction websites as a way to trim their portfolio or get rid of names that they have been trying to sell to end users but have not yet been successful. These names may be nearing their end-of-registration date. You should check the domain name's registration date (through a Whois search) so if you win the auction you will know how long you will have the domain name until you need to renew its registration. Some auction sites will automatically require you (or the seller) to pay for an additional year of registration.

4. Buy Domains Directly from Owners

What if you have your eye on a name that is already registered but it's not for sale on an auction site or other online marketplace? One way is to contact the owner directly and make an offer. Sometimes they may bite, other times they may not. But you'll never know until you ask.

If there is already an active website on the domain you want, you will most likely have an impossible task in buying it (unless you are willing to pay a very high price). If there is not a website and you can't find the name on any market places, then performing a Whois search is the only way to find out who owns the domain name. But you still may end up not finding the owner if they are using privacy on their domain name registration. If this is the case, it is probably best to move on to another name.

It is always important to remember, you should not just try to buy any domain name that you can think of. It is better to be patient and do your due diligence for each and every name you may consider buying.

Figuring Out Your Investment Strategy

When looking to buy domain names, you should consider how best you want to strategize your purchases. For instance, with a thousand dollars to invest, you could register one hundred new domains at about ten dollars each. With these new "hand regs," you have the opportunity to make a good profit on each of them if you choose your names wisely. Unfortunately, most new registrations are hard to re-sell, and you might be lucky to sell five out of the hundred in your first year.

With that same thousand dollars you could look in the secondary market and find names that have already been registered that are for sale. Although they, like you, are looking to sell for a profit, they may not see the same value in certain domain names as you. For instance, they may have bought a hundred domains and now, six months later without any sales, have reduced their prices (and expectations) and are seeking whatever profit they can out of a good chunk of their domains. This is where you may be able to find an opportunity.

On the secondary market you can also find short names for investment. As previously mentioned, these names are likely to gain in value over time so they are safer investments, although they probably don't have the potential for a large profit in a shorter time span.

As a new domainer, it is probably best for you to invest in a range of domains, with a combination of new registrations, secondary market values and short names for investment. By having these different types of domain names in your portfolio you will be able to see for yourself which types of domains you would like to build your business around – and there is no better way to learn than by experience.

Buying a Domain Name from a Third Party

What happens if the domain name you want is already owned by a third party? It may be offered for sale but not for a particular price or at auction, or maybe the domain name is just not being used. Either way, it would be up to you to contact the owner and either ask an open-ended inquiry as to whether the domain name is for sale, or to make an offer to buy the domain name directly from the current owner. Most likely, if you simply ask if a domain name is available, the current owner will say "Yes" and ask you to make an offer.

While nothing can guarantee the success of any particular transaction, much will depend on the current use of the domain name and at what price the current owner values the name. Using the right approach can increase your chance of completing a successful transaction, while maybe at the same time reducing the amount you'll have to pay to secure the domain name.

Negotiating as a Buyer

When buying domain names, your negotiating skills can be essential in not only securing a good domain name, but sometimes necessary so the deal doesn't fall apart. If you are dealing with an unreasonable seller, you may need all of your best skills if you really want to buy a particular domain.

A good negotiator for a domain name will try to get to know the seller's name if possible. You can perform a domain search on a Whois page of a Registrar, you can go to the website shown on an email address, or you might try random searches on a search engine to find a name. You are always in a better negotiating position if you know more information. This research can always influence the price you might want to start with to make an offer.

Making an Offer
Once you have identified the owner of a domain name you want to buy directly, there are a number of ways to reach out to the owner. Your approach may vary

depending on the market value or uniqueness of the domain name. But you should always be professional in all of your dealings.

Here are three basic approaches to making an offer:
1. Making Relaxed Conversation
2. Starting with a Low Offer
3. Making a More Realistic Offer

Making Relaxed Conversation
You might begin with an approach to simply find out if a domain owner even has any interest in selling the name. It's your first contact with the domain owner so you want to stay short and to the point. Here's one way you could word a relaxed email:

> Hello,
> Are you the owner of Zelks.com? I don't see a website associated with this domain name and was wondering what plans you had for the name.
> Regards,
> (Name)

The relaxed email should be different if the domain name has an active website, and could also be tweaked based on some particular circumstance. The main point of this relaxed approach is that you don't state any interest in buying the domain name. If you just come out and say you want to buy the domain, you either might not get any response or they may fire back with some high outrageous amount.

However, you also run the risk that the domain name owner may not take your relaxed approach seriously, so they could also either ignore your email or respond with an inflated price anyway.

If you don't get a response following the example above but are still interested in pursuing that domain name, you can always wait a few weeks and then send another type of email, maybe using a different email address or even a different identity to see if you get a response.

If you do get a response that is something other than a quoted price, you can then email back with one of the following offer approaches.

Starting with a Low Offer

This approach also doesn't work if there is an associated website with the domain name. If it's a good domain and has a current, functioning website, then it is most likely not for sale. If the owner does want to sell, it will most likely be at a high website price. But if it's a good domain and you'd rather start with an offer rather than a relaxed email, you can craft a more specific email while suggesting a price which is lower than what you would really pay, but not too low where you might not even get a response. You're just not going to get something like shoes.com for $1,000.

So if you want, you could try a low offer email, something like this:

> Hello,
>
> Are you the owner of Zelks.com? I don't see a website associated with this domain name and am looking at names for my business. Zelks.com is on my short-list.
>
> I have a budget of around $500 for a domain name and could quickly complete a deal. Are you interested in selling Zelks.com and, if so, at what price?
>
> Regards,
> (Name)

Although it's unlikely the seller will accept your initial offer, sometimes an offer for a domain name that's been sitting in their portfolio for a while is tempting. But since you're first offer is well below what you might really pay, you have room to negotiate if the domain owner counters with a higher number.

Making a More Realistic Offer

If you have a larger budget and are looking to acquire a higher value domain name, you may have a better chance at closing a deal by not sending a lowball offer. A more realistic offer will get the domain owner's attention. This, of course, ruins any chance of buying the name at a discounted price, but when you are dealing in premium domain names, domain name owners typically know the value of their domains.

However, it's also true that most domain name owners, when they receive a very good offer, won't just turn it down. They may still insist on an unreasonable price and, in these cases, you're not going to get the domain name anyway unless you over-pay. But for many domain owners that are truly interested in selling their names, a more realistic offer in your first email may give you a much better chance at getting the name.

Again, you want to be short and somewhat to the point. Here's one approach at a more realistic offer in an email you might send:

> Hello,
>
> Are you the owner of Zelks.com? I am building a website for a client and am looking for a good domain name. We have a $2,000 budget and came up with a list of names that might fit the style we are looking for. I am contacting the domain owners for the names on our list, which includes Zelks.com.
>
> Please let me know if our $2,000 offer is acceptable and I can either send you the funds direct through PayPal or have it wired to your bank the next day. Just let me know your PayPal address or bank information.
>
> Regards,
> (Name)

Let's take a look at the language in this email:

1. You did not say you will be the 'owner' of the domain name. Instead you said you were working for a client on a website. If you figure the domain owner is going to counter with a higher price, you have already set yourself up with your next response, which would be something like "My client says he has a set budget and your price is too high." With this, you are trying to see if the domain owner might come back with a lower price. If they won't come down as far as you want, you could further reply with "I will see if I can get the client to approve a budget increase ..." This again makes the domain owner think they

are just dealing with someone who is working for someone else, without any emotional investment in the deal.

2. You also said you had a list and were reaching out to the owners of the domain names on that list. This could lead the domain owner to think there is competition, and if they don't respond quickly the buyer may instead buy another name on the 'list.'

3. By including methods of payment with your offer it makes you a more serious buyer in the eyes of the seller. And the way you word this using 'direct" and "next day" helps by having the domain owner think they can actually have this amount of cash in their hand that quickly.

Using this type of approach in your first offer email can be very strong, so it is important what you say. It could be the difference between continuing a negotiation or being ignored.

This approach also won't get you the next shoes.com for $10,000, but it should be good enough to complete a deal at a reasonable price on most unused domain names.

Negotiating and Counter Offers

As an example, your first offer on a very good domain name was $2,000 (using the "working for a client" strategy) and the domain name owner responded with, "I have already had other offers which were higher. The lowest I will go is $10,000."

Since you don't know exactly who you are dealing with, and aren't with them in person to see their body language, you should not fully anything they say. Once you've been in a number of negotiations, you'll most likely hear the "I have already had other offers" quite a bit. If they had other offers, then why didn't the name sell?

Continuing with this example, unless you think $10,000 is a good price, you could instead reply with something like "Sorry, that figure is outside of my client's budget. I may be able to get him up to $5,000, but he may not even agree to that. Thank you for your time."

By saying "thank you for your time" you are essentially ending the negotiation. But the seller will most likely respond back to you nine times out of ten. There are times in negotiations you have to take risks, as well as being patient. With this experience you will learn to gain confidence in your negotiating skills.

Also remember to play up the competition. "Thank you for trying to make this deal happen but that price is too high for my client's budget. I think he will instead consider one of the other domain names he has asked me to look at. He still likes your domain, but he doesn't want to pay that much." This is definitely not what the seller will want to see in an email response.

In many deals, about a third of the initial asking price is where many agreements end up. There have been many successful transactions for very good names where a domain owner was first asking for $30,000 and the final price was $10,000.

There are a number of factors you should consider when negotiating a deal to buy, or even sell, a domain name:

- What is the most money you want to spend (or are able to afford) for the domain name?
- How important is that particular domain name to you?
- How did you initially contact the buyer or how were you contacted as a seller?

Since domain names do not have any set prices once they are registered, in most cases the final price that is agreed to will largely depend on your skills as a negotiator. As a buyer, you want the seller to agree to the lowest price possible, ideally lower than what you were actually willing to pay. And as a seller, you want the buyer to agree to the highest price possible, ideally higher than what you think is the domain's market value. And although you would like to have a smooth negotiation and come to a price that both parties agree is fair, this does not always happen.

If you have a project for a particular domain, say an e-commerce website in a trending niche, then in the end you may end up paying above market value, with the goal you can recoup your investment many times over with your website's success.

How an initial contact was made is also an important factor. If you use a general contact form on a domain owner's website and simply state your interest in the domain name, you may be in a better negotiating position from the start as opposed to sending a direct email to the seller from a company account that may suggest a larger budget is available to be spent. And it's also a good idea to be less formal in your emails – using "Hi …" instead of "Dear …"

The negotiation methods outlined below may be able to be used, either as a buyer or a seller, for a domain name. You should modify the language for your particular situation, but the ideas here could be helpful in either securing a very good domain for a reasonable price or selling a domain for above market value.

Negotiation Methods for Domain Names

There are a few methods you can use in domain name negotiations depending on the circumstance:

- Seek More Information
- Accelerate the Timeline
- Simplify the Transaction
- Reference Your Partners

When you use one or all of these different methods, you may find yourself in a better bargaining position than based on negotiating on price alone.

Seek More Information

While negotiating, a good tactic to use to break up the back and forth pricing is to ask for more information. What you want to do is get the other side to focus on something other than the money, and can be particularly helpful to your position if what you are asking for is something the other party doesn't know or isn't readily willing to tell you. As a buyer, this could lead to lowering the final price.

As an example, if you know the domain name doesn't have a live website attached to it, you could still ask them about how much traffic the domain receives, stating that information could help you better judge the name's value.

When the seller responds there is no website then you may have changed the thinking about the domain's worth from a *potential* value to an *actual* value.

This then would allow you to re-start the negotiations with something like this:

Hi (Name),

Without knowing what sort of traffic Zelks.com could receive, I am still interested in the name if a deal can be quickly closed. Without any current traffic or backlinks, I think $800 is a fair price. My offer is good for the next three days and I look forward to your reply.

Regards,
(FirstName LastName)

Accelerate the Timeline

Another way to break up the back and forth price negotiations is to place a deadline in your offer, as shown in the previous example. While doing this, you can also inject competition for other domains as well if you didn't already use this tactic in your initial offer:

Hi (Name),

I would like to move forward in securing Zelks.com for a new website that I am developing. I have a number of domain names on my list and need to make a decision in the next 3 days. I have an $800 budget to work with. If this is acceptable I can move forward very quickly with payment.

Regards,
(FirstName LastName)

Placing an impending deadline and inserting some competition might be enough to influence a seller to let the domain go at a lower value, particularly if they have owned the domain for some time and haven't received much interest. The seller might think he or she might lose out on the deal if you say you are looking at other domains for the same project, whether you are actually going to develop a website or not.

You want to be sure you use language that isn't too demanding or absolute. You don't want to say anything like "take it or leave it" or "this is my final offer" because those types of statements could just end the negotiation right there without a deal.

When selling a domain, you sometimes want to do just the opposite and slow the negotiation process down, particularly if the potential buyer is still below what you are willing to accept for the domain. With time, they might consider a better offer or have more time to think that you are not willing to quickly offload the domain at any price. But you don't want to move so slowly where the potential buyer can re-think their offer and decide it might not be worth it.

As a seller, at any time during the negotiation you can introduce competition by stating you have other offers, although most experienced buyers usually discount that kind of statement.

Simplify the Transaction
When negotiating a deal to buy a domain directly from a seller, the best leverage you have is money. How the transaction takes place could influence a seller to accept a deal for a lower amount.

One way is to avoid an escrow service and offer to pay all or some of the money up front and as quickly as possible. PayPal, for instance, is accepted by most and is an instant payment method, with safeguards in place that you will receive the item purchased. This avoids the additional cost and time of using escrow, unless the domain name is of such a high value (or over Paypall's upper limit) where you want to be completely safe with no risk. Here is an example:

> Hi (Name),
>
> I can immediately pay you through PayPal if you accept my offer of $1,000 for Zelks.com. We can then work out the simplest way of transferring the domain name to me.
>
> Regards,
> (FirstName LastName)

As mentioned, there is some risk in this approach. Most secure domain deals that are direct between buyer and seller are done through escrow or with a contract. But even with one of these safer approaches you can still use language in your negotiations that you will either quickly set up a wire transaction through escrow or accelerate the payment of funds upon a signed contract.

Reference Your Partners

When negotiating, another method of shifting the focus from the back and forth price exchange might be to introduce a third character or set of characters into the conversation. As an example, you could reference a partner as someone you need to talk to in order to continue negotiating:

> I am going to need to review your last counter-offer with my partners in order to decide if we will increase our last offer or not. I should be able to get back to you in a few days or so once we've discussed this amount.

Let a few days go by and then you can send another email like this example:

> I've discussed your counter-offer with my partners and although we'd like to make a deal for this domain name, our $1,000 budget is pretty well set. Can we do the deal for $1,000?

This doesn't keep you from eventually going higher, but at least gets the seller to think this might be the maximum amount you (and your partners) are willing to spend. You also don't have to wait until near the end of negotiating to mention your partner or that you are not doing this domain deal alone.

If you can't get to an agreeable price on a domain name you really want, you can always refer the deal to a domain broker, knowing you are going to have to pay a commission. A broker can serve as a fair mediator to bring a negotiation to a close, and can lead both sides to believing they are getting a fair price in the deal. There is more about domain brokers covered in Chapter 7.

Finishing the Deal

Once you've ended the negotiations and there is a price that is accepted by both the buyer and seller, it is time to finish the deal. To complete the transaction, it is a good idea to send a follow-up email with the deal terms, then discuss the payment method (if it wasn't already negotiated) and receive payment, transfer the domain name and confirm, then finish with a "thank you" email.

Follow-up

There may have been many emails back and forth throughout the negotiations. Specific parts of the deal, including domain transfer or method of payment, could be embedded in separate emails. Therefore it's a good idea to repackage the deal into one follow-up email that summarizes the terms of the deal:

> Hi (Name),
>
> Just wanted to follow up and make sure we've got the details straight for the purchase of Zelks.com. We've agreed I will purchase the domain name Zelks.com (of which you are the current registered owner) for $1,000. I will first send 50% of the sale price ($500) as a deposit.
>
> Once you receive the deposit, you will transfer the domain name Zelks.com to me. Once the transfer of Zelks.com has been completed and is in my account, I will send you the remaining $500 within 2 business days.
>
> Please reply to this email to confirm our agreement.
>
> Regards,
> FirstName

If the domain transaction is for a premium domain for a large sum of money, it is better to write out a contract, use a broker, or at least use an escrow service to hold the money (final sales price) until the domain transfer is completed. Generally, for good faith, it is best to split the fee for any 3rd party service in half between buyer and seller.

Payment

If you didn't already negotiate how the payment for the domain name is to be made, this finishing email is the time to do it. Most smaller transactions are simply a PayPal payment for the full amount from buyer to seller, then the domain is transferred to the buyer. Again, for larger transactions, an escrow service should be used.

However, since domaining is an international business, some methods of payment are not as easy to make. For instance, buyers and sellers in some countries cannot use PayPal. Also, if you live in another country beside the US, you may have a hard time setting up a wire transfer to a US bank or bank in another country. And even when using escrow, the escrow service could have restrictions on methods of payment. Most domainers have already worked through payment issues for their particular country, but they still must be clarified, preferable during the negotiations.

Transfer

How a domain name is transferred usually depends on whether the domain will stay with the same Registrar or the registration will be transferred to a different Registrar. Although the basics for most Registrars are similar, certain Registrars may have different processes for domain name transfers.

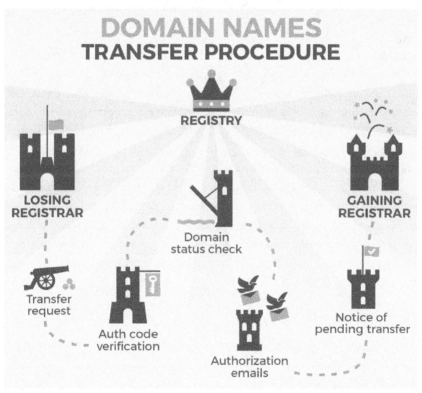

Source: gandi.net

Typically, the transfer of a domain name is done following one of these paths:

1. Within the same Registrar: this is known as a "push." The Buyer either creates an account at the same Registrar where the domain name is currently registered or already has an account there. Creating an account at a Registrar does not cost anything. Then with the passing of either a user name or number and/or an email account, the domain can quickly transfer from the seller's account to the buyer's account within the same Registrar.

2. To a different Registrar: this is a transfer between Registrars. In this case, the buyer does not want to keep the domain registered with the same Registrar where the seller currently has the domain name. Some Registrars have built-in processes for transferring to another Registrar, but in most cases transfer codes are typically used, as long as the domain name is out of a 60-day lock.

Confirm

Once the buyer has the domain name in their account, they should email the seller that the domain was successfully transferred as a confirmation. The buyer should make sure the registrant information has changed and, if not, manually change it so their contact information, as the new Regsitrant, shows up in the Whois record for the domain name.

Finish

Once the seller receives confirmation from the buyer that the domain has been successfully transferred, it is a good idea for the seller to reply to the buyer with a final email thanking the buyer for a smooth transaction. You never know when you might be making another deal with the other party, so it's good to be polite and courteous, regardless of whether the final price was what you wanted in the end or not.

Building a Worthy Portfolio

Building a high-quality domain portfolio can take years to accomplish. Often, the key is looking forward to what domains *may* become popular in the future and hedging through numbers by purchasing hundreds of domains. Others choose to purchase a few already high profile domains and sit on them, waiting (and sometimes hoping) that they appreciate in value.

In the domain names market, it is not uncommon for resellers or traders to buy hundreds of domain names in a short period of time. The logic is that it is easier to find the rare domains that will sell for a lot by registering a large quantity of names. But this method requires significant investment, as well as the additional time spent managing so many domain names.

For beginners, one suggestion is to start out with a mix of domain names. Not only should you hand-register some names you think have value based on keywords in a trending or future market, but you should also find a few good domains on domain marketplaces, be it in an auction or make offer/buy now situation. From there you can slowly build your portfolio. You should be conscious of the fact that it takes time (sometimes years) to build an impressive domain portfolio. The best strategy is to look for those potential big hitters. But you could also hedge your bet by progressively buying up more and more lesser priced domains, as long as you are following the rules, such as only registering names you believe will have interest to a business owner, would make a good company name, and be in the .com extension.

Another strategy is to only acquire domain names on the secondary market (or that have recently expired and are being dropped) that seem to have already gained some traction, and keep your fingers crossed that the value could appreciate even more. You should carefully research each potential name – what kind of traffic is directing to the domain name and what sort of website, if any, was associated with that name in the past. You should also check to see if that particular name has been sold before, along with checking recent sales of names that are similar.

In the next chapter we will discuss short-term domain flipping strategies, and in Chapter 7 will concentrate on longer term domain name sales. But to end this chapter on buying domain names, you should remember that it is very easy to buy a domain name, but quite difficult to sell that same domain name for a profit.

This means you do not want to just go and register tens (or hundreds!) of domain names that don't have direct potential business or website uses. Instead, you want to slowly build up a domain name portfolio with only quality names, concentrating on .com TLDs. At the same time, you want to create a name for yourself, either as a domain name business or under your own name, complete with a professional-looking website or attached to a third-party domain name platform.

Over time, once you have an established domain name business, your portfolio of domain names can give your business credibility. And with experience selling domains, you will learn better strategies in locating future potential domain name purchases.

Chapter 5 – Domain Flipping

Domain flipping is the business of buying and selling domains online in a relatively short amount of time. Keeping domain names for a longer period of time, as in many years, is more like domain investing, and selling domain names with this longer term in mind will be discussed in Chapter 7.

With domain flipping, the domainer is looking to make a nice profit with each sale so that money can be re-invested into purchasing new domains to flip. The bigger your profit from the previous domain sales the better domains you can pick up the next time, with maybe a little cash left over for yourself.

Domain flipping is very different from flipping websites. Website flipping is more involved and more complex: website hosting, adding content, finding ways of monetization, possibly outsourcing some work, and then finally backing up and transferring the website to a new owner. Website flipping takes a lot more work than domain flipping, and in short periods of time the margins for website flipping can be slim.

Domain Flipping Expectations

If you are starting a domain name business and want to flip names for quick profits, you should first have a better understanding of what to expect with domain flipping.

Domain Flipping Is Not A Get Rich Quick Business

There are many stories of people who have made millions selling domain names. The truth is, this is rare in the industry. There are not many domains that sell for over $100,000 and most domainers do not have the funds available to invest in such high quality domains.

Is it possible to make big profits through domain flipping? Yes – or people wouldn't do it. Most large sales of premium domain names are done by investors who have bought domains for large sums and sell them over time for even larger. This is called high end domain flipping. However, these high end domainers usually have years of experience and have gained much knowledge of the business along with relationships with domain brokers and other top buyers.

Shorter-Term Goals

With domain flipping, the goal is to keep the domains in your possession for a short period of time by only registering each domain name for a year. Your goal is to have it sold for a profit before the domain name renewal fees are due. This is a relatively quick turnaround from the time you first bought it to reselling it on the market. The intent of this approach is to find domain names that are undervalued or relevant to current events or trends in order to find buyers interested in capitalizing on those same current trends.

In order to be successful in domain flipping, you should get into a daily routine, possibly an hour or two per day. Your routine will include domain name research, looking at recently sold domain names, checking out drop and expired domain lists, and keeping up with current news and events. Domain flipping is also an active process. You will not be successful if you buy domains and sit on them waiting for a buyer to come to you. Instead, you will need to have good marketing, networking and negotiation skills to quickly sell domain names.

Unfortunately there is still a misconception about domain flipping, as many people think buying domains with the sole intent of trying to sell them to someone else for a lot of money is unethical. This goes back to the early years of the internet where domain flippers were buying names of popular companies and 'squatting' on the names with the sole intent of selling them to those companies for large sums of money. Trademark laws have ended the domain squatting practice. Since then, many multi-million dollar domain and website companies thrive on the business revenue of the buying and selling of domain names. As long as domain flippers aren't doing anything illegal, there is nothing wrong with taking advantage of a market of supply and demand.

In the last five years more than 200 million domain names have been registered, but many of these are not being used for websites. A good percentage of the unused domain names are held by domain flippers (and investors) who are trying to sell these domain names for a profit.

Although there are domain names that have sold for millions of dollars, these are generally names that have been held for a long time, or purchased for large sums of money and then re-sold – a sort of high end domain flipping approach. However most domain flipping is based on less expensive names as that is what most domain flippers can afford.

For those that would like to take a domain flipping approach to their new domain business (as opposed to investing in names and holding them for a long time), you most likely have a small budget to start with. Like domain name investments, it is best to not start out by registering many domain names without first doing research. With this approach you are more often than not bound to end up with a list of domain names you will not be able to sell. It is better to start with targeted domains with a particular niche or focus and gain experience with those before moving on to a wider field of domain names.

Finding Domain Names to Flip

Registering a domain name is simple. However, finding one that you can actually flip for a profit is much more difficult. There are many factors that determine a domain name's value, but the major factors for domain flippers are memorability and keyword/SEO optimization.

With experience, you will be able to determine what makes a good name to flip and what doesn't, just by name alone. Understanding markets and trends is important. With that knowledge you should be able to find good domain names that are memorable as well as marketable, whether it be a new registration or on expired domain name lists, dropped lists or auction sites.

Expired name lists are a good place to find domain names that are already search engine-optimized. This strategy can be beneficial in two ways. First, any domain that has already been purchased was probably already researched for potential benefits (for good or for bad). Second, and more important, is that many recently expired domains still retain some of the search engine optimization attributes that were built up by the previous owner. For example, a recently expired domain name may still have active backlinks on the web, and the page rank of the domain could still be high, giving the purchaser instant SEO recognition with minimal effort.

Using keyword research tools is another great way to find out which domains could prove to be valuable, as many webmasters use such tools when deciding which domains to buy. If you can obtain a domain name that contains a popular keyword, then you can find a buyer in most cases.

Flipping Domain Names

Buying what you believe may be a valuable domain name is the easiest part of the equation. Finding the right buyer for your names is much more difficult. Using auction sites and forums is perhaps the best way to find qualified buyers that are interested in your domains, and using auctions will take some of the stress away from establishing the value of a domain name yourself. But auction sites and forums consist mostly of other domainers, so you most likely will not make large profits.

If your domain name is related to a particular niche, then you may find success by advertising in forums that are related to that niche. Simply placing a link in the signature of your posts can tremendously speed up the selling process. While it may be possible to find prospective webmasters on niche-specific forums, it is generally better to advertise on webmaster forums where there is a high volume of potential customers.

As a domain flipper, quickly selling a name takes work. In most cases a name will not sell if you don't put in the extra effort. There is much more to cover regarding domain name selling, which is discussed in Chapter 7.

Volume Selling

Unfortunately, most domain names minimally take a couple of months to sell, and many times years, even with an attached website. Sure, there are stories of domainers registering a name and flipping it for a profit in less than a month, but this is rare. There is no need to become discouraged if your domain name does not immediately sell. Remember, if you just hand-registered a domain name, that means it had been available for anybody else to hand register before you did. The chances of you being able to turn that domain name around and sell it quickly for a profit isn't so easy.

Many domain flippers rely on volume to make a profit. They typically buy portfolios on auction sites or domain name forums, or seek out low-priced names that they think have more value. These volume domain name flippers often pick up domain names in large portfolios, sometimes for less than a dollar each from other domainers that have given up on those domains and didn't plan on renewing their registrations. They then turn around and quickly market them on other marketplaces, often with less than a month left on their registrations. They also may have other contacts and connections where certain names may have markets where those domain names may sell. Even if a volume domain flipper buys 100 domains for $100, all it takes is ten sales at $10 each to break even, but they often are more successful than that.

For the average domain flipper looking for quick turnaround sales, if they only buy a few domain names then the chances of selling any percentage of them is low. But if they buy domain names in bulk, then for the few they sell they have at least made some money, hopefully at least enough to pay for their other domain name registrations. The trick is finding what percentage of names they can sell in a given month and how quickly domain name renewals are coming up on the domains they buy. It is a balancing act that requires some skill, so they need to have tools in place to track their domains, as well as having strategies for how and where to sell different types of names and extensions.

Domain Flipping Tips

Because buying and selling domains can be a fun business, and chances of making good profits are there, many enter this business thinking they can easily make money. However, as mentioned before, you should first research all you can learn about the domain flipping business before investing large sums of money. If you start buying multiple names in extensions other than .com, without knowing where or to whom you are going to sell them, you are simply throwing your money away.

So to get you started, here are some domain flipping tips to consider:

Get Experience
When starting out, most domainers end up losing money buying useless domain names they cannot resell, or get caught up in the hype of a trend (like LLLL's or 6N's) after the peak and end up selling names for a loss.

Even if you intend to buy and sell names as a hobby or side-business, it is still a business and you need to learn all you can and get experience before you can be successful. For most domainers, it takes a year or two of selling domains before understanding how to make profits. Again, anybody can buy domain names – it is the selling of domain names where you get the experience you need to best understand this business.

Don't Concentrate On the Big Sale

With a domain flipping approach (as opposed to domain investing), you should be looking at turning over domains by volume. This will take time and effort on your part to develop a strategy for making profits. Looking for the occasional big sales is not the domain flipping strategy – that's more like domain speculation and is an entirely different approach. Sure you may find a particularly good name you may want to keep as an investment. But as a domain flipper you want to learn how to make multiple sales each month to keep the bulk of your inventory of names turning over.

Identifying Good Domain Names

You may hear others in the domain business say that "all the good names are taken." However, with so many new websites being created all the time, there is an ever-expanding market for domain names. It is true the single English word domains in the top extensions have all been registered, so people tend to think that there are not many good domains left. But that isn't true as the domain market has expanded into two- or three-word domain names with targeted keywords as well as pronounceable "brandable" names, which are becoming more popular by new companies, such as etsy.com, zillow.com and mynt.com.

When looking for good domain names for flipping, here are some ideas:

- Depending on your budget, generic names are popular as there are always new businesses (and other domainers) looking for these types of names. The so-called "brandable" names are not good for flipping as it might take years for these to eventually sell.
- If you plan far enough ahead, time-related domain names associated with sporting events or other popular gatherings can be profitable in a short window. Once the event has concluded, the domain name has little to no value.

- In order to help with search engine rankings, professions combined with the city, state, or province where the business is located rank well in search engines. More and more, even local businesses can increase their customers by using search engine optimization with a domain name with their locality. So, for example, a domain name that links chiropractor with Boston, like bostonchiropractor.com, has an end user market list of chiropractors where a domain flipper can offer perhaps a better domain name than what the business is currently using.

- Again, depending on your budget, identifying better-quality domain names that you find for sale on the secondary market that are under-valued can be a great opportunity. If your budget allows, you could buy a domain name for $1,000 and turn around and sell it for $2000-$3,000 if you think a re-seller value is at that level. Of course, if it is an exceptionally good name, you might want to instead invest and hold for a number of years, and then possibly sell for $10,000 or more to an end-user.

You Don't Have to Always Stick with .coms

Despite other advice in this book, profits can be made in other extensions than .com. The .com approach is best for domain speculation. However, if you have a good understanding of the markets for other TLD's or even country or new extensions, then this can be a good domain flipping strategy. There may be more risk with these names, but there can be profits to be made, particularly if you are able to find good names in other extensions that others are selling as part of a portfolio. You can many times find names for a dollar or less each by buying in bulk. If you find a few gems, even in other extensions, you might easily be able to make your investment back with just a sale or two.

Good names in extensions other than .com have the potential of being sold at higher values. Certain names in .net or .org can also be profitable, as well as country extensions like .io or .co. But you should only buy in these other extensions if it is a high value generic word, as well as finding one where the same name in the .com extension is not being used.

Hand-Registered New Domain Names

Even though flipping hand-registered domain names for a profit is possible, it's still unlikely. A new name has no age and no traffic. And because it is new, if somebody else wanted it, they would have been able to hand-reg it themselves before you did. And with a new name, you will have to put in a considerable amount of time and energy to market it, and still probably won't be able to sell it in less than a year.

Instead, domain flippers should be looking at domain drop lists to see if there are good names about to expire. Other avenues are auction marketplaces or domain forums – on each of these there could be good value in names that another domainer may not see, or maybe there are a few gems that are part of a portfolio or lot of names another domainer is selling in bulk.

If you have a higher budget, then you can search through Buy It Now listings or higher end auction marketplaces for better .com names. You should particularly look for .com names that are being sold that are also registered in all of the other TLDs, as these will already have built-in value based on demand.

Don't Develop Websites
It is true that just about any domain name is worth more if there is a popular website built on it with high levels of traffic. However, that traffic does not come overnight. It takes time to develop a good website and post original content with good SEO strategies in order to build traffic and thus increase the value of the domain name.

If you are a domain flipper, trying to develop a website on one of your domain names, with the intent of trying to re-sell the domain name in less than a year, is not a good use of your time. There are so-called website developers that have built businesses based on this strategy alone, but the websites they develop usually consist of duplicated (and many times years-old) content, rehashed over and over again, looking to make small profits on each sale.

If you enjoy searching for good domain names and then selling them, it is best to concentrate on domain names alone and not get sucked into trying to develop websites for re-sale.

Domain Flipping As A Business

Aside from the buying and selling of domain names, there are other factors to consider for domain flipping. This is where you identify your domaining as more of a business enterprise. What is it you want to accomplish with domaining? How will you set yourself up to differentiate you from other domainers? How much money do you have to invest and how will you make a profit?

Below are some tips that look at domain flipping as a business that you might find helpful.

Setting Up Your Finances

If you already have some experience buying and selling domain names, then you have a better understanding how important it is to budget how much you spend registering domain names. It is best to log each purchase on a spreadsheet so you can carefully follow your finances. This way you will always know how much you have spent with registrations. And as you begin to sell domains, you can track those sales in another column and begin to see your profits (or losses). It is better to clearly know these numbers so you can adjust your strategies as your business moves forward.

By knowing your domain flipping finances, you will be better able to set budgets for both how much you want to spend registering more domain names, as well as your targets for domain sales. Too many domainers start out registering many domain names (even hundreds!) without yet having a strategy of how they will sell the names. Profits and losses are important to understand in domain flipping, just like any other business.

Choosing a Niche

With so many domain names available, the worst thing you can do is just start registering names because they sound good, regardless of what the names are about. For example, if you have a large variety of names in industries as diverse as artificial intelligence (or AI), marijuana, porn, finance or bitcoin, you will be spread out across many different niches. However, you may not really know enough about each niche to understand what could make a profitable domain name or not. You should instead try to concentrate on more specific areas for the domains you register, hopefully in niches where you already have understanding or you've done your research.

Also, as a business, how do you want to represent yourself? Do you want to have a website or landing pages that have porn or adult-oriented names? How will you know where or to whom to sell your domains if you are spread across so many different niches? If you want to be successful domain flipping, it is better to be able to have an identifiable business with a more targeted approach so you can more easily market yourself and your business in order to make more consistent sales.

Building a Domain Portfolio

In order to be profitable in domain flipping, you will need to trade in volumes. What this means is you will need to build up a sizeable portfolio of good names in order to make money in any given year.

If, for instance, you have a total of 100 names, with good marketing efforts, landing pages and located on secondary marketplaces with reasonable prices, you may be able to sell five of the names, maybe ten if you are lucky. If that is all you sell, you want to be sure the profit on those 5-10 names exceeds the yearly registration costs for the one hundred names.

However, if you also target outbound marketing to specific companies based on better geo- or business-related names, you could sell much more than that. As long as you don't overprice these domains, you could find yourself making decent profits with good turnover. And with experience in sales, you will get a better understanding of good price points based on the type of marketing and audience you are targeting.

You may also find some domain names you bought for a quick flip end up increasing in value due to more demand in that market niche. If these don't sell in the first year, you will most likely renew these registrations and look for higher profits in the future.

For the rest of your names that don't sell within 9-10 months, it is a good idea to try and at least get your registration fee back by selling in bulk on a domain name marketplace or forum. There may be other domainers that think they can flip these names and you have nothing to lose to at least recoup the money you already spent, in which you can use that money to invest in maybe better domains. You don't want to find yourself in the situation of renewing hundreds of domain names without having a specific market or targeted end user in mind.

Strategizing Sales

The domain flipping business is based on sales, and you most likely are not going to sell all of the domain names you register. With experience, a domain flipper begins to understand which domains have the potential for quick flips and which may take several months or even years to sell for a profit.

Once you build up a sizeable portfolio, you will need to budget your time wisely. Each and every domain name has the potential for a sale and profit. But if you spend your time trying to push domains you just hand-registered instead of working on names you've held for a while, you may be wasting your time.

With a good domain name sales strategy, you will know, with experience, how to effectively price different types of names in your portfolio. You will also know how to better market your generic, niche and geo-based names.

Understanding Risks

As in any business, it is important to also know the risks involved with flipping domains. Chapter 8 goes into more detail about the overall risks involved in buying and selling domain names. For domain flipping, or domains you are looking to turn around faster than domain name investing, the main risk is financial. As you are most likely looking to buy more domains to flip than you would if you were investing, you have more names to manage, work on selling, and then after a year, decide if you want to renew each remaining domain's registration or not.

As your domain business grows, it will be even more important for you to keep your names well-managed. As you add more names to your portfolio, you need to be sure to keep up with your spreadsheet (or whatever tools you use to manage your domain names) in order to log all of the names you bought, how much you paid for them, their end-of-registration dates, and where you have them listed for sale. Being organized will only help save you time, which you could better use marketing and trying to sell your names as opposed to searching through multiple Registrar websites to see if you had listed this name or that name there.

The spreadsheet is also where you would log all of your sales and any other business-related expenses, including domain name renewals, auction listing fees, website hosting, etc. Running a domain flipping business is just that, a business. And you will need to track profits and losses on a yearly basis as for most domainers there will be tax implications for your business.

So Why Domain Flipping?

As discussed elsewhere in this book, most of the large profits domainers find are through locating quality names that are undervalued then selling them for considerable profit, oftentimes holding them for many years. But finding very good names to hold can be a challenge. And the longer you have multiple names in your portfolio, the more you have to spend on renewal fees. With domain flipping, you are working on smaller profits per sale, but will be making many more sales. You are essentially working on volume.

Domain flippers have a better sense of where and how to sell domains because they do it much more often than other domainers. They often have a network of contacts set up or else just know where to sell certain domain names based on what type of name it is. Through a higher volume of sales the smaller profits often add up to an acceptable overall profit margin.

Chapter 6 – Monetizing Domain Names

Just buying and selling domain names isn't the only way to make money in the domain business. Although the highest potential to make money from domains is by selling them, you can also make money by simply holding on to them.

There are several different ways you can monetize domain names while you own them. Some methods are easier than others and some can have higher returns than others. They all have their pros and cons, and they all take time and work to utilize effectively.

Affiliate Websites

Of the different ways to make money from domain names, affiliate websites are often the hardest and take the most time. It also requires knowledge of search engine optimization techniques and additional money to invest in PPC campaigns, which could end up outweighing the amount of money made from the affiliate links.

How Affiliate Websites Work

With an affiliate website, you'll first need to research a good domain name in whatever market you plan on building a website for. Once you find your market and available domain name, research web hosting plans before registering the domain. This is important because you might find a Regsitrar that also has web hosting, and will let you register a new domain name for free when you purchase web hosting. Or perhaps you can plan on setting up multiple websites, where a cPanel hosting setup might be your best option. If that is the case, then you can register a domain through any Registrar.

Once you start developing the website, you should look for companies selling products related to the domain you registered and sign up for their affiliate programs. There are also affiliate networks such as ClickBank and Commission Junction where you can find companies offering different advertising programs. These networks gather online companies into one place making it easier for you to find appropriate merchants for your site. They also make it easier to add links to your site and track click-throughs and conversions. Finally, they can consolidate the money earned from multiple companies into one monthly payment to you.

Once your website is live, you will need to start generating traffic to your site. Usually, this involves a mixture of search engine optimization (SEO), link building, PPC advertising, and social media postings. As your website's traffic increases, the website will inevitable begin to convert visitors into money, hopefully to at least pay for your web hosting and any other initial investments. And when it comes time you want to sell the domain, not only will the domain name have more value, but your website may add to the overall value and make you even more profit when you sell.

The Best Domains for Affiliate Marketing
The best type of domain name for an affiliate website is using a keyword-rich name in the same market as what the website is about. The domain name 'TheWebsiteDesigner.com' won't do much to help increase the page's ranking in search engines. However, a name like 'WebsiteDesign.com' is much better. If you want to target local traffic, a name like 'WebServicesNewYork.com' would work if you want to concentrate in one geographical area.

If you look to buy the domain from an online auction or sale, you might find a domain name that already has had some traffic and/or backlinks. If the website associated with the name already has a good amount of traffic, you will probably need to pay more for that domain than you normally would if the same domain name did not have an associated website with traffic. There are other smart people in the business who know the value of website traffic and won't give up an established domain name for a low amount.

You will often have to rely on what the seller tells you as far as how much traffic a domain name gets. So you should always do your own checking. Alexa may be able to give you an overview of the amount of a traffic a domain receives. Estibot is another source, which could include the popularity of related keywords and an estimate of the domain name's value with the associated website traffic. Most good website owners already have Google Analytics integrated into their website, so you should always ask to see these reports. You can also look at Google's Advanced Search to see how many sites link to a certain domain name and how old those links are.

If you're registering a new name and are just developing a website for it, then the extension won't make too big of a difference, although the .com is still preferred. If you think your traffic will come from a particular geographical area, then you may want to register the corresponding ccTLD and forward it to the main website's URL..

Developing an Affiliate Website
Website development is not easy. To start with you could use an online web-building tool offered by your web hosting company. Although these are easier for beginners, they are limited in terms of final layout and design and may not give you all the options you need for a successful affiliate site.

In viewing online resources for beginning web developers, there are some great videos and tutorials to get you started, but it takes a lot of work to get a complete website set up. There are so many little things that need to be done, from logos and graphics to social media integration and your first web content – and this is before adding the affiliate codes. There are professionals that can help you with your website, but this is an additional cost that you would need to recoup based on your affiliate revenue.

HTML (Hyper Text Markup Language) is the basic coding language for websites. You don't necessarily need to learn HTML in detail, but some HTML coding helps. There is HTML editing software like Dreamweaver that can help you with your website design. The main advantage of an HTML website is that you have much more control as to how your website looks.

Another option is to use a Content Management System (CMS) like WordPress. CMS companies are continually working to make websites easier to get started. It's also much easier to add and change content with a CMS website than it is with an HTML editor. WordPress, for instance, continues to add features that make their websites very dynamic, but this approach isn't always best for an affiliate site. Dynamic WordPress sites tend to look alike and many take a long time to load. There are hundreds of free templates available on Wordpress, many of which are stripped-down versions of templates for sale to buy. The full templates typically have more features than the stripped-down ones, but for an affiliate website you are looking to sell, the free templates are good enough.

113

Promoting an Affiliate Website

There are thousands of websites and books related to website promotion. If you have never set up a website before, it is advised to read as many different approaches as you can into both website development and how to market your website and build traffic. The end goal is to draw as many people with interest in your content to your website as you can, as the more quality visitors you get the more likely someone is to buy something through one of your affiliate links, thus earning you revenue.

The quickest way to start to increase traffic to your website is through PPC campaigns. But you have to choose the keywords you want very carefully in order to generate the right traffic while keeping the money you pay for clicks to an affordable rate. It could end up costing you more for the PPC than the money you can make through affiliate revenue, so you should be knowledgeable about the costs and effectiveness of a PPC campaign before getting started.

Effective Search Engine Optimization (SEO) is a requirement in order to rank well with the search engines. When building your website, there are available tools to help you when adding content so that you are creating web pages that aren't too short or too long while integrating appropriate keywords into each page or post. While good SEO doesn't cost you up front money, it is much more focused on long term results and takes a longer time to realize traffic. Another challenge comes from the search engines themselves, which won't rank affiliate sites without original content. So to optimize your site and increase your website ranking, you'll need to continue to add original content and links from other sites. Over time, these efforts will pay off in rankings when someone uses your keywords in the search engines.

You may find it best to promote your affiliate site with a combination of PPC and SEO strategies, making sure the long term and short term campaigns are both receiving the proper amount of attention. Also adding corresponding accounts in the top social media platforms allows you to potentially reach a different audience and garner more traffic to your website. A website with good, original graphics and/or photos should be on Pinterest, with each image pinned from its corresponding web page. Regular tweets on Twitter and posts to Facebook pages are also a must.

PPC Websites

A PPC website is almost the same as an affiliate-based site, except you earn money every time someone clicks on one of the ads on your website. This differs from affiliate marketing where you are typically only paid when someone actually makes a purchase. If you want to gear your website to more of a PPC approach, you will set things up a little differently from an affiliate site. Just beware there are a lot of scammers out there selling PPC websites or systems that are just trying to get you to give them money for their so-called expertise.

How PPC Websites Work

Unlike affiliate links where you typically only earn revenue if someone buys something, Pay Per Click (PPC) ads will make you money, albeit less per action than an affiliate site, whenever a visitor to your website clicks on one of your ads. An effective PPC website usually has a combination of informative articles, visually appealing graphics, and some type of networking system, like a forum. Once the site is complete, sign up for a PPC program, like Google AdSense or Bing Ads, and place the ads on your website. Many of these ad programs will automatically inventory the content on your website and then display related ads to the content.

For example, you publish an article on your website about lawn maintenance. You then take the code provided to you in your Google AdSense or Bing Ads account and put it somewhere on the same page as your article on lawns. The PPC system will see the keywords used throughout the article and, when your page is loaded, ads from lawn maintenance companies or other yard-related services will automatically be displayed on your page.

Using the same PPC code in the previous example, you now put it on a page with an article about finding the right shoes to match a new dress. When that page is displayed, your visitors will see related ads from shoe or clothing stores. Every page will display a different set of ads based on its content. And every time your website visitor clicks on one of your ads, you'll make money. The amount of money that you make per click depends on the popularity of that keyword and how much money those advertisers are paying to the PPC program to host their ads.

Many ads are also able to display different ads to each individual user based on their previous purchases or searches. More and more visitors are noticing ads directly related to searches or purchases they recently made.

One word of warning – don't be tempted to click on your own ads or have your relatives or friends click on your ads. Advertisers and PPC networks are constantly monitoring for click fraud. Clicking on your own ads could get you banned from your PPC program.

The Best Domains for a PPC Website

For a PPC website, you would be looking for the same type of keyword-type domains as for an affiliate site. You will also need to develop a website and promote it like you would for an affiliate site. And nothing is to stop you from including both PPC ads and affiliate links on the same site, if applicable.

Domain Parking

Registering a domain and then parking it with a parking service is one of the easiest options for a domainer when it comes to monetizing a domain name. But there are pros and cons to parking domains and only certain domain names should be considered for domain parking.

How Domain Parking Works

Domain parking is when you point your domain to a parking service via your domain's nameservers. That parking service usually has templates which have a number of PPC ads that are then placed on your parked website. You will then earn a percentage for each ad click-through that your parked domain generates.

As with affiliate websites, your means of making money relies on people landing on your site and clicking on one of the ads. If you have a domain name that doesn't attract any traffic, the name will gain nothing from being parked. Some parking companies won't even accept domain names that don't already have traffic.

The Best Domain Names for Parking

A domain name needs traffic in order to make money through domain parking. A new domain name isn't going to bring any kind of search engine traffic, especially once it's been parked, so these domain names would not be good for parking. You can always build search engine traffic by building a website, like an affiliate or PPC website. But then you are creating the traffic for your own ads or affiliate links, of which you will earn a higher percentage when compared to parking revenue.

So why would anybody choose to park any of their domains? There are several types of domain names where parking makes sense:

1. Maybe the name was once a developed website that search engines still remember. And the domain might also still have backlinks – direct links from other sites that pointed back to the previous website on your domain. If you buy a dropped or expired domain that was previously a website, parking it is a good idea. However, over time, the domain will lose its ranking in search once the engines see there is no longer a website. But backlinks can remain active for a long time, depending on how often the other sites' webmasters check their own links.

2. The domain name once had a popular website that people were used to typing into the browser (type-in traffic). This traffic can also be short-lived as once people see that the website they used to visit is gone, they'll likely stop typing it in, and you'll get less traffic.

3. People type-in a generic product name or keywords into their browser and add a .com, hoping they'll come to a site that's useful to them. The likelihood of this happening is slim, but it does happen. Single generic word domains are very expensive and there's usually more money in their resale value. Two- or three-word keyword domains are much less expensive and may have more value as an affiliate website. The reason people park such domains is to give them a 'resting place' and gain residual income until they develop a website or find a buyer.

4. People try to type-in a popular website name into their browser but mis-type the name. This is known as 'typo-squatting' and will be discussed as a Domain Name Risk in Chapter 8. For the purposes of monetizing domain names, it is best to steer clear of mis-typed names.

For most domainers, the keyword domains usually offer the best results with domain name parking. While single word domains would obviously yield better results, these types of names are very expensive and not typically available to most domainers.

To find keyword domain names to park, the best online tool to use is Google Keyword Planner. Once on the Google keyword planner site, you type in a keyword and the tool suggests various relevant key phrases that are often used in Google searches. Similar sites also provide an approximate view of how often those phrases are searched for, how many competing sites exist, and how many existing advertisers there may be for that phrase.

You could also use a short, common phrase for an effective parked domain name to draw in type-in traffic while it's parked. Any type of name that brings in any sort of traffic will work. But as with any of your websites with ads, don't click on your domain name parked site's ads ether. Doing so may lead to you getting banned from your parking service.

Domain Leasing

Domain leasing is when the domain name Registrant allows someone else to build a website on the domain in exchange for money. This is similar to a house owner renting out their house to a tenant.

For a domain owner, domain leasing has the main advantage of allowing the domain to increase in value over time while earning enough revenue to pay for renewal fees, plus extra if you have a high value name.

To advertise you have a domain name you want to lease, you can list the domain name in one of the popular leasing directories or you can market your domain name for lease on your own.

How Domain Leasing Works

Domain leasing websites, like NameForest.com, try to match advertisers or startups with domain name owners. On some sites, domain owners set the leasing prices for each of their domains, so they know they will be making more money through leasing than say parking the domain. Other sites have set fees for leasing and the domain owner has to judge whether what they can make on a monthly basis is worth it. Either way, the domain owner can make parking revenue on the domain while waiting for a lease.

One of the best things about leasing a domain name to an advertiser or business owner is that they will put content on the site, which will most likely increase the value of the domain. Lease terms generally have limitations of use to avoid a renter from filling the site with adult content or click bait ads. If your renter decides to end the lease, they leave you with a domain that now has traffic that other renters or buyers may want. Even if you end up re-parking the domain name, you will now earn more from parking revenue than you did before the lease.

It is also possible that a company or individual starts renting your domain and builds a profitable business. If their brand depends on the domain name as an important part of their business, they may offer to buy the domain name from you. You can either negotiate a sale, keep the domain and the lease terms, or better yet, try and sell the name on the market, now with a competitive buyer already in your pocket.

Why would a business rent a domain instead of purchasing one?

If you are thinking of leasing one of your domain names, it may help to better understand why a business would want to rent a domain instead of purchasing one. In many cases, a business owner may want to test a domain's viability before purchasing it. By renting it first the business owner can see what types of visitors and conversion possibilities a certain domain name has as opposed to relying on data collected by other parties. A business could avoid spending thousands of dollars by sampling a few different domains and deciding on a purchase after seeing real results.

A business might also have a spin-off product or other short-term plan for a domain that would end before they could recoup their purchase price of a high value name. And if your domain already has type-in or backlink traffic, even better for the renter, and you may be able to charge more, too.

Startup companies also like to use leased domains as they are typically bootstrapped for money and leasing a good domain name costs much less than purchasing an equivalent high value name. Additionally, startups sometimes have multiple ideas which they can much more easily test on multiple domains that are leased rather than investing in multiple domain names with a higher purchase price.

Making a Website

Developing a domain name is to make a website for it. Although there are some website developers that make multiple "starter" sites with the same content and sell them as businesses, real domain development is based on getting the most value for a domain name with a unique website with original content. The goal of making a website for a domain is to receive income from the site itself, keeping the domain name for a long time as the website becomes the main money-maker.

There are some domain names that can literally sell themselves by the name alone. Other domain names might sell for a large amount if you find the right buyer, but that could take years. If you have a good domain name but don't want to just earn residual parking or PPC income, developing a website on the domain is an active way to increase the domain name's value, but it takes time.

What types of websites might you develop and how do you make money from them? A lot depends on the domain name itself. Sure, you can take a domain name that isn't really a word but is pronounceable (like zelks.com) and develop it into anything. Other domain names may have keywords that will guide you to a certain type of website.

The type of website that has perhaps the greatest chance of making the most money is an e-commerce site. This would be an online store where you sell goods. You could sell things that you make (either physical or digital goods) or you could set up a dropshipping business where your store accepts the orders but the goods are stored and shipped from a third party.

Another type of profitable website is a membership site where you build an active forum and sell advertising space. You could also set up a news and information site on a particular topic or niche that is trending or has a growing interest. With this type of site you can make money through memberships which unlock additional content as well as advertising revenue. And then there are affiliate and PPC sites which were described earlier in this chapter.

How you choose which type of site might work best is based on a combination of things. First, you should consider what you would enjoy. You don't want to spend a lot of time making a website for something you aren't the least bit interested in. Your website will be much more successful, no matter what type it is, because of your interest in that market or niche. Then you should consider the domain name itself. Based on the name, be it a keyword name or something more generic, do a quick online search with the name itself, before it is developed, and see what comes up. What types of websites are ranked high based on the domain name alone? This may give you an indication of the type of website that might be most popular with that particular domain name.

Websites Aren't Easy to Make

Developing a website isn't easy. Even if you have already set up a website or two, each new website can be a challenge. To make a good website with the most potential to be profitable, you don't want to just copy something else that is already out there. You instead want to design something new and unique, be it an idea that has not yet been tried or a much better way to do something that someone else is trying but is not so successful.

Again, you start with the domain name and your interest. Designs for different types of sites have basic structures. If you are designing an e-commerce site, you first need to think about how your goods are going to be displayed, how your pricing will work, and how you will collect money. These are just the first three of many decisions you will need to make as you design your site. For a news and information site, how are you going to gather and then display the stories you want to publish? RSS feeds are no longer popular, and you shouldn't "scrape" stories from others' websites. The search engines will not rank you very high if you don't have original content, so to make a successful news or information site will take a lot of writing or, if you want to invest, you can hire writers to generate content for you.

There are many many decisions to be made as your website starts to take shape. Colors, logos, and graphics should all be unique. If you simply use a template (like a basic Wordpress site), there will be other sites that look just like yours. Instead, you might be better to start with a template you like (again, based on the type of website you are developing) and then customize it across the board. At least then you aren't starting from scratch and can begin to see the end result quicker.

While developing your website, you should also be planning on how you will integrate social media. It is never too early to begin to think about how you will promote your website, and the easiest (and cheapest) is through the main social media companies like Facebook, Twitter and Instagram or Pinterst. These, of course, may change over time based on popularity, but setting up separate accounts for each social media outlet is a must. It would be ideal if you were able to make your user name for each account be the same as your domain name. This may not always be possible, but you can build a much stronger brand if your social media names are the same as your website's domain.

Once your website is launched, you should plan on spending as much time promoting and adding content to your site than you spent developing the site. A developed website is now an active business. Without your involvement, the site will just sit there with no traffic. This can involve anything from updating store details and products to filling orders and answering phone calls from customers if you have an e-commerce site. For a news and information site, you will need to be continually adding new content or moderating others' content. And no matter what type of website it is, promotion is the key to success. This also takes time, as you make posts on the various social media platforms and, as your website begins to attract attention, setting up your own ad campaigns. It is a lot of work. Depending on how successful your website becomes, you have the potential to take what was a hand-registered domain name and turn it into a domain worth tens or hundreds of thousands of dollars.

Selling Developed Websites
The challenge in selling developed websites is in what profit you can attain. For instance, if you create a starter website for a domain name (a starter site means there won't be any developed traffic or sales/ad revenue/profit yet), then when you try to sell it you will need a certain amount from your final sale to make a profit. Let's say you sell your new, starter website for $100. Well, your costs so far are: let's say $10 for the domain name registration, $5/month for website hosting, at 2 months (one to develop and get the site started, and one while you are selling the site), so that's $10. (You could get your hosting costs for less per website if you use cPanel and have multiple websites going at once.) Then, it might cost you $29 to list your website for sale on one of the popular website sales marketplaces. Upon sale, the marketplace might take a 15% cut of the sales price for their commission if the buyer uses PayPal, so we'll use $15 in this

example. So $100 for the sales price, minus $10 for the domain, minus $10 for hosting, minus the $29 listing fee, minus $15 for the marketplace commission leaves you with $36 in profit! In the end, that's not a lot of money for all of the effort you put in developing the website, promoting its sale, then all of the time it takes to get it transferred to the buyer.

There are some sellers who have multiple sites for sale at once, many of which are 'stenciled' sites, so are relying on a quantity of sales to make a profit. But these are small margins and you would need many sales to make a decent profit. Additionally, not all starter sites sell the first time, and it costs to re-list an item, which will make your profit margin even less, if the website sells at all.

If you take a longer view as an investment, then you will want to develop a website and run it for a period of a year or two in order to develop traffic and financial earnings, either through ad revenue or e-commerce sales (like a dropshipping business for instance). Websites that are "aged" and can show real traffic (through Google Analytics) and profits through financial data can sell for much more ... but it takes a lot of time and effort to promote websites once they are up and running through social media and possibly even spending on ads to get your site noticed.

If you find yourself making money through domain development, you could decide to spend your time developing websites instead of buying and selling domains names. That approach would change your business plan from making profits through the buying and selling of domain names to developing profitable websites. There are many books and online resources regarding successful website development, so this book won't go any further into that topic. But you can easily see how a domain name's value can increase with a successful website, as long as you understand the time and effort it will take to get there.

Risks in Monetizing Domain Names

This book will cover the many risks of buying and selling domain names in Chapter 8. But for domain monetization, there are particular risks that should be considered.

Click Fraud

There are several forms of click fraud. The main one concerning this chapter is the kind PPC sites or parked pages would use to make fraudulent money. In this case, a website owner clicks on the various PPC ads on their own site in an attempt to generate more revenue. Sometimes software is used to automatically click through links from different IP addresses. Either tactic will get you banned from most PPC networks or parking services.

You would also gain a bad reputation with other domainers since the high click-through rates would make your site seem more valuable than it really is. If someone were to buy a name from you that vastly under-performs, word could spread and damage your ability to make future sales.

Website Content

When you are planning to develop a new website on your domain, be sure to only populate your site with original content. Don't be tempted to copy and paste (or scrape) content from other websites.

With original content, your pages and/or posts will rank higher than if you copied content. And copied or scraped content could get your website banned or blacklisted by companies such as Google. Having the ability to earn advertising income through Google AdSense makes a website attractive for re-sale. But if Google has banned the website, it is no longer worth very much.

Cybersquatting

This term will also be covered in more detail in Chapter 8, but it is worth mentioning here as well. If you buy a domain name that includes a company name or trademark and develop it into a website, or try to re-sell the name for a higher price, that is considered Cybersquatting. You will find many of these types of names on dropped or expired domain name lists – there is a reason for this. Other novice domainers thought they could make money registering a name related to a popular company, only to later find out about trademark laws, so either deleted the domain or let it expire. Registering dell.ru and using it to sell computers is obviously a bad idea, and it could likely land you in deep legal trouble. Even having a domain name that includes a branded company name as part of it could get you in trouble. It is best to stay away from trademarks, no matter what extension.

You should always be careful to stay away from possible trademarks and company names and the legal risks involved. There are so many domain names available to register that have the potential to be profitable, so why chance getting into potential legal and financial troubles by getting involved in copyright infringement?

Typo-Squatting
Like cybersquatting, typo-squatting is also best to avoid. Typo-squatting is when you buy a domain name that is similar to a popular domain or trademark, maybe off by a letter or two. The hope is that an Internet user makes a typo when inputting a website address for a common domain into their browser and ends up on your site instead. One of the most famous cases was goggle.com, a typo-variant of google.com. It was a phishing/fraud site for many years before an agreement was made for it to redirect to Google. In most cases, typo-squatted domains are full of PPC ads.

The owners of well-known websites are obviously opposed to this practice. Some might work with the website owner to quietly shut them down while others will take on legal action. There have also been cases where a UDRP was filed with the World Intellectual Property Organization (WIPO) against a Registrant who was using a similar domain name to a trademarked name in bad faith and lost their domain. Regardless, the practice of typo-squatting is still used and many domainers can make some profit off of this practice. But if your business goal is to be a reputable domainer and are seeking higher profits on domain name sales, it is best to stay away from typo-squatting.

Why Not Monetize Your Domain Names?

If you have a portfolio of domain names just sitting there not doing anything, you are basically throwing money away. Not only are you missing the opportunity for potential buyers to find your domains, but each domain name you own has the potential to at least make some money while you are holding it.

Let's say you have a portfolio of 300 domain names. If you were able to park all of these domains and just make two cents per day (on one click) at a parked site, you would make over $2,000 of revenue per year, paying for over half of your domain renewal costs. And if that parked site also had a banner advertising that each domain name was for sale, you would also have the opportunity to sell your domains through that same parking site, without doing anything. Of course, as a domainer, you should take a more active role in selling your domains, but at least you know that each domain you own has the potential to earn some revenue.

How this affects the buying of new domain names can be of some concern. Most of the good keyword domains that make larger profits through parking (and re-sale) are taken. But if you do your research and keep up with trends, you still may find good, affordable domain names with good keywords. If you are fortunate enough to buy a .com domain name before some cultural event makes it valuable (like "fake news"), you could make thousands on selling the domain name alone. But while you are waiting for that event to take place, you can still earn some revenue from that domain.

Additionally, there are new TLDs coming into the industry every month. This gives domainers an opportunity to purchase some of the highly-desired generic domain names with a different extension. Although these new extensions make it a long shot to make money reselling these domains, you can still monetize non-.com domain names just the same. This means that you may need to work a little harder to make your domain name profitable, so doing things like making parking revenue or developing a website can only help increase your possible earnings from each non-.com domain.

Chapter 7 – Selling Domain Names

Now that you have bought some domain names and are looking to sell, how do you do it?

Domain flipping, or working towards re-selling your names in volume, under a year, was covered in Chapter 5. For domain investing or speculating, you are instead looking at getting the highest return for your domain name investments, which could involve holding on to domain names for many years.

Upon purchasing a domain name, the first thing you will need to do is to place your domain name on a landing page or parking site. If you own a domain name and just have it sitting in your account, without placing it on any sales or parking sites, the only way a potential buyer will find you is by doing a Whois search on the domain name if they are interested in that particular name. Although the chances someone will send you an offer through your Whois contact information is very slim, it does occasionally happen. And even if you plan on holding a domain for a long time, putting the name on a landing page or parking site (with a "this domain is for sale" banner), you may get lucky and be contacted by a buyer willing to pay a premium price for your name.

After some time of holding on to the name, when you are ready to start marketing your domain name for sale you should determine the price range you want for your domain name and what your marketing strategy is going to be.

There are some simple things you can do that don't cost money to tell the world your domain name is for sale. And then there are other efforts that will cost you some money. You also have to think about what your timeline is – are you willing to wait a longer period of time (even years) to get a good price on your domain name, or are you wanting to sell it faster? Just remember, typically to make high profits on domain name sales, you usually have to sit on them for a while as you wait for the right buyer to come along. It is not very often you own a domain name for less than a year that you can flip for thousands of dollars of profit, although it occasionally happens.

The number one thing you should think about when looking to sell a domain name for its highest potential price is how you can find an end user to buy your domain. It is the end users that will most likely pay the most money for a domain name as they will want to run a profitable business with it. End users will also be the ones who will know how important it is to have a good domain name to represent their business on the internet. So in order to get end users to buy your domain names, you need to let them know that you have your domain names for sale. For most domainers, sending "outbound" emails is the best way to sell your domain names to end users.

You can also create landing pages for your domains on a website to let everyone know that the domain names are for sale, or use parking pages with for-sale banners. Then any interested buyers can contact you.

However, you shouldn't only rely on your outbound emails and type-in traffic for your domain names. It is a good idea to also list your domains for sale on websites that specialize in domains. If you bought a domain from a domain Registrar with a marketplace, you can list the domain(s) for sale on that same marketplace, or you could choose from any number of other marketplaces and 3rd party websites – but it is highly recommended to have your own landing pages as well.

You should also have multiple social media accounts, either in your own name or, if you have one, your domain-selling business name. The power of social media has been well-proven. As you grow your domain business, networking through social media is easy to do. And the more followers or "likes" your domain business social media accounts have, the more people will see your domain names for sale when you post.

The point is that when you are ready to market and sell one of your prized domain names, you should use as many resources as possible to "get your name out there" so it is seen by the most eyes.

Novice Seller Mistakes

Almost every domainer has made mistakes when selling domains. Each and every transaction is its own deal, and typically the only way to learn is by experience. But here are a number of pointers that can help you not make some of the most glaring mistakes when selling domain names.

Thinking Your Name Is Worth More Than It Is

Whether you run your domain names through online valuation tools or just believe you are sitting on the next big thing, you could end up losing a sale by simply believing your domain name is worth more than is being offered.

Try not to get "attached" to your domain names. They are simply investments you are trying to sell for a profit. You need to take an objective look at what they are really worth. Study and research recent similar domain name sales and get your names appraised if you need to. Either way, if you price your name too high, nobody will buy it.

Bad Negotiating

There is almost an art to offers and counter-offers, whether it is involving real estate or domain names. Learning how to effectively reach an acceptable price takes practice.

As an example, let's say you receive an email from a potential buyer for one of your domain names you think is worth $1,000. The email has a very low offer of $50. You might be tempted to either ignore the email or reply in a rude or insulting manner that their offer is not even close. However, before replying in any manner, you should take your time and ask yourself the following questions;

1) How long have you owned the domain?
2) How much did you pay for the domain name, initially and in renewal fees?
3) Have you received any previous offers for the domain?
4) Are you receiving any parking or affiliate income from the domain? (See Chapter 6 - Monetization)

With every offer, you should always reply in a positive manner, no matter how low you think the offer may be. It doesn't hurt to start a negotiation because you never know how it may end up. There have been many sales in the thousands of dollars that started out with a lowball inquiry.

After thinking about the offer, you may end up changing your expectations on what you believe the domain name is worth to you. Let's say you initially hand-registered the name three years ago so have paid about $40 in fees. Although you think you should sell for $1,000, maybe lowering your expectations to $500 (or even lower) should not be out of the question, especially if you've not received any other offers in the previous three years.

Expecting Quick Domain Sales
As discussed earlier in this book, the average domainer only sells about 5% of their domain names in any given year. So what makes a novice domainer believe they will register some domain names and immediately expect to re-sell them for thousands of dollars?

For the most part, newbies begin to register domains to sell but haven't done the proper research to understand the business. They get easily frustrated that nobody has made them offers and then find a domain name forum and ask why their domain names aren't selling. Happens all the time.

Ways to Price Your Domain Name

What to price each domain name you have for sale is always a tricky process. If you set too high of a price, it may sit in your portfolio and never sell. If you set too low of a price, someone will buy the name at a discount and maybe even re-sell the name for a higher price.

There are generally three different avenues for how a domain name's price is determined.

1. Set Your Price
If there is no pressing need to quickly sell your domain names, the desired approach is to simply set a specific price on the respective domain names. This is how many domain sellers operate.

When setting the price for what you want to sell your domain names for, there are many factors to consider, depending on how you intend to market and sell your domains, and your overall domain business strategy.

2. Domain Name Auction Pricing

If you seriously believe that there is a lot of interest in a domain you own, put it up for auction. This is the best possible approach to fetch the highest possible price when you think there is interest from many parties.

Auctioning your domain name is only recommended if you are domain flipping or have a name that is something other than an English word or high-value keyword name. These could be short names, like a 4L .com or a 5N .com, which may not have an end user business looking for the name, but has value based on its scarcity.

For auction listings, there is an art to setting your pricing, which includes both an auction start price as well as a reserve price (if applicable). This requires some work on your part to not only understand what the value of your domain name is, but also have knowledge of how the particular marketplace works where you are listing for auction.

Some sites, particularly those that deal more with premium names, have a set minimum price, like $69, for all domain names. With these sites, the initial start price is set and you don't have to worry about that. On these premium auction sites, you can usually choose whether to have a reserve price or not. If not, then the initial start price (say, $69), is the minimum amount for the sales price if there are any bids. You will also need to know what the marketplace commission will be (usually a percentage of the sales price), along with any additional registration or other fees that might be applied, to find out what you would actually get as a net dollar amount upon a completed sale.

If this minimum net amount is not enough for you, then you can set a reserve price. When setting a reserve, you should consider an amount you think is realistic. If you set a $10,000 reserve price on a domain name you just registered that might be, at most, worth $100, it will most likely never sell and you would have wasted your time listing it. Therefore, you should consider a reserve amount that you think is attainable through bidding and an amount you will accept.

Other domain auction sites don't have minimum start prices, so you can set it to be $1, $10, $100 or even more if you want. There is a skill to setting the start price amount. If you are running an auction with no reserve which some sites, particularly on forums, require, then the start price is the lowest amount the domain will sell for. You will need to be careful to understand what commissions or fees are taken out after the sale to determine your net dollar amount.

But if you have a reserve price set, then there isn't much risk in setting a low start price. In fact, in many auctions, setting a $1 start price can be an advantage, as it gets the auction bidding started, which can draw interest and have a larger number of watchers or followers for the auction. With more bids placed, your auction may also end up getting better placement on a home page or in searches for most active auctions.

3. Make Offer (or not setting a price)

This method lets a potential buyer start a price negotiation without a start price or reserve. If the domain name under your possession is a "niche" name in nature, chances are it is not going to create mass interest. In such instances, you may have to list it as a "make an offer" as there may not be useful guidelines to determine the value of your domain name, or you are willing to sit on it for a while without having a set price.

When you list your domain name for sale without setting a price, you are essentially looking for offers. Sometimes you may get an offer from a potential buyer that is more than you thought you could sell the domain name for, and this is great if it happens. But more often than not, you will receive "lowball" offers or no offers at all. This also depends on where the domain name is being sold. For instance, some domain name listing services allow you to not set a fixed price and instead have an entire section (or the whole site) is for make offers only with no set or minimum price. Some sites (and even forums) have different sections for domain names of different values, so the domains worth over $1,000 aren't lost in the "make offer" domain names that are valued for less than $100.

Using the Make Offer method also will require you to use your negotiating skills. By having your potential buyers start with an initial offer, you typically will need to give them a counter-offer such that they don't go away. Unless, of course, they first gave you such an unreasonable lowball offer that it might not even be worth your time to counter. However, there have been many claims where an initial offer was only a few hundred dollars but the final sale ended up being well into the thousands.

Where to Sell Your Domain Names

If you are interested in selling on a domain name marketplace, you have many options. The different websites seem to specialize in different areas. For instance, one website may be marketing towards more international buyers (including end users), while there are others that have buyers that seem to target specific names, such as short names (3L, 4L or 4N, 5N) or certain extensions like .io names.

It takes some time and research to find which marketplace may work best for your particular domains. Some of the best advice, if you are looking for some help, can be found on domain name forums. Within these forums you will find many other domainers willing to give advice – some helpful and maybe some not-so-helpful. But the forums generally do support those looking to sell domains – because with every domain name sold, it only helps everyone else in their domain name sales pursuits. As more domain names are sold on the secondary market, it only increases the viability of third party domain name sales as an industry.

Forums are also good places to sell domain names which, after trying to sell them elsewhere, may be the last place to sell names that are coming to their end of registration, or you have decided that you maybe shouldn't have bought in the first place. You generally will not get good prices on your domains in a forum. But if you are thinking you are just going to let a domain name expire, you may be able to at least get something back, even if it is at a loss from what you originally bought the name for.

Selling a Domain with No Upfront Cost

When you first buy a domain name, it is typically best to not start spending additional money to market your domain. There are some simple things you can do to get you started that don't cost money, and also don't lock you into paying a fee or commission on a domain name sale:

- No privacy. Do not pay for (or select, if offered for free) domain name privacy. By having your Whois information public, potential buyers who are interested in your domain name can find you. If you have your registration information set to private, there is no way that someone interested in your domain name can contact you through Whois. But this comes at a price. By having your registration information public, you will most likely get spam emails and phone calls selling domain services, from website creation to SEO services. These can be an annoyance, but they typically die down a short time after you have registered the domain name. Overall, this is a small price to pay for the potential that someone who really wants your domain name can contact you directly.
- Domain Parking or Forwarding. You should also, at a minimum, park or forward your domain name to a site that in one way or another tells people who type your domain name into their browser that the domain name is for sale. If you just leave the domain name in your Registrar account and don't change the nameservers or use domain forwarding (and the domain is not set up as a website), then anybody typing the name into a browser will just see a promotional page for your Registrar or, if they don't have that, the domain will not resolve and someone who might be a potential buyer will just get a "did not resolve" or "server not found" error.

- List your domain name for sale on a domain name forum. Most domain name forums have a place where you can list domains for sale that don't tie you to a specific price or auction. You can simply post that you have your domain name for sale and you are accepting offers. The chances of getting high offers through an online forum are pretty slim, but it doesn't cost you anything to try.

- Post your domain name for sale on social media. You can post on domain name pages or marketplaces within Facebook that your domain name is for sale. And if you have a Twitter account (as you should), you can tweet your domain name for sale adding hashtags such as #domains, #domainnamesforsale, etc. And other social media sites, such as Instagram, Pinterest, and others, can also serve as free marketing for your domain name. Through these and other social media platforms you can also create an online presence for yourself as a domainer – whether you use your real, personal name, or create a "business" name for yourself. Either way, you should find a unique name that is available on all platforms so you can have a consistent user name across all accounts. You should also use a name that is available as a Gmail account so your email address and online Google accounts are all in the same name.

Domain Sites with No Fee

There are other places you can list your domain name for sale that won't cost you any upfront money, but these sites will take a percentage commission if the domain name is sold through their site. Some of these websites are very popular with domainers and are active marketplaces. Others may cater to more of the general public which may lead to a potential end user buying your domain name through that site. These domain sites generally require you to post a price you want to sell your domain name for, which will be covered later in this chapter. If you place your domain name at one (or more, if allowed) of these sites, you should at least set your nameservers or domain forwarding to the site so any direct type-in of your domain name in a browser will take that person to a domain name sales page.

As mentioned earlier, it takes both research and experience to find which of these domain name marketplaces may be best for each of your domain names, but you have the potential to make decent sales on your domains through these avenues. Also, if you post your domains at any of these websites, you should also use some of the free marketing mentioned above to help promote that your domain name is for sale.

Selling Domain Names with an Upfront Cost

There are some domain name marketplaces that will only allow you to list your domain name if you pay a fee. Some of these sites are very popular and have a lot of traffic – meaning more eyes on your domain name. Some of these sites are purely domain name auction sites, some have your domain name as a fixed, classified listing, and some offer both. Either way, you are risking additional money on listing your name for sale, so it is only recommended you do this when you are looking to sell your name after other avenues have been tried.

These sites also take a bit of research and experience to find what sells best on which marketplace. And if you use an auction-type listing, you might not get as much for your domain as you would like - but you also have the potential to make more if your domain name is in demand. There is more to read about auction sites later in this chapter.

Selling Domain Names on a Fixed Price Marketplace

In earlier chapters in this book, how to price your domain names and how to estimate the value of your domains was discussed. This section will go into a little more detail on how to get the most from your domains and how to effectively market them on listing services.

Domain Listing Services

Domain name brokers, domain listing services, and parking services can all be used to sell your domain names, and each of these can usually perform at least one other service. For example, most parking services allow you to put a 'this domain is for sale' banner on your domain name along with the ads. Many domain listing services also provide parking services. And most brokers list the domains their clients are selling. But not all companies do all three and some only do one.

Many domainers use companies that both list and park their domains. You can make extra money through perking ad revenue when listing a domain for a lengthy period of time. In addition, the services that both list and park are not only good for the seller, but can also be used to find a buyer.

When listing a domain name, you shouldn't price the domain at an unreasonable level. A domain name valued for less than $1,000 isn't going to be taken seriously if the listed price is over $20,000. But you don't have to start with your market value either. It is best to choose a price somewhere in between to give yourself a chance for a good profit if the right buyer comes along, while also allowing for some negotiating room above the evaluation price.

One thing to avoid is lowering the price every month. If someone sees a domain name's listed price gradually being lowered, they will think either the domain owner is inexperienced and wasn't sure what to set the initial price at or the owner is desperate to sell the domain. A potential buyer could simply wait for the domain name to drop to a below-market value and then make an even lower offer for your domain. Make sure you don't make this mistake and end up devaluing your domains - pick a price and stick with it.

Some domain listing services offer the ability to use keywords or tags in the descriptions making it searchable for a particular interest or industry. When listing a generic name like shoes.com, keywords aren't really necessary as the domain is self-explanatory. But, if you list a name like workboots.com, good description and keyword tags would definitely help you find the right buyers. People looking for a domain name for a specialty shoes site might not have thought of searching for the term "boots." Choosing good keywords can help potential buyers find your domain.

Domain Name Auctions

Listing your domain name on an auction site is only recommended after exhausting all direct end user options. When putting a name up for auction, you are essentially ending your desire to hold onto the name for an extended period, and no longer seeking the potential top dollar from an end user. Domain name auctions also have advantages and disadvantages.

Auction advantages:

- Puts your domain name into a marketplace where there are many potential buyers.
- If a popular or desired name, you may be able to get a final sales price for more than you thought you would get.
- When an auction is completed, the site generally provides a payment mechanism (or escrow service if a higher-priced domain) so you do not have to work directly with the buyer to receive payment.

Auction disadvantages:

- The domain name might not get any bidders so if you paid a listing fee you will have lost this amount of money.
- If you set a reserve price, the bidding may not meet the reserve. You also would lose your listing fee unless the domain name sells during a re-list if you choose that option. Some auction sites also charge (sometimes a smaller amount) for a domain name re-list.
- Even if your domain name "sells" on an auction site, sometimes the sale doesn't go through. The highest bidder may end up not paying.

With domain auctions, it is recommended that you don't just sit there and watch the auction. You should also use some marketing strategies of your own to promote the auction. During the auction, many of the sites have places where you can enter comments during the auction. You can add additional "promotional" details about the domain name in the comments periodically during the auction, such as recent similar sales or potential uses of the domain name. Don't put all of this good information in the initial domain name auction listing – save some of it for comments during the auction.

It is also recommended to promote your domain name auction through social media and domain forums. Sites like Facebook and Twitter are good places to post that your domain name is in auction. And domain name forums generally have a section where you can post that your domain names are for sale on another platform.

Additionally, some domain name forums have sections where you can run an auction within the forum. You should keep in mind that these forums typically don't have end users, so the final price you get in an auction may not be very good. But if your domain name is nearing the end of its registration and you no longer think it has the potential for a big sale, auctioning it on a domain name forum (with no listing fee) will most likely at least get you something back for your domain name.

Domain name auction sites are also a good place to list a portfolio of domain names that you may want to sell in bulk. Whether they are nearing the end of their registration or you have similar domains, either with particular extensions or in a related category, a portfolio sale is a good way to possibly sell multiple domain names in one listing. This saves you on listing fees (as opposed to paying a listing fee for each domain name separately), as well as your time spent in promoting the auction and final payment for the domain name sale. You still have to transfer each domain name individually to the buyer, but if you have a lot of domains you want to sell in a short period of time, portfolio sales can work well. You also may not make as much (or any) profit on each individual domain name when compared to their combined registration cost plus the listing fee for the auction, but sometimes some money in return is better than nothing.

Bulk listings can also be an advantage if you are selling different extensions of the same name. For instance, if you are able to register the .com, .net and .org extensions (plus possible others), it may be of particular interest for buyers (and end users) to know they are buying the domain name as a brand, where they control many extensions of the same name. This can come at a risk for

139

domainers though, because you are taking a chance by registering multiple extensions with the same name that the name will be of interest to someone and you will be able to sell them for a good price.

With domain name auction listings, you may also have the option of adding listing enhancements, such as a premium listing, placement on the front page of the website, or included in email marketing from the marketplace. Before paying extra for either (or all) of these enhancements, you should not only have a quality domain name, but get a better understanding through the marketplace as to how effective these enhancement will be in driving additional traffic to your auction. For some types of domains, the extra cost for additional exposure may be worth it.

Selling Domain Names on Auction Sites
When selling domain names via auction, sellers can sometimes be at an advantage as a final sales price could end up being bid well above the name's actual market value. However, at the same time, a decent domain name might not even get one bid, which might leave you worse off if you had to pay a fee to put your domain name up for auction.

There are many different auction sites for domain names. For instance, if you have a premium or "top" domain that you have decided to put up for auction, you should choose an auction site that specializes in only domain names, not a more general consumer auction site that sells everything. By putting your name with a domain-only auction site, you are mostly marketing to other domainers who are more likely able to understand a domain name's market value or worth, or perhaps an end user who know to go to a domain name marketplace to find a good quality domain name for their business.

But if you have a domain you just want to put out there with a high reserve and see if you can get bidders who don't understand the domain name market, then a more general auction site may work. This is good if you have domain names that don't really have investment value but are attractive to potential buyers in other ways, such as relating to popular culture or news events. Also, if you have a domain name that has a developed website you might find a general auction site, or even sites that specialize in website auctions might be better.

How you set a starting price for your domain name auction is important. If you set a very low start price, it may create a lower value for the name in the eyes of potential bidders, but could also get more bidders interested and you could end up with a bidding war. If you set too high of a start price, you may discourage anybody looking at your auction and you might not get any bids. More experienced investors won't look at the starting price and, if interested, will place a higher bid near or at the most they will pay in order to weed out other potential bidders. And many experience bidders won't even place a bid until the very end, known as sniping. Although some auction sites re-set the auction end-time an additional fifteen or sixty minutes if a bid comes in near the auction's end, there are other sites that don't re-set and a winning bid can be placed in the last few seconds of the auction.

Auctions of any type can create a psychological response in people that can lead them into bidding higher than they might normally want to go. If an auction doesn't have any bids, many times the auction might be ignored. But once an item has some bids, it can attract more attention. Then when people see that there is interest in something, they may take a look at it themselves. And once they place a bid, then they are invested and may feel committed to then increase their bid when somebody else bids higher.

But if you have an auction that isn't getting any bids, do not be tempted to bid on your own domain names. If the auction is through a domain forum or website where it didn't cost you anything to start the auction, you would have no reason to bid on your own auction as you have no money at stake. Domain name sales and auction websites make most of their money off of the commission on a sale, so it's better to have no bids than a number of low bids below the domains market value.

And if there are bids but not as high as you like, just accept it for what it is – again, don't be tempted to bid on your own auction. Not only is it against the rules of all auction sites, it leaves you in a questionable state as other domainers may identify you as a shill bidder.

Shill bidding is where sellers use friends or family members, memberships of people they know, or fake memberships they have created to put false bids on auctions in an attempt to bid up the price of a domain name they are selling.

This dishonest type of bidding, when done, is usually on auctions with a set reserve price, or the minimum price a seller is willing to sell the domain name for. Shill bidders mislead other bidders about what that reserve is by gaming the auction and trying to bid up to a price just below the reserve.

However, most auction sites have built-in mechanisms to detect shill bidding, such as looking for similar IP addresses or tracing email or payment accounts for various users bidding on any one auction. Other legitimate bidders may also sense shill bidding is going on and alert the moderators or auction management.

When selling domain names at auction, how you set a reserve price (or not) is kind of an art form in itself, and takes experience as well as a good sense of the true market value of your domain in setting this minimum accepted price. With a good marketable domain name that will have a lot of interest, sometimes setting up an auction with no reserve has an advantage. This type of auction will generally attract a lot of bidders and as the domain name gets a lot of bids, it may get additional attention on the auction site, maybe even on the front page, because of its popularity. However, a no reserve auction also runs the risk of selling for less than its market value, so there is some risk involved.

You can also auction off a number of your domain names all at once as a "portfolio." This is a good way to sell many domains at once, particularly if you have exhausted all other methods of selling those names first. Many domainers end up buying names that, in hindsight, maybe they should not have purchased – don't worry, it happens to everyone. Yearly registration fees will require further investment in your domain names, and sometimes you may decide that keeping particular names for a long period of time may not end up being worth it. So selling names in bulk allows you to trim your portfolio and concentrate on other more marketable domains you own. You might not get a good price per domain selling this way, but sometimes something in return is better than nothing – which is what you will get if you just let the domain name expire.

Overall, selling domain names via auction can get you a great price for your domains. There are many domainers that only use auctions as a last resort, after trying all other types of outbound marketing and other methods of sales. You may not always get the most profit for domain names through auction sales, but selling at auction can earn you a good profit in which to invest in other domains.

Selling Your Domain Names Yourself

As a domainer, you do not have to rely on other businesses' online marketplaces to sell your domain names. Although marketplaces give you an opportunity to get your domain name in front of many potential buyers, the fees and sales commissions for these sites can take a chunk out of your profit. Additionally, many of these marketplace sites are populated by other domainers, not potential end-users who may pay more for your domain name.

When trying to sell your domain names yourself, your best potential profit is to reach out directly to end users. But before doing that, there are three relatively easy methods for potential buyers to find you: wait for a buyer, set up a simple web page, or make an active website. The method you choose depends on how quickly you want to sell and how much effort you may want to expend to market your names.

Wait for a Buyer

Just by registering a domain name you could have someone contact you. This "do nothing" approach takes no effort on your part – you just wait for a potential buyer to look up your domain name through a Whois search (once they see the name is already taken), and can send you a direct offer to buy it from you. The odds of this happening are very low, but there are many cases where a domainer sold a name for a large profit without doing anything other than registering the name.

As mentioned earlier, it's essential that you keep your Whois record (the registration ecord of your domain name) updated at all times, free from errors, and not set to private. You never know who might be trying to contact you.

Make a Simple Web Page

Another easy thing to do is to create a very basic web page with simple text stating that the domain name is for sale. You should also provide your email address so a potential buyer can contact you. With some simple html code or whatever site creation tools are available on the platform you choose to use, you could also include a contact form on the page so anybody interested in the name wouldn't need to leave your page to access their email account in order to contact you. The advantage of this simple approach is that you don't have to spend a lot of time and effort creating a good looking web page, and it gives any potential buyer who types your domain name into their browser a so-called landing page with an easy way to contact you if they want to buy your domain name.

How this simple page best works is for you is for you to use domain forwarding on all of your domain names to this one page. There are a number of different sites that offer free basic web pages, although some put ads on these pages as well. The disadvantage is these types of free sites don't rank well on search engines, so you shouldn't count on search engine traffic with this method. If you also want to rank in search engines and capture traffic through web searches, then you should create an active website.

Create an Active Website
If you are willing to spend more time and effort in attracting more potential buyers to your domain names, the best way is to create a complete web site, with pages or posts set up for each domain name you are selling, and simple contact forms so potential buyers can easily get in touch with you. The main home page, along with the individual pages or posts, should clearly indicate that your domain names are for sale. Good, professional-looking websites take some work in developing. And if you want to rank in search engines, you will need to create content-rich pages with keywords related to the domain industry and any particular niche that may be your specialty in order to attract visitors to your website.

This is not the same as creating a content site to increase the value of the domain name (as covered in Chapter 6), but rather a more formal domain name sales site, which could even be under a business name if you want to go that route.

There are two main benefits in having an active website. Firstly, a website which attracts many visitors will get your domain names in front of the eyes of more potential buyers. Secondly, if the site is popular enough, you may be able to make additional revenue through advertising, or possible consulting services for domain name brokering or website development. Having a popular web page can build your brand as a domain expert and carry over onto social media platforms and the like.

There are many options you can use to create such a site and you will, at a minimum, have to pay a small monthly fee for website hosting. If you want to go this route, a simple Wordpress site with hosting for as little as a few dollars a month is recommended. With Wordpress, you can easily create a great, attractive home page (with plugins to help with SEO and widgets to add other features, such as advertising). And you can also create individual pages or posts (depending on how you set up your site) for each of your domain names so they each have an individual landing page for you to use for domain forwarding for each domain. This way, when someone types in a particular domain name you own in their web browser, they will be taken directly to your web page for that particular domain.

Through your Wordpress site, for example, you can add a contact plugin so a potential buyer can contact you directly (inquiry goes directly to your email address), or you can add an e-commerce plugin and set up each domain name as a product, where buyers can purchase your domain name directly from your website. An e-commerce setup has the advantage of possibly receiving a quick sale of a domain name without having to take the time exchanging emails back and forth to negotiate and complete a transaction - extra time which, unfortunately, could lead to the buyer backing out and not completing the sale.

When creating an active site, you should also have it on a domain name that becomes your "brand." This way, once you have established yourself as a domainer, your website name matches your social media names (and email address), making it easier for you to market both your domain names and yourself, while also giving yourself credibility as a domainer.

Selling Domain Names to End Users

The best way to sell a domain name for the highest profit is by finding end users for your domain name and approach them directly – either by email or phone. Selling a domain name to an end user will most likely get you the highest price because the right end user/buyer has a business along with the desire to own your domain name.

The bigger question often asked is, how can you find end users?

The key is to find some websites that relate to your domain name. For example, if you have CarParts.com you may offer it to the owner of websites in the car part-selling niche. People who have online car part businesses more likely will want a domain name like this.

You can use search engines to find such websites. You will find many online stores related to your domain. And there will also be some advertisers shown on the search result who could be a potential end user/buyer too.

After you have a list of related websites to your domain name, find the owner for each site. You can do it by checking directly on the website through a contact form page. Another way you can see the ownership is by checking the Whois of their current domain name.

However you find a company's contacts, it is always best to reach a CEO or senior decision-maker for a company. Sending emails to generic contact addresses or administrative personnel rarely succeeds, and you typically have only one chance to reach out to each company.

Contacting end users directly is called "outbound" marketing. Since this is similar to cold-calling, you should use caution in contacting end users. This is why most domainers don't make phone calls. Phone marketing is typically frowned upon and the chances of making a sale based on a phone call is practically zero.

That is why most initial outbound contacts are through email. By using email, you give the end user the basic information that a domain name that you think may fit their business is available. Or you could use the reason that your domain name might be a better name than the one theyy are currently using. For the most part, your email will be ignored. You may even get a reply telling you to remove their name from your email list or never contact them again. You can't take these kinds of responses personally, just move on to the next company.

Your email address should also be on your own business or domain-sales name. It is not recommended to use a free email service like Gmail or Hotmail. Many people have spam filters and your email could end up not even being seen. One alternative to consider is to set up an email address on the domain name you are trying to sell. This may indicate to the potential end user that the domain has value. The potential buyer might also think they are dealing with another company that was using it rather than a domainer, and feel better about making a purchase.

Any time you send outbound emails you should be contacting these companies individually by email. That is, sending each contact an individual email. Send one at a time. You can write your email first as a draft in your email program or in a Word document that you save on your computer (which you can then easily reference at a later date). Then you can simply copy and paste the text (with a direct hyperlink to your landing page) into each individual email, making sure you change the salutation on each email.

You should make a plan as to how your potential buyers might benefit by owning your domain name. Use a good subject line for your email. Many of your end users are busy people and may only single out emails to read by the subject heading, so don't make it read like a spam email. A subject like, "You Need To Have This Domain Name!!" will most likely be deleted without being opened. Just try and be unique and business-like – something that might pique the end user's interest in opening your email.

If the domain is RunningShoes.com and your potential buyer manufactures or sells running shoes, then you might use a subject line like "Running Shoes Business Opportunity." Business owners may not delete an email that directly relates to the line of business they are in.

You want the potential buyers to feel like you are only writing directly to them – so no generic statements such as "Dear Sir/Madam" or "To Whom It May Concern." Do everything you can to find out the names of the people that are your potential buyers. Then write a short, polite and well-written email, personalized for each potential customer. You do not need to do a lengthy sales pitch. Also don't mention the value of the domain – save any dollar amounts for the negotiations.

You should end your outbound email with a professional signature which includes your real name, your domainer website (if you have one), your real address, your telephone number and your email address. You should always use your real name. Don't hide behind a generic company name. Buyers for premium domain names will want to know who they are dealing with. And you should always include your real phone number. Many buyers do not like to do negotiations over email.

When writing your short email message, do not include anything other than the facts. The potential buyers don't need (or want) to hear a story about why you are selling the domain name. An example of a message might be something like this:

> Hello,
> I am (Name), owner of the domain name Zelks.com. I am currently offering this domain for sale. Should you or your organization have an interest in acquiring this domain name for your business, please feel free to contact me.
>
> Regards,
> (Name)
> (Domain Business Name, if any)
> (Address)
> (Telephone Number)
> (E-mail Address)

Remember to have patience. You might send out 30 emails and only receive 2 responses, of which one might be "Remove me from your mailing list." Don't take it personally. Business people are busy and may not want to be troubled. You might also receive a phone call. For either a reply email or phone call, many users may ask questions related to how the domain name gets transferred so you should be ready with those answers.

Think about how many emails you get each and every day from people selling web development or SEO services for the domain names you have registered. Then think about how many marketing phone calls you might receive every day. Add to that any people coming to your door trying to sell you stuff. There are many people who might immediately dismiss your email, no matter how good you might think it is for their business, because they don't want to be bothered.

If you don't receive any responses through this set of emails, be sure you still have your domain name on a landing page with domain forwarding for any potential type-in traffic. Then try again with emails to a new contact list after a period of time goes by – could be months or years, depending on the particular domain name and the market.

Negotiating as a Seller

In the selling of domain names, your negotiating skills are an essential part of making money. Unless you list your domain names with a fixed price on a website or marketplace, or in a domain auction where the final bid becomes the final sales price, almost every other sale of your domain name will require you to negotiate the final sale price. Sometimes you may be negotiating with another domainer, sometimes with an end user.

Look at Domaining from the Viewpoint of an End User

Since the end user is most likely going to get you the most profit on a domain name sale, it might be a good idea to look at a domain name transaction from the end user/buyer point of view. For this example, let's say your potential end user is looking for a domain name for their new startup business.

Your end user has a great online business idea, has a completed business plan, and is funded. If they don't already have a domain name for their website, they will probably start looking at what's available. What they will find is that practically every .com domain name that is short or has their top keyword is already registered. They will also find it hard to just "make up" a pronounceable domain that isn't already taken. Once they realize English words and short, pronounceable "made up" words or top keywords are not available in a .com extension, they have two choices: register a domain name in some other extension, or find a good domain name for sale from a website or from someone who sells domain names.

If the business owner is smart, they will quickly rule out other extensions. The .com is the only way to go. And, more often than not, the end user will not want a domain name with a number or hyphen in it. So they start looking around online at the domain name market. For the most part, they will find a lot of available domain names that are for sale – many of which are very, very expensive, much more than they first thought they would be willing to spend for a domain.

So what they will possibly do is start to type keywords related to their business into Search and see what comes up. The keywords will tell them what other businesses are doing. But let's say this business owner wants a short, unique name, not a string of keywords linked together. What they might do is make a list of fun-sounding made-up words that might make someone think of their business. They will type these possible names into their browser's address bar (without going to it) just to see how names might look and feel. Some words, like with repeating letters, can look a little confusing as a lower case word (which domains are used as), but they might find adding a double letter at the beginning or end of a word could not only be memorable, but also very marketable for their business.

Let's say they find a name they really like – let's call it zelks.com - and you are the owner of that domain name. They see you have the domain name posted on a website with a "Make Offer" listing. If this end user is good at business dealings, they will NOT immediately send you an email, saying something like "I see you are not using zelks.com. I have a little project I'd like to use it for ... would you be willing to let it go?" People in the business world know better than to start a negotiation like this. And you, as a domainer,, aren't sitting on a good .com domain name just to "let it go."

Be Realistic About Your Domains
Many domain owners think that one day someone is going to come along and give them millions for their .com no matter what it is. The fact is, domains are only worth what someone is ready, willing, and able to pay. There are many great domains that never get sold, mostly due to price, so you should always keep that in mind. Many domain owners will not list a price – believing that the "Make Offer" approach is best for two reasons:
1. If you list a domain name with a price that is too high, it will just sit there, year after year, with no inquiries.
2. If you list a price that is too low, it will most certainly sell, but not for what you could have sold it for.

It is important to remember that you will NOT sell each and every one of your domains, even if you are careful and selective when buying. You will inevitably have a portfolio of names with some duds. It just happens. And these duds will not sell. So the names that you *do* sell need to not only make more money than you have paid for them (plus any renewal fees), but also must cover the registration of your domain names that are not going to sell (which you most likely will end up dropping). And that's not including your other business expenses, such as any web hosting, marketing, or other fees you might be spending on your domain name business.

Even if you are not going to list your domain names for a set price, you should still know the market and have an idea of what they may be worth. This information will help you when it comes time to negotiate a sales price.

Most domain name owners are most likely hoping a buyer is going to come along and offer some ridiculously high price that they will either accept or counter with an even higher ridiculously high price. But that doesn't generally happen. If there is a business owner (end user) who is interested in your domain name, they could consider not making an offer in their first contact with you. But if they use an approach like "would you be willing to sell zelks.com? If so, how much?" they may not even get a response. But you should already know how to respond if you do get such an inquiry.

If they understand the domain market they may know that domain owners of decent domains get many fishing emails all the time and probably ignore emails that don't seem to be legitimate. Domain owners with very good domain names routinely receive offers of $100 (or less!) for domain names worth well into the thousands - or more. These lowball offers can be from people who don't understand the value of domain names or those on a fishing expedition. And if the domain owner has a large portfolio of names, they are less likely to even respond to such an offer, or even any casual inquiries.

So good negotiators for domain names will follow a few simple rules:
#1: The end user will start out by making an offer in their initial email.
#2: The offer must be good enough to get the domain owner's attention, and make them at least think the end user is a legitimate buyer.

Of course, offer amounts can vary wildly depending on the value of the domain name. But a $100 offer for a name the end user knows is worth well over a thousand dollars will more times than not kill any chance of making a deal. Domain brokers have bought many $100K+ value domains for clients for $15K-$20K by starting with a $5K or $7K offer. By starting with at least something that gets the domain owner's attention, the owner of the domain name will take a potential buyer more seriously.

Receiving an Offer

You've had your name listed on a website or parking page with a "This domain name is for sale – make an offer" statement (or placed a reasonable, yet somewhat high, asking price on the name). You've waited patiently for a buyer (or marketed to them). Then finally you get an email from a prospective buyer.

In any response, it is best to remember two things:
1. Do not lie
2. Keep a professional disposition

If you have an asking price of $1,000 and someone offers you only $50, don't reply with something like "What an idiotic offer!" Instead, you can send a more polite response, something like, "Thank you for your offer but I am looking for something in a higher price range." Kindness may be the biggest key to a sale. You always want to be professional in your domain name business dealings. Whenever you are trying to sell something, you should be polite and courteous. Using good manners will help make the buyer feel better and could lead to a much easier negotiation.

You also don't want to lie about anything. If the buyer asks how long you have held the domain name, then tell them. If they ask if there is any traffic, tell them. The truth is always much better than a fabrication.

Lowball Offers

If you receive an offer for one of your domains that you think is unreasonably low, your first reaction might be to just delete the email without even replying. You should instead try to respond with something, it doesn't take too long. Just because the prospective buyer started at a low price doesn't mean you can't negotiate towards something agreeable to both parties. As was covered in the chapter on buying domain names, a smart buyer will most likely open with a low initial price to give themselves room to bargain.

You also won't know much about the prospective buyer. They could be a college student wanting a domain name for a class project they are working on. Or they could be an IT Director for a Fortune 500 company pretending to be a college student – you don't know.

If you think the price is unreasonably low, just write a simple email back explaining the price you are asking and that you aren't interested in offers below a certain amount. Many times a lowball offer came from a buyer willing to pay much, much more because they really wanted that particular domain name – and that they were just playing a game to see how little they could get it for. If you use common sense and stay professional, and stick to the value you think your domain name is worth, an initial lowball offer could end up turning into a big sale.

High Dollar Offers
Although this isn't likely to happen, you might get an offer for one of your domain names for a very high price. If this happens, you should proceed with caution and do your research, not only more on your domain name (and any associated keywords), but also try and research the potential buyer if you can. While it's possible a high initial offer could turn out to be legitimate, take your time and be patient. Research your own domain name and see if there is a reason this high offer came in before responding.

Also, you should make sure that you don't give any unnecessary information in your response. If the prospective buyer asks for anything unusual or tries to get any kind of information from you that isn't necessary, there is a chance they might be attempting to scam you out of your domain. Proceed with caution. If you're still unsure, seek the advice of a domain broker or ask for advice on a domain name forum. And always receive the money before you transfer the domain name, or use an escrow service.

Escrow Services and Domain Brokers

It's hard to believe that someone would steal a domain name, but it does happen, so sellers want to be careful with whomever they are dealing with in a prospective domain name transaction. At the same time, buyers may be unsure as to whether they are actually going to get the domain name transferred to them once they send the seller their money. This is when escrow services are a good idea in a domain name transaction.

But even before that, buyers and sellers may be wary of the other party, or just not want to deal directly with another party in either negotiations or the transaction. This is when a domain broker is a good idea in a domain name transaction.

Using an Escrow Service

An escrow service for a domain name transaction works in a similar manner to a real estate escrow service. The money for the agreed-to price from the buyer, and sometimes the item(s) from the seller, is transferred to a 3rd party service. When all of the deal's conditions have been satisfied, the 3rd party then releases the item(s) and money to the respective parties.

For a domain transaction, if the buyer and seller decide to use an escrow service, the seller can sometimes transfer control of the domain name to the escrow company. The escrow company would also receive the money from the buyer. The escrow company would then transfer the domain name to the buyer and release the money to the seller.

More often, money is first put into a holding (escrow) account with an escrow agent by the buyer. Once the money is in the account, the seller is notified the escrow company has the money so is then able to transfer the domain name to the buyer. Once the buyer acknowledges the domain name is in their account, they instruct the escrow company to release the funds to the seller.

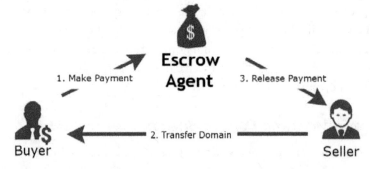

Escrow services aren't only used for high dollar transactions. You might think using escrow for a mid-$xxx transaction might not be necessary. But many times one or both parties in the deal want the added safety that an escrow service provides, as long as the dollar amount is above any minimum the escrow company will support.

How the escrow fees are paid can become a point of contention. If one party doesn't feel using escrow is necessary but the other party is adamant about using escrow, then it sometimes can be negotiated that only the party that wants to use escrow pays the fee. Many times the seller will insist that the buyer pay the fees since it is the buyer's money that is to be protected until the deal is done. Usually it's best to split the escrow fee in half between buyer and seller.

Many auction websites have escrow services built into their site, where the seller has the option for every transaction to be done through escrow. This is usually a fair way for the buyer to be protected since they usually don't know who the seller is. Other websites require an escrow service to be used if the final bid or buy now price is over a certain dollar amount. In these cases, the escrow fee is normally the responsibility of the seller, taken out of the funds sent to the seller after the domain is transferred to the buyer.

For a domain name business, you should have an account already set up with an escrow company and understand how it works. This way, if you are negotiating with an end user, you can describe a safe method of payment through escrow and get the process started as soon as possible.

Using a Domain Broker
Domain brokers can work for a buyer to help secure a domain name. But more often than not, domain brokers represent sellers in advertising a domain name for sale and helping to negotiate and close a deal. This can be particularly useful if you have a premium domain name you want to sell. One advantage most brokers have is they have many contacts in the domain industry, as well as experience selling high quality domain names, many to end users. But many brokers with a lot of experience and a good track record often won't deal with a novice or anyone without a large number of premium names.

If you are interested in using a domain broker, the first thing to do is to explore their website to get a feel for what they offer and how they work. You can also look at or post on domain name forums to get some feedback on brokers.

When you have narrowed your broker choices down to about three, send an exploratory email to the contact address on each site. Explain your interest in selling your domain name(s), and ask any relevant questions, including what percentage commission they take and whether they have any domain name exclusivity requirements. Check how long it takes for a representative to contact you and how appropriate their reply is to your questions.

Domain brokers normally work on commission, so they are paid after the deal is done as a percentage of the final sale price. You can rationalize the use of (and payment to) a domain broker in that by using a broker who is a good negotiator, you may be able to sell a domain name for more using the broker than you would have trying to sell the domain on your own.

When you have a domain name being sold through a broker, the broker will keep in touch with you regarding how your domain is being marketed and any contact he or she receives. When there is an offer for your domain name, the broker will discuss the amount and compare it to the current market and recent sales, and usually offer recommendations as to whether to accept the offer or counter with something higher. However, when looking at the offer amount, you should always remember to deduct the commission the broker will earn on the sale so you know what your net amount will be once the deal is done.

If you're selling a domain name yourself and are contacted by a broker who is representing a buyer, you should take your time during negotiations. Because there is a broker involved, that usually means you have a serious buyer. Since brokers specialize in negotiations, they will be trying to get you to agree to the lowest price possible, and will use all sorts of comparables from market trends to recent sales (which may or may not be directly applicable) to persuade you to accept their offer. Again, if you find yourself in this situation, try and have patience and take your time, and hold to your price if you think that is what your domain name is really worth. But also be professional and courteous in all of your correspondence with the broker as you never know when you might be dealing with that same broker again.

Chapter 8 – Risks Involved with Domain Names

As in any business investment, there will always be risks for potential investors.

There are many risks that would-be domain investors should carefully consider before buying and selling. Not every domain you buy is going to sell for more. Domain names can be appraised for wildly different values by different people. And with any transaction, there could be legal issues you have to deal with.

As far as domain name risks, the three to be most concerned about are liquidity, subjectivity and legality. But there are also many others, ranging from questionable Registrar practices to not receiving payment for your domain name. Would-be domainers should carefully consider these risks before investing in domain names.

Liquidity of Domain Names

Both stocks and bonds are traded on fairly liquid markets and there are always brokers you can count on to facilitate your transactions. But this is not the case with domain name trading. Most stocks and bonds can be bought and sold with ease through a broker, but domain names can be much harder to sell. Finding the right buyer is often a matter of listing a domain name for sale and/or contacting potential buyers for several months or even years, which means that investors should have a lengthy time horizon.

The first thing is to do your research before buying any domain name in hopes of selling it for more. But you will also need the patience to be able to hold a domain name for a long period of time if that is what is needed to make a profitable sale.

There are some domain names that inherently go up in value, typically the short names in the .com extension. Even the "worst" two-letter .com domain name is worth tens of thousands of dollars, just by the name alone. Three-letter .com domain names continue to escalate in value, and certain "Chinese" four-letter .com domain names have risen like a commodity. These types of names are not necessarily worth their high figure because they are a word or directly related to a business, but rather due to the scarcity of short names in the .com extension. Of course, if you have a short name that is an English word, it could be worth even more. However, typically only the most wealthy domainers have these types of names in their portfolio.

In the 2015-2016 time frame there was a rush on four-letter .com domain names due to Chinese investors, until all of the four-letter .coms were registered. Their value continued to increase, but then in 2017 when crypto currencies took off, many investors pulled out of domains, leaving many holding four-letter .coms that weren't related to any business name or acronym, and they could no longer sell them even for what they were bought for.

Other names can be worthless (or "hand-reg") one month, then worth much, much more the next month because of current events. Other domain names could actually go down in value because of a negative connotation to some event where nobody wants to be associated with the name.

One must also consider renewal fees. The "non-liquid" domain names that might be a good investment may take a good number of years to finally sell. But with each year another renewal fee needs to be spent, unless you first registered the name for multiple years. These yearly fees can put additional burden on the price of a domain name, and could be the difference as to whether you sell it for profit or not.

Subjectivity with Domain Names

Unlike stocks and bonds where transactions are well regulated and the respective values conform to certain rules and regulations, domain name evaluation can be more subjective and difficult.

Because domains are not traded and regulated like the stock market, each domain name ends up being worth whatever someone is ready, willing and able to pay for it. There is no set standard for evaluating a domain name's worth. Even domain appraisers can only make an educated guess as to what you might sell the domain name for, if at all.

There are also automated domain name appraisal websites that use scripts to analyze recent sales with similar keywords, name length, extension, etc., or whether the domain is attached to a website with traffic. These online automatic appraisals are often high or overvalued for lower value domain names (say, up to $10,000), but are also often low or undervalued for higher value domain names (say, $20,000 and up). One must be careful when using these appraisals to value a domain name.

That said, subjectivity also comes into play based on an association with a domain name. If a domainer has a name that is tied to a certain niche that they know very well, they may see more value in that particular name than someone who doesn't know that market. The domainer may be asking more for the name than anybody is willing to spend, and it may take much more of the domainer's effort to educate or influence a potential buyer to pay more for the domain name.

Many times when looking at the recent sales lists, you might see names that were sold for a high amount and wonder how that name was ever sold for that much. Sometimes the names are sold by experienced domainers or brokers who "work the deal" to get it sold. Other times the name is sold to a buyer who has a specific interest or business tied to that name and was willing to pay top dollar for the domain. Either way, one domainer may look at a domain name and not see much value while another may look at the same name and see a great opportunity.

When it comes to subjectivity with domain names, you should remember that any domain name purchase comes with a risk that it may not be worth more to anybody else, no matter how good you think the domain name is.

Legal Issues with Domain Names

Domain names can be a sticky business from a legal standpoint. Choosing names that are too close to a trademarked name can result in a lawsuit and a court order to forfeit the domain name. In other cases, stolen domain names can be sold before the buyer has the ability to discover that the person selling them the domain is not the true owner. Understanding legal issues is important for anybody buying and selling domain names.

Here are some legal issues to consider:

Cybersquatting and Typosquatting

Domain names and how the trademark laws are applied to them seem to now be much more straightforward than in the earlier years of domaining. But there are still many questions about trademarks with domain names, and even looking at recent cases there are many controversies and inconsistencies. The main point regarding domain names and trademark laws is basically to stay away. If you are looking at registering or buying a domain name where there is any question about whether the name infringes on a trademark, why open yourself up to the risk in the first place? There are so many available domain names that have great potential where there is no question regarding trademarks, so it's best to stick with being safe.

Cybersquatting

In the early days of registering domain names, there were many people jumping into the domain business registering names that belonged to companies and businesses that already existed but had not yet developed websites. These early domainers were then trying to sell the domain names to those companies. Before trademark laws were interpreted and applied to domain names, many of these same people made a lot of money selling trademarked names. Many of these sales were publicized and the term cybersquatting was invented. This in turn gave domain buying and selling a bad reputation, and many to this day still believe the domain business is questionable.

The same questions also apply to registering domain names that are people's names. There is a blurred line as to whether trademark laws apply to a person's name, particularly if that person is a celebrity of some sort. Many domain names have ended up just being handed over because of all of the legal issues involved. Unfortunately, this could apply to a person's name that is not a celebrity, but you could end up being labeled as a cybersquatter for even owning a domain name that is a FirstnameLastnae.com for anybody, celebrity or not. It is best just to register your own name (you never know whether you will become a celebrity or not!) and stay away from other people's names.

Let's look at a few possible examples of cybersquatting and how trademark laws may apply:

- You see the name AmazonProducts.com is available and you register it. You then try to sell it to Amazon. The trademark law applies simply by owning the name, even if you are just trying to recoup your registration cost and are not making a profit. You could end up paying a hefty fine as well as legal fees, and you will lose the domain.

- You see the name AmazonProducts.com is available and you register it. You then start a website that discusses Amazon products and even have a huge disclaimer on your site stating that the site has no affiliation with the Amazon company. The risk here is that Amazon could still make a case against you by using the Amazon name, even if your website explains and promotes products that are sold on Amazon.

- You see the name AmazonProducts.com is available and you register it. You then start a discussion forum based on Amazon's pricing tactics and how the company treats its employees. Even if you don't earn any profits from the website, just by using the Amazon name it is still considered trademark infringement.

- You see the name AmazonProducts.com is available and you register it. You then start a website selling products related to the Amazon River. Even though this may not technically be trademark infringement, there have been many cases where a large company has sued smaller companies simply by having part of their name being used. If you wanted to spend money on legal fees fighting the large company, you could still end up losing the case if it went to court.

161

The previous examples show how trademarks can be applied and how much risk you take on by just registering a name that has the trademarked word in it, whether you plan on making a profit from the name or not. And even if you are doing everything legally, a large corporation could still march in and you could not only lose the domain name, but also pay a fine or end up in court.

Again, it is best to be cautious regarding trademarks. There are many names that end up on the expired and dropped lists that include company trademarked names or words in them. They look tempting, and even rate high in CPC or SVG rankings, but you should avoid registering them. There is a reason they are being dropped and you will be wasting your money and opening yourself up to huge potential risk by registering them.

When in doubt, do a trademark search first or don't register the name.

If you are unsure whether or not your domain involves the use of a copyrighted name, check a database. The World Intellectual Property Organization (WIPO) maintains a searchable Trademark Database that covers various international trademarks.

If you still want to venture into the territory of trademark names, you should at least consider the following:

Understand the Anticybersquatting Consumer Protection Act (ACPA)
The ACPA is a US federal law that addresses trademark disputes regarding domain names. Many times trademark claims aren't black and white. If a company is suing you over a trademark and you believe your domain name is not a trademark infringement, you could still lose the case. Whenever dealing with a lawsuit (or even a cease and desist letter), it is recommended you consult with a copyright attorney to review your case.

When faced with a claim against you for cybersquatting, you should review some of the basic domain name trademark guidelines and ask yourself the following questions:
- Did you register the domain name before the other company or individual registered their trademark? You will not have acted in bad

faith if you already had the domain name before they obtained their trademark.

- Does the other party really have the trademark rights they claim to have? The first place to look is on the US Patent and Trademark Office (USPTO) website to see if there is a registered trademark. (https://www.uspto.gov/)

- Is the domain name in question a generic or descriptive word? Just because the name sounds generic enough does not mean someone won't try and file a claim against you, especially if it sounds close to a trademarked name.

- Do you have your own legitimate business on the domain name that is in no way connected to the copyright holder? Although you may not legally be in the wrong, many times you will end up having to give up the domain name in these cases.

Keep It To Yourself

If you registered a domain name with the thought of resale and find out later it is a trademarked name, it is best to simply delete the name instead of contacting the copyright holder. Especially do not contact them with hopes of selling the domain name to them – this will most likely start a legal process.

If you have set up a legitimate business website on a name you first checked but didn't find a trademark on (in good faith), but later found out the name is trademarked, it is best to transfer your business website to another domain name and either delete the questionable domain name or let it expire. No need to contact the trademark holder, just keep it quiet and move on.

Hire a Lawyer

Although intellectual property laws regarding the Internet and trademarks can be open to interpretation, if you are being sued or receive a cease and desist letter, it may be best to seek out an attorney that specializes in trademark law, particularly if you have a profitable business and don't believe the other party has a right to your name.

You may also seek out the help of the Domain Name Rights Coalition, especially if it is a large company threatening you but you think you are in the right.

Typosquatting

Typosquatting is similar to cybersquatting, except the domain name is actually a misspelling of a popular trademark. Mis-spelled domains can get a lot of internet traffic due to mis-keying of letters when typing in a domain name to visit. These sites can generally make money through advertising, especially if the correctly-spelled website gets a lot of traffic.

There isn't much case law regarding typosquatting cases. But even if you don't think what you are doing is illegal, with a mis-spelled domain name set up only with the goal of making money from traffic meant for a different website, you could still find yourself in a trademark lawsuit. Many companies are aggressive in protecting their trademark, even with mis-spellings.

Continuing with our set of examples:

- You see the name AmaznProducts.com (without the o) is available and you register it. You then do any of the examples that were discussed in the cybersquatting section above. You still run the risk of being caught up in a trademark suit, and could lose the domain name, have to pay a fine, and could even end up in court.

The practice of typosquatting is typically frowned upon by other domainers. However, there are still many typosquatting websites still being used, more often than you would think. Those website owners are doing it at risk and they probably know it, but are often located in countries that may be hard to reach if a case is brought up. Overall, it is much better to be safe and avoid typo-squatting. Even if you think you could make some easy money with it, you could also find yourself facing some big legal trouble.

UDRP

The UDRP (Uniform domain name Dispute Resolution Policy) is the policy ICANN passed to resolve cybersquatting domain name disputes. When you register a domain name, you are agreeing to the UDRP policy (usually in the small print). The UDRP process is an easier and much less expensive way to resolve domain name disputes when compared to legal actions.

How UDRP Works

When a UDRP complaint is filed, a panel consisting of 1 to 3 reviewers will look at both the complainant's and the respondent's documented evidence. The panel will then come to a decision to either transfer the domain name to the trademark holder or let the domain name stay with the respondent.

The UDRP process is more like mediation than a trial. The final decision is not an official legal document. But the UDRP does involve panelists with deep knowledge of the domain name industry, unlike a judge who might not be familiar with cybersquatting. However, if after UDRP the dispute is continued by one party or the other in the courts, the side that had the favorable UDRP ruling may stand a better chance at winning the court case.

The UDRP process has many advantages over an official legal proceeding, the first and most obvious being cost. But another main advantage is that ICANN is international, so trademark owners are able to have a proceeding regardless of what country the domain name owner lives in. Because ICANN controls the domain name system (DNS), they have the ability to enforce a domain transfer depending on the panel's ruling.

However, what the UDRP process does not include is any monetary damages. Upon a favorable ruling for the trademark owner, the Registrar holding the domain name will receive instructions to transfer the name to the complainant (trademark owner). If the complainant also wants monetary compensation, legal action would need to be pursued.

Although there are many ccTLDs that have not adopted the UDRP policy, the main TLDs like .com, .net, .org, .info, .biz and .name (among others) has adopted the UDRP process as the method to resolve trademark disputes.

The UDRP Complaint

If a trademark owner wants to file a UDRP complaint, they need to use an approved 'Dispute-Resolution Service Provider.' Usually an attorney for the trademark owner does the filing, but a lawyer is not required. But it's still a good idea for the trademark owner to hire an attorney who specializes in domain name cases. The case will need to be presented to the UDRP panelists so a good understanding of the law will certainly help. The trademark owner becomes the complainant in the proceeding.

After a UDRP complaint has been filed, the owner of the domain name being disputed will receive a copy of the complaint from an accredited provider. The domain name owner becomes the respondent. The respondent will have 20 days to provide an answer to the complaint. If an answer is not submitted, within 20 days, the UDRP panel will review the complaint without a response, which most likely will end up with a favorable ruling for the complainant, which leads to a domain name transfer order to the Registrar. There could be circumstances where the 20 days could be extended if the respondent requests such an extension.

In filing a complaint, the trademark owner has to prove the domain name that is being disputed is either identical or similar to the complainant's trademark. The complaint should also show the domain owner does not have a legal interest in the trademark or domain name. Additionally, the complainant must prove the domain name was registered and being used in "bad faith."

What does bad faith mean? Although defined by the UDRP policy, there may always be cases where the circumstances don't exactly fit and could be open to interpretation. In the broadest sense, "bad faith" is when someone purchases or registers a domain name that is clearly a trademarked name, with the intent of selling it to the trademark owner for a profit.

For example: Jane registers the domain name AmazonSolutions.com and tries to sell it to Amazon for $10,000. Even though the domain name could be used by someone in South America at the Amazon River, Jane instead tried to sell the domain name to the Amazon company for a profit. This is clearly bad faith on her part.

Jane could also be guilty of bad faith by registering a domain name of a new company in her town before that company's owner registers it. If she then reaches out to the new company owner offering the domain at a profit, the UDRP policy has been breached, even though the name isn't technically a trademark. In the early days of the internet this was done all the time, and many early domainers made a lot of money by selling domain names to either already established businesses or new companies, until legal action and finally the UDRP was created put an end to this tactic.

Bad faith can also be described for a situation where web users can be confused into thinking that a domain name is related to an actual trademarked website or domain name. Continuing our example, even if Jane registered the domain name AmazonSolutions.com and developed a website which included a statement that the site is not in any way associated with Amazon or an Amazon Affiliate, she could still be guilty of bad faith. Of course, this would not apply to websites that are part of Amazon's actual affiliate program. Additionally, this type of bad faith could also pertain to typosquatting.

Just like legal cases in the United States courts, in a UDRP complaint the burden of proof rests on the complainant who must prove all points of their case. The respondent is seen as innocent until proven guilty, so to speak.

As for the cost, a UDRP complaint can end up well over $1,000 US. The final cost depends on the number of domain names involved as well as the number of UDRP panelists who review the case and how long the case takes.

The UDRP Response

When the owner of a domain name that is being disputed for a trademark breach receives a UDRP complaint, the owner has 20 days to provide a written response. In answering a complaint, the response should carefully detail each point made in the complaint and why the domain owner does not believe there is a trademark violation.

Although an attorney is not needed by the domain owner, one with domain name experience is highly recommended. A well-crafted response siting domain policies has a better chance of providing a strong defense.

The response does not need to be lengthy. In a UDRP complaint, the respondent should be able to prove the domain name was not itself already trademarked before the respondent registered the name. If the registration occurred after the trademark date, the respondent could prove they were already a business or known by that name before the complainant registered the trademark. The response could also be that the domain owner has a use for the domain name that won't be used for profit and will not mislead web users into believing the site is affiliated with the trademark owner and won't tarnish the name of the trademark holder, but this defense may be harder to win.

The UDRP Decision

Following the UDRP complaint and response (if submitted), the panel either rules for the complainant or for the respondent after deliberation. There are no rulings where there is a "hung jury" so to speak.

If the ruling favors the complainant, both parties are notified and a 10 day ICANN process starts. Essentially, this gives the respondent the opportunity to file legal action in order to keep the domain name from immediate transfer. Once it is transferred it may be near impossible to get back. If there is no legal suit filed, then ICANN notifies the Registrar to transfer the domain name to the complainant. If ICANN receives notice that a lawsuit has been filed by the respondent, then transfer is delayed until the legal case is resolved or dropped.

If the UDRP panel rules in favor of the respondent, then both parties are notified and the domain name stays with the respondent.

Once a UDRP ruling is given, either party could pursue legal action to try and overturn the UDRP decision if the panelists did not rule in their favor. There have also been cases where the UDRP panel found in favor of the respondent and the respondent followed with a civil suit against the complainant in order to recover their legal costs in defense of the complaint. The complainant could also sue the respondent in court for trademark infringement, even though they did not win the UDRP ruling.

Other Domain Name Risks

There are other risks in domaining that you should be aware of:

Not Receiving Payment

When selling domain names, there could be times when receiving the payment might be a challenge or, perhaps, not received at all. Or you might find when you are buying a domain name after an agreement has been reached that you don't receive the domain name after paying for it. There are some steps you can take to help avoid either of these from happening.

As a domain name seller, when you list your domain name for sale on any marketplace, or even your own website, you should always list the conditions of how you can receive payment and when the domain name will be transferred. Some marketplaces already have set rules and policies about this, so if you list on one of those, then the transaction simply follows their pre-set policy. Keep in mind to set up your business or accounts as best you can to be able to receive many different types of payment. If you solely rely on PayPal, for instance, there are many buyers that either can't or won't use PayPal as a form of payment, and you could potentially lose a sale if you don't have alternate means of receiving payments.

When you are selling on a domain name forum or on your own website, it is best to explain as clearly as you can what forms of payment you will accept and when the domain name will transfer to the buyer. For low-priced domains, it is typical to only transfer the domain name once you receive the full payment from the buyer. Some buyers may be hesitant, but this part of domaining relies on honesty and integrity. And since domainers can post on forums about anyone in the business who does not follow through on a sale, it is not worth risking your reputation on a small dollar domain name sale.

You may find yourself in a situation where you have an agreed-to price, but the seller is delaying sending payment, even if after a set period which you may have posted as a condition of the sale (24 or 48 hours after end of auction or accepted BIN for example). It is best in this situation to be patient and continue to communicate with the buyer. If the buyer starts sending you excuses which begin to raise red flags in your mind, then you should proceed with extra caution. If the sale is through a marketplace, you can always reach out to the marketplace for assistance in completing a sale. However, in the end, there are times when a sale does not go through. You should learn to accept this risk and move on if it happens.

To possibly avoid losing a sale due to a hesitant buyer, there is always the option to have the buyer first send half of the payment to the seller. Then after the successful transfer of the domain name, the buyer then sends the rest of the payment. This is not often done, but can be a good compromise for a buyer with whom you think this may be the only way to get the sale to go through.

And remember, never push or transfer a domain name to a buyer without first receiving at least half of the money.

As a buyer, when paying for a domain name, most times you will send the entire payment directly to the seller relying on good faith the seller will transfer the domain name to you. One of the best ways to ensure this happens is to only buy domain names from reputable sellers or on reputable marketplaces. If you are on a domain name forum and a seller has a domain name for sale, you can typically see how many transactions the seller has made on that forum, or else see reviews for that seller. If you have any questions about the seller's practices, you can ask them before you place a bid or make an offer to buy a domain name from that seller. It is always prudent and wise to not be hasty and place bids or offers from a seller you have not first vetted.

For higher priced domain names, using an escrow agent is the safest way to transfer both the money and the domain name. For the most part, escrow companies provide a reliable 3rd party service in collecting money, holding it until the domain name transfers, then releasing the money to the seller.

However, some complain that escrow companies hold on to the money too long and may cause the seller some heartache. Escrow companies also, in most cases, have no control over the transfer of the domain name. Just because funds were sent and are being held in escrow, sometimes the seller decides not to complete the transaction and doesn't transfer the name. This can happen when a seller may get a better offer during the escrow process, or else for some reason decides they can still get more for their domain so pulls out of the sale. Unfortunately for the seller, the potential buyer can always post on domain name forums what happened and tarnish any good reputation that seller might have had.

If you do not want to have a chunk of the sale amount go to a third party like an escrow company, you can always execute a domain name sales agreement. This can be a somewhat short document that is signed by both parties regarding the price and terms of transfer of the domain name.

Here is an example:

DOMAIN NAME SALE AND OWNERSHIP TRANSFER AGREEMENT

This Domain Name Sale and Ownership Transfer Agreement ("Agreement") is entered into between *seller* located at *address* ("Seller"), and *buyer* located at *address* ("Purchaser") on this *date*. This agreement sets forth all terms and conditions under which Seller agrees to sell and transfer to Purchaser all ownership rights in and to the domain name *name* ("Domain Name").

Seller and the Purchaser hereby agree as follows:

1. **Purchase Price**. In consideration for payment of *sale price in words* ($*sale price in numbers*), the sufficiency of which is hereby acknowledged ("Purchase Price"), paid by Purchaser to Seller, Seller hereby assigns, sells, transfers and conveys to Purchaser all of Seller's right, title, and interest in and to the Domain Name. Payment will be made in US dollars (*or other currency as agreed*).

2. **Seller's Representations**. Seller represents and warrants that it is the lawful and exclusive Registrant of the Domain Name and no other party has any right to registration of the Domain Name or has otherwise made any claim to the Domain Name. Seller further represents that it has the exclusive authority to enter into this transaction and transfer the Domain Name, free of the claims of any third parties.

3. **Transfer of the Domain Name**. The Domain Name is registered with *Registrar* ("Registrar"), an ICANN accredited Registrar system. Upon confirmation of receipt of Purchase Price, Seller shall push the Domain Name to Purchaser's account at Registrar within 2 days of receiving payment. This enables Purchaser to modify the registration information as desired and/or transfer the Domain Name to a different Registrar, in order to take full control of the Domain Name. If any additional funds are required to properly transfer the domain name from Seller to Purchaser, the cost shall be the responsibility of the Purchaser (*or other agreement*).

171

4. **Further Assurances**. Seller shall take all necessary actions, including providing all necessary documentation to Purchaser in order to transfer Domain Name to Purchaser.

5. **Counterparts/Fax**. This Agreement may be signed in counterparts. Signed counterparts of this Agreement transmitted via Fax or Scanned Document are equivalent to a signed original of this Agreement.

6. **Governing Law**. This Agreement is made under and shall be governed by and interpreted in accordance with the laws of the *agreed-to place*, without regard to that state's choice of law principles, which may direct the application of the laws of another jurisdiction.

7. **Entire Agreement.** This Agreement constitutes and contains the entire agreement between the parties with respect to the subject matter herein and supersedes any prior oral or written agreements. This Agreement cannot be changed, modified, amended, or supplemented, except in writing signed by all parties hereto.

IN WITNESS WHEREOF, Seller and Purchaser have caused this Agreement to be executed by their duly authorized representatives.

_____   _____
[Purchaser's name, signature above]   [Seller's name, signature above]

_____   _____
            Date   Date

Domain Name Tasting and Kiting

Although these practices have become limited due to newer regulations, in the early days of domaining, domain name tasting and kiting were often used as ways to test out domain names without actually paying the registration fees.

Domain Name Tasting
Tasting a domain name is when someone registers a name and, sometime over the following five days, contacts the Registrar to delete the name from their account and get their money back. Many Registrars allow this five day (or

thereabouts) return. Sometimes a website developer might register a good name for a website and then, a day later, find another name that will work even better. By being able to give up the registration on the first name (and have the fee returned) - no harm, no foul.

But a domain name investor might first want to test whether a certain domain name might have value due to backlinks or other associations, and can more easily test this out by registering the name. Once registered, the domainer could put the domain on a parking site and see what kind of traffic might still be associated with the name. After five days, the domainer has the option of either deleting the name (and having the registration fee returned), or keeping the name if he/she thinks it has monetary value. And even if the domain name is deleted, any revenue the name made in those five days belongs to the domainer.

Another reason a domain investor might want to use this domain tasting tactic is that by registering the name, particularly if it just appeared on an expired list, it keeps other investors from registering that domain name. Then the investor can take five days to decide whether to actually keep the domain name or not.

At a much larger level, a domainer could use this tactic for hundreds or even thousands of domain names every five days and only keep the ones that are worthwhile. This method was used very heavily in the mid to late 2000s, where it is reported that in one month alone (February, 2007), there were 55 million domain name registrations but during the same month there were 51 million domain name deletions. That is a rate of almost 93% of the domains registered that month being returned! However, most Registrars now place limits on how many times (and/or how often) the five-day return policy may be used.

Domain Name Kiting

Domain kiting is a term used for re-registering a domain name that was just deleted by the same domain investor. Essentially, it is domain tasting a second time. After five days of "trying out" a domain name, an investor could delete the domain name and have the registration fee refunded. Then, immediately re-register the domain name, thus starting another five day period in order to further taste the domain name.

Once these practices got out of hand in 2007, the Registrars reached out to ICANN with their complaints. The Registrars were having their resources tapped by domain name investors without earning any revenue as they were refunding so many registrations.

Because domain tasting was still very prominent through 2007, in 2008 ICANN set up penalties for deleted domains. The new regulations would allow up to 10% of registrations for a particular Registrar to be deleted without penalty – and anything above that would incur an ICANN fee per domain name. The Registrars, of course, passed that fee on to domain name investors, affecting those investors that were deleting a large percentage of their domains.

Once the policy was adopted, in the matter of a month the number of deleted domains decreased from about 18 million domain names in June, 2008 to under 3 million domain names in July, 2008. The penalty was soon raised to equal the price of the domain name's registration, and a year later in July, 2009, there were only about 50,000 domains deleted.

Domain tasting isn't used much anymore as revenue from ads on parking sites has seen a sharp decrease over the last few years, so a domain investor won't be able to make much money in five days by parking a domain name.

Domain Front Runners

Unlike domain tasting, the front running of domains is a practice that many domainers still believe is happening on a regular basis. A front runner could be another domainer or even a Registrar (or someone who works for a Registrar) who collects data from Whois searches or queries regarding the availability of a domain name and registers the name before the person who was doing the search has the time to complete their registration.

As a domainer, you might see a news story on TV about a new technology. You immediately go to your computer to check about the availability of the domain name. To do that, you might just go to your favorite Registrar's website and query the name in the search box on their website. Once the search is implemented, the Registrar's software checks to see if there is a Whois record for that particular domain name. If there is a record, then the search returns a statement to you saying the name is already taken. If a Whois record is not found, then the search returns a statement to you saying the name is available.

You think you've found a great name that is available. You go through a number of steps to put the name in your cart, determine how many years you want to register the name for, review your payment information, and then submit your order to buy ... only to see a message now saying the name is taken. How did this happen? Only a few minutes ago the name was available!

It could be that someone else had the same idea at the same time and, by coincidence, was registering the name at the same time that you were. But what are the odds of that happening? Or perhaps the name had actually already been registered but there was an error by your Registrar saying the name was available when it actually wasn't. Not very likely, but it happens.

It may also be possible that someone hacked into the Registrar's server, or even your computer, or maybe is an employee or consultant for the Registrar who saw the search happening on your great name and went and registered it before you could. One might think someone would have more important things to do with their time than sit around and watch domain name searches, but stranger things have happened.

Once something like this happens to you, what can you do? The first thing would be to do a Whois search on the domain name. You might find out that the domain had been registered for some time and so it was a mistake in your initial search. But you might see the domain was just registered, and through the same Registrar you were doing your search. If this is the case then front running could be the cause.

Other cases of possible front running have been discussed regarding URL browser searches. Some have reported that after typing a domain name into a browser and finding the name did not resolve, they went to register the name only to find it was registered just minutes earlier.

Avoiding Front Runners
If front running is really happening, there really isn't much you can do. Whether the culprit is at the Registrar, the Registry, or even your own Internet

Service Provider, if the domain name is already registered when you press the "Buy" button, you will not be able to register it.

So instead of continuing to blame others, what can you do to try and avoid suspected front running from happening in the first place? One is to only do your domain name searches at a Registrar you trust. If you are new to domaining you might not yet have a trusted relationship with a Registrar.

If you suspect front running is happening, you could try and type in a different domain name or two that you know have been available, then check to see whether they become registered in about the same time frame. The chances of seeing something like this happen are pretty slim. You can also ask for other domainers' input in a domain name forum. You might be amazed at the stories you hear, but this still doesn't stop suspected front running from happening.

The best advice is to be ready to make your purchase when you are making a domain name query. For instance, many domainers make lists of domain names they are interested in on a separate spreadsheet. Then, when they are at their computer with payment options ready, they can immediately register and pay for each domain. If you wait and look up multiple domain names, putting the available ones in your "cart" without actually completing the payment process for each one, there is a chance that one or more of the domain names in your cart could be registered by someone else before you make your payment.

If A Suspected Front Running Happens
One thing you can still do if a name becomes registered just before you are able to register the same name, is to wait five days and check the name again. You may find that the domain name was "tasted" and then deleted by whomever registered it just before you tried. If this is a domain name you really want, you can continue to run Whois queries from a trusted Registrar. But you should always avoid entering a desired domain name into your browser. If it is indeed a case of domain tasting and they see some type-in traffic to the site, they will most likely keep the domain name.

Alternative TLDs

If the .com domain name you want is not available, there are alternative extensions you can choose from. We covered gTLDs and ccTLDs earlier in this book. Generally, you are safe when registering domain names with these extensions, although there may be times with some ccTLDs where a country may block or take over access to domain names.

There is also a set of extensions called nTLDs. These are "new" TLDs and include names with endings like .SHOP, .APP, .NINJA and .BUZZ. In these extensions you have a wider availability of desired names, and new extensions keep getting added

However, not all Registrars support every extension, so you may be limited where you can register and keep alternative types of domain names. Also, how these domain names are governed could sometimes be shady, and have much different rules and fees associated with them than the Top Level Domains. And, if you don't see the extension that you're registering on the ICANN/IANA recognized list, you should proceed with caution.

It is also important to note that names with these "new" extensions are extremely difficult to flip. Many companies and businesses register names in these extensions and market their business with the alternative extension proudly displayed in all of their marketing. But for a domainer, names with alternative extensions don't have much of a resale market, and registration and renewal fees in many of these extensions cost a lot more than gTLD extensions.

Domain Stealing

So you've registered a great domain name and even created a nice landing page on a website on that domain. Then one day, you log into your domain control panel and see that the domain name is gone. And the website does not resolve. You then check the Whois record for your domain only to find it is either now showing a different contact name, most likely from someone in another country, or the Whois contact is now set to Private. It looks like your domain name has been stolen, and there are a number of ways this could have happened.

Through Your Email Account
One of the first recorded domain name thefts involved an email spoof. This means that a hacker gains control of an email account and uses it to steal domain names. There are different ways someone can hack into your email, but

once this is done they may be able to make changes through the Registrar and use your own email account to verify the changes or even send emails without you even knowing.

Domain stealers have also been known to gain control of an abandoned email account that was once used for a Registrar. They might be able to contact the Registrar posing as you asking for a forgotten password on the old email account. Once they have your Registrar password, they could go in and change all the domain name information or transfer the domain to their own account at another Registrar, and the original domain owner is unaware their domain name(s) have been stolen until it is too late.

Over the Phone

When you call your Registrar about your domain name account, what sort of information do they ask you for verification purposes? Do they ask for your name and address? Do they ask for a PIN number? Or might they send you an email or text with a verification code?

You might think this verification process is annoying, but for the safety of your domain names (and information), it is best to be with a Registrar that has strict policies as to how they verify your information to be sure it is actually you that is talking to them.

It has been known where a domain stealer called a Registrar pretending to be upset about their account, demanding passwords or other account information over the phone, trying to be so annoying to the Registrar's phone personnel where they end up giving in and releasing the information or making an account update on a domain name. This is another reason to use a Registrar that has good verification processes in place, even if they can be annoying at times.

Third Party Seller

Some domain marketplaces have excellent procedures for sellers to verify they are the owner of the domain name before it is listed for sale. However, there are also some domain sales websites that don't require such verification.

It sometimes happens where a domain name is put up for sale by someone who does not actually own the name. Maybe they are looking to see if they can make some quick money. A good indicator of this is if you see a premium domain name on a site selling for a low "Buy Now" value. You go through the process of starting to buy the name, and even make your payment, only to be notified by the domain sales website that the seller was not authorized to sell the domain and your money is returned. But there is a risk the marketplace does not do a good job of finding out the seller did not actually own the name and a payment still goes to them. Then the marketplace may be out the money, but it could take a long time before you get your refund.

However, for the person who does actually own the domain name, the name could become at risk. It has happened where someone sells the domain name without being the actual domain owner, and the buyer ends up pressuring the Registrar to give them the domain. If for some reason the Registrar is not able to immediately contact the real owner, the domain transfer might happen without any payment to the actual domain name owner.

Preventing Domain Stealing
Keeping your contact information current at your Registrar is the best way to prevent someone from stealing a domain name. You should always check to be sure you have a current email address in your account and if you ever migrate to a new email, be sure to change your contact information at each Registrar where you have domain names.

The email address you use should be one you often check. This is because there could be suspicious emails from hackers or others wanting to steal your information, and the sooner you can see and flag emails asking for passwords or other information, the less likely the chance there could become a problem.

As mentioned elsewhere, you also want to be sure you have your domain names with a trusted Registrar. You should always check your Registrar's policies regarding their security measures, particularly if you are notified there is a change to any of their policies.

Within your domain names' control panel, you should always have your domains set to the "locked" position. By having domain lock on, domain names cannot be transferred. And if you are just a suspicious or careful person in general, then you can spend extra money for domain name certification and privacy when registering your domains.

What You Should Do If A Domain Name Is Stolen
It is always a good idea to regularly check your domain name inventory with each Registrar. The sooner you notice something isn't right, like one of your domain names is missing, then the better chance there is of getting the problem resolved.

If you do see there is a problem, you should immediately call your Registrar. Wait on hold for as long as you have to. If they are not taking calls, then you should go through whatever online support system they have, be it opening a ticket or just emailing their help desk.

You should then check the public Whois database. If the domain is still in your name, then it's probably just a mistake with your Registrar. But if the domain is set to Private (if you didn't have it private before), or it is in somebody else's name, then you have had your domain name stolen. And even if the new contact information is private, you should still be able to tell which Registrar the domain name has been changed to, if indeed that changed as well. If it's still at the same Registrar, then you may have a path to getting the domain name back. But if the domain is at a different Registrar, you will have a much more difficult time getting the name transferred back. Although it's a long shot, it can't hurt to call that other Registrar and explain what happened to see if there is anything they can do.

If the domain name in question is premium and worth a lot of money, you may want to also contact an attorney familiar with the domain industry (if you don't already have one). You may be asked to send a certified letter to either or both Registrars so that you have written documentation stating your case.

As you are reading this without having experienced something like this before, you may be wondering how a domain name can be stolen in the first place. Back in Chapter 2 domain registration was explained. The most important point is that a domainer does not actually "own" domain names. Instead, domains are registered giving you the right to use that domain name for whatever period of time you have purchased. And when a domain name is renewed, you are simply extending the time period of your agreement to use the name. Domain names are not "property." So stealing a domain name is actually more like hacking into your personal information in order to change the domain name's registration and contact information without your permission.

If you are able to get your domain name back into your account with your Registrar, then you will want to take extra precaution in the future to protect your domain name. And even if you are not able to get it back, you should still be extra vigilant and follow all the steps you can think of to keep your other domain names safe.

Protecting Your Domain Names

The domain industry, just like any other online endeavor, has its share of hackers, thieves and scam artists. If you have a domain business, there are precautions you can take to help protect your investments.

Registrars

The first place where you might be vulnerable is with your domain name's Registrar. In order to register a domain name, you have to give your Registrar personal information, as well as credit card information. If you are using a Registrar that is untrustworthy, then one quick way to protect yourself is to transfer your domains to a better Registrar.

We discussed Registrars and how to choose a good one back in Chapter 2. With regard to security in particular, you can search online for reviews of Registrars and see how they rate. Be careful when reading some of the negative reviews, though, because they aren't always a truthful account of what really may have happened. One of the best resources for finding out more about Registrars and how well they may be trusted are to simply post questions on one of the domain name discussion boards/websites.

Another reason a trusted Registrar is important is that they are the ones actually holding your domain names for you. If something were to happen and one of your domain names disappeared from your account, it is your Registrar who you contact. If you think something malicious has happened, only by having a trustworthy Registrar will you feel better about getting whatever issue is happening successfully resolved.

What sort of protections are there with your Registrar just to access your account or, better yet, make changes to your account? If all it takes is a PIN number to make changes over the phone, that probably isn't secure enough. There have been many stories of domain names being transferred out of an account via a phone call, and once the domain name is gone it's next to impossible to get it back. So the next time your Registrar is asking for two or three different pieces of information in order to access your account, say thank you very much, take the extra few seconds to give the extra information required, and know that your domain names are being guarded as best they can be by your Registrar.

Passwords
Most online users get sick of passwords. One company requires a minimum of 12 characters, including a capital letter, a number and a special character. Another company requires less, but is very careful about screening consecutive digits or letters, and will only approve a password if their system determines it to be a good password. Oh and you may also need to change your password every so often.

Domainers typically have accounts at many, many sites. From the different Registrars where you have your domain names, to all of the marketplaces and online communities, there's easily a dozen or more passwords to remember just for your domain business.

So here's some tips: pick a theme for your domain business passwords and have all of your passwords somewhat related to that theme. This will at least help you keep some sort of order to your domaining passwords, but never use the same password on any two sites, be it a Registrar, marketplace or online community. Next, don't have your passwords listed in a document or spreadsheet on your computer – easy target for hackers. A better way to store your passwords is by using a secure password software or a secure app on your phone. Of course, don't forget the password to get into your secure app!

If passwords are emailed to you, immediately input the password into your secure app and then delete the email from both your inbox and the trash folder. And with regard to the password to your email account, never ever ever give it to anybody. Your email account, the one associated with your domain name Registrars, is a hacker's gateway into stealing your domains. When you request a domain change what is the first thing you get? An email from your Registrar for you to confirm whatever change it is that is being requested. If a hacker gets into your email account, they may be able to find all of your saved emails regarding your domain names and then methodically work to steal them from you. You may also want to consider setting up a secure email account on one of your own domains. Free email accounts such as Hotmail or Yahoo are well known for security risks.

Keeping Domains Safe

In your domain business you will inevitably get a lot of phone calls and emails regarding website design, app design, SEO support, etc. from individuals or companies, many in other countries, trying to sell you their services. You will also get emails throughout the year warning you that your domain is going to expire and if you just click on this link they will make sure you do not lose your domain. Of course you know not to click any links in emails you get from any company you are not already working with. And you should never give out any information to anybody over the phone regarding your domains.

These individuals or companies may have legitimate businesses or they may not – you don't know. So how do they get your information? The information they are using usually comes from the Whois contact information when you register a domain name. As discussed elsewhere in this book, setting up Whois privacy on your domain names has pros and cons, and you must weigh these before taking this step. But if you place a higher value on security over the possibility of selling a domain name through your Whois contact information, then enabling Whois privacy will prevent both these annoying companies and any potential hackers from having your contact information.

Another thing to remember is to always keep your Registrar Lock enabled on every one of you domain names. In your domain account, you can set each domain to be locked or not. With the Lock set to ON, any unauthorized changes to your domain name can be prevented. Then, only when you are ready to make a change to your domain, such as transferring it to another Registrar or pushing it to another domainer if you sold it, would you turn the Lock to OFF.

Legal Actions with Domain Names

The UDRP process described earlier in this chapter is only used for cases involving cybersquatting and trademarks. And the result is only the transfer of the domain name to the complainant if ruled in their favor with no monetary losses or penalties.

A civil suit is the legal path either a complainant or respondent could take following a UDRP ruling to recover any monetary losses. Domain name owners can also file a civil suit if they feel a company has misused the UDRP process to "reverse hijack" a domain name. Suits could also be filed against other domainers for non-payment for a domain name, against a Registrar for unfair practices, or practically anything involving domain names.

Any legal actions will look to jurisdictional laws. In the United States, as mentioned earlier in this chapter, the federal law that protects trademark owners against cybersquatting is called the Anti-cybersquatting Consumer Protection Act (ACPA). Not only does the law prohibit misuse of domain names through "bad faith" (described earlier in this chapter), but also covers typosquatting and the misuse of misspelled domain names or names that are similar to a trademark.

Of course, legal actions can get very expensive, unlike the UDRP path. Not only are there large legal fees, but per the ACPA the court could award up to $100,000 in penalties per domain name violation. This could mean that if a domain owner had ten misspellings of Amazon and showed bad faith in the use of these names (like trying to profit from ads), the domain owner could end up being liable for a million dollars in penalties.

Legal cybersquatting actions have a similar burden of proof to prove as in the UDRP process, but quote ACPA law as well as any other case law. Many legal actions also bring additional information into the case, such as past history of the domain owner (if they have acted in similar "bad faith" manners before with regard to domain names), or if the Registrant name on the domain's Whois record is false or misleading.

The other challenge with the legal system is the power large companies can bring to a legal action, including the threat of millions of dollars in damages. If you don't have the funds to go up against a large corporation in court, then it would be best to not do anything that could have even the most remote possibility of being misconstrued as trademark infringement.

Cease and Desist Letters

A so-called "cease and desist" letter is not something you want to receive. Although better than having a legal case filed against you, this type of letter is generally used by companies asking you to transfer your offending domain name to them (or just simply deleting it) or they will take further legal action against you. Many times this may be just a scare tactic, but if there is even the most remote association between your domain name and this company, you will typically follow whatever they are asking.

If you have the domain name listed on any marketplaces, you should immediately remove the listings. And by all means you should stop any other attempts you may have in trying to sell the name. If you have a website running on the domain name, you should either take it down or else consult an attorney and get a legal opinion before continuing.

The best advice is simply to stay away from trademarked names. It's not worth the potential hassle and risk for the domainer. There are many, many different niches in which to make profits in domain names, so why would you want to risk your entire domain business with tempting trademarks?

Also, when browsing through dropped or expired domain name lists, you will see many names with trademarks. Most of these were registered by inexperienced domainers thinking they found a great name, only to later learn about trademark law and cybersquatting. Then the name just sits in their account until its registration runs out, or it can be deleted at any time through the Registrar. If you have a question whether there is a trademark on a name or not, there are online resources for searching for active trademarks. After reading all of the above legal risks, you should not be tempted to register any domain names that include a trademark, or do anything else illegal with regard to your domaining business and practices..

The Future of Domain Names

Although the domain name industry is alive and well at the present, could there be a time when the internet transitions to something else? As in anything else in life, there is always a risk regarding what might happen in the future.

Social Media Profiles

Many advertisers and marketers are concerned that social media will soon replace domain names completely and make them go obsolete. This fear is even more real nowadays because many online businesses and startups are using the power of social media to connect to their target audience, and their websites are secondary. The main social media companies are working on strategies to lead the online presence of global industries, and how this evolves could lead to domain names being less important for businesses.

New Technologies

With the growth of mobile devices, the URL of domains is becoming less clear. And at the same time, we are witnessing change and growth in technologies that have been unprecedented. The cryptocurrency market is a good example. How this affects domain names is still unknown. There is much research going into solving some of the limitations of the domain name system. For instance, if the server that your website is on goes down, then your site is down. Why rely on a server for your online presence? Are there other ways files, and websites, can be stored and accessed? If a new technology for file systems gains traction, the domain name system as we know it could cease to exist.

The Bottom Line with Regard to Domain Name Risks

As in the case of any normal business, buying and selling domains for profit has its own advantages and disadvantages. And, like any investment, domain names come with their own set of risks.

However, at this time, diligent investors who consider the risks and follow the right steps can be profitable. Keeping your domains and online information safe, while also minimizing the chances of getting involved in any legal dealings, security fraud or threats, only help with your business success.

Chapter 9 – Making Money Selling Domain Names

Now for the good part – how to buy and sell domain names for profit!

Have you heard the following expressions?
- Money doesn't grow on trees
- If it sounds too good to be true, then it probably is

The first means you are going to have to put some effort into the buying and selling of domain names to make a profit. The second is to follow the advice in the previous chapter and be wary of scam artists or others who are trying to take your money.

If you really want to make money buying and selling domain names, then you should think of it as a business, not a hobby. Yes, treating something like a business can, at times, take some of the joy out of it. And domaining as a hobby, for the most part, is just not profitable. If you are treating domaining as a hobby, there is always the possibility you may get lucky and sell one of your domain names for a lot of money, but the chances of that are very slim.

One of the first rules of a commercial business is to know your customer. In the case of selling domains, your target should be on finding an end user for each and every one of your domains. Sure, you may be able to sell domain names to other domainers. But for the most part, any profit you make selling to others in the business will be much less than selling to someone (could be a person or company) that wants to use your domain name for their business on the internet.

And this, of course, means that before you buy a domain name, you need to first decide whether you think someone would want to use the domain name for a business. A long, unpronounceable domain name with a bunch of random letters generally will not make for a good business website. Also, most business owners are not willing to invest in new TLDs or, in many cases, anything other than a domain name with a .com extension.

Sell to End Users

Again, you should look at who your best customer will be – the end user. You can always try and sell your domain names to other domainers, and you might make a small profit. But, for the most part, other people in the domain name buying and selling business are looking to buy at "discount" prices, not "retail" prices.

Let's look at an example. You think you have found a good deal on a domain name. It is in a market that is selling in the mid-XXX range (that is, around $500). You are able to buy the domain name on a website for $400. Wow! You think you have made an instant $100!

But wait, who are you going to sell this great domain name to? It may not be a single word or brandable domain name that a business owner will want to use. You only bought it because of a "market" you saw as profitable based on the sales of similar domains. If you look at that market more closely, for the most part, those reported sales are domain names being sold from one domainer to another, not to an end user.

So you put the domain name on one of the online marketplaces. And after a couple of weeks, you have a $500 offer. WooHoo! You think you just made a profit! But wait. The marketplace takes 20% of the sales price as their commission. That's $100. You just flipped a domain for no profit. Buying domains and selling to other domainers is typically not a successful business model.

Of course there are exceptions, particularly if you happen upon a domain name in a trending market, before domain name prices with keywords in that market start going up - think Bitcoin or fidget spinners. Keeping up with the news and lifestyle trends is a good idea as a domainer, but may take some risky speculation on your part. Each Fall you can read about trends for the upcoming year. But when you start searching for domain names with the keywords for those trends, you will most likely find the best domain names are already taken. So being one year ahead of the trend may not be good enough – you will need to think with a longer view, which will inevitably have some risk as well as patience. The end users for future trends may not be there yet. Sure, registering domain names before a trend becomes a "thing" can be risky, but that's what makes domain speculation so much fun. Those that bought the best Bitcoin and cryptocurrency domains before that market took off made a lot of money selling domain names they originally registered as "hand regs." But those that held on to fidget spinner domains for too long paid a price, as fidgets were a fad that lasted a very short time.

So for the marketing of domain names for current end users, there are a few important rules to follow:

Rule #1: Be Patient - .com is What You Should Focus On

Patience is a great attribute for everybody in the domain name business to have. Except for a small percentage of sales, most domains sold through direct sales take a long time to complete, from initial query/offer/contact through negotiation and payment, then finally the transfer of the domain name.

For the most part, domains with a .com extension are easier to sell. You don't have to go into any long explanations as to why the non-.com domain name will work for them or their company.

The .com extension is 'king.' Do not be hasty and register a bunch of non-.com domain names. To maximize your efforts and potential profits, you should concentrate only on .com domain names. And you should take your time finding only the best names that have the potential to be a website for an end user. Randomly registering names in .com doesn't typically work either. You will usually end up with a long list of names that you cannot sell.

From the beginning, the commercial aspect of domain names was established with the .com extension. That is where most of the Internet's money is and it doesn't look like that is going to change any time soon. All other extensions (including future ones not yet created) do nothing but cause more confusion. The most successful companies in the world use .com. The .com extension is already established. Sure, any domain extension could work for a website, but any online business using any domain extension other than .com is at a major disadvantage. Even if a company using an extension related to their business, say a video startup that uses a .TV domain, is still at a disadvantage.

The disadvantage the non-.com domains face is that they all send traffic to the .com version. Most web users only think in .com names. When trying to remember a website or company, most users will type in the company's name followed by .com.. So if a business has their website on a .net domain, they will need to know that whoever owns the .com version of their domain is getting some of the traffic meant for their .net version. And, more importantly, if someone types in the .com looking for your company (which has the .net extension) and they instead get either another business' website or a parking page (or even a 'domain does not resolve' error), many will not even try looking for your business under another extension. People are fickle ... and lazy. If it is too much of an effort for them, they won't put in the extra effort.

A business running a website with a .com extension implies credibility. This gives any business, even a startup, an advantage over a competitor on a non-.com domain name. Which in turn means that a good domainer is going to concentrate on investing in domain names with the .com extension.

You may hear and/or read about domainers having successful big sales with .net or .ca domain names. Sure, it can happen – occasionally. For every one of these big sales, there are many more small sales in those extensions with narrow profit margins (or losses), and even more never sell and are eventually dropped. Don't let the few reports of big sales fool you. Even if you think you have found the best name under some other extension than .com, it is most likely not going to make you the money you think it will. To be successful in the domain name business, at least in your first year, stick with the .com extension.

Rule #2: Be Patient - Find Potential End Users

You've just bought what you think is a great domain name. You have found a gem in what you believe is a growing market, and it's never been registered. You should not think you can buy it and then be able to turn it around and sell it for thousands in a week or a month. Remember, just before you registered it, anybody else could have also registered that name for just $10, so why do you think it is worth thousands? So your goal is to be patient and start doing your research into which end users might want your domain.

Putting your domain name on a professional landing page (whether on your own website or a 3rd party's site) is the next step in selling to an end user. Sure, someone may type your exact domain name into a browser and, with you having forwarded your domain name to your landing page, they will end up on your lander. Because you have a contact form plus email address on your lander (you do, don't you?), the end user may contact you, make you an offer and buy your domain!

Sounds easy, right? Well, it's possible and there are many stories from successful domainers of this happening. But the "build it and they will come" approach will not work for most of your domains. This is the exception rather than the rule.

So, you should plan on doing a little work to find potential end users. But remember to be careful and be patient. Don't hand register a domain name one day, then blast a thousand emails to potential end users trying to sell your domain name to them for thousands of dollars. This approach simply will not work.

Instead, take your time and be patient. If you have carefully selected your .com domain names, each one should be treated separately as a unique opportunity. Look at the market for each domain name and what is trending. If you see one of your domain names has potential but the timing isn't yet right to maximize your profit, then you should plan to sit on the domain for some period of time – could be months, could be years. Being a successful domainer takes patience, as well as timing.

Once you determine the time is right to actively market one of your domain names to end users, go through these steps to begin to compile information related to your domain name:

1. Go to whois.domaintools.com and find owners of other TLDs of your domain name, as well as the domain name history. You will also see current auctions of domain names that are related to yours. Take the email addresses from the Whois records of the respective site owners.

2. Go to your favorite search engine and search for keywords either part of or related to your domain. If you are selling CarParts.com, search for "car parts"; if selling RunningShoes.com, search for "running shoes." Make a list of all the

paying advertisers that appear in the 'Sponsored Links.' You can then visit these advertisers' sites and copy the contact emails (or links to their contact form if that is all they give you).

3. Go to Alexa.com and search for the keywords contained in your domain. Make a list of all the paying advertisers. (Click "View Advertisers' Max Bids") At Alexa.com you can also find similar sites based on shared audience and keyword overlap. You can ten perform a Google search for these websites and copy the contact emails (or links to their contact form).

From here you should have a list of potential buyers for your name. You can then begin the steps to reaching out to these buyers through outbound emails.

Rule #3: Be Patient and Professional Contacting End Users
How you present yourself could mean the difference between a large sale or nothing. You do not want to be seen as a spammer, so look to send individual emails to each potential buyer on your list.

In Chapter 7 we covered how to conduct yourself using outbound emails. Having a good email address, either from your domain name company's email or from an email client built directly on the name you are trying to sell is the most professional. Sending an outbound email from Hotmail or Yahoo may just end up in the potential end user's spam folder or just be ignored. As stated earlier, you might only receive one or two replies for every thirty emails you send, so don't be upset if you are not getting responses.

But there are times when you might receive a response. Many times these will just be questions asking who you are or why you are contacting them. In either case, you want to be courteous but business-like in your communications, where hopefully you can get to the negotiating phase for selling your domain name.

If your end user strategy doesn't work, you will have to decide whether you want to sit on the domain name longer and try the end user approach again at another time, or look to a marketplace to sell your name. You will usually have the best chance at a high price sale if directly to an end user. But if you've run out of patience and you have a name that has value for just the name alone (single English word, great keyword domain, or short domain name with a .com extension), then using a good auction site that has many successful high price sales may be your best bet.

Running a Profitable Domain Name Business

Now that you are ready to choose domain names for investment (or already have some in your portfolio) and are thinking like an end user, it's time to run your business with the goal to make a profit. This includes how you operate your business and budget your time.

Set Up Multiple Accounts

If you are not already in the domain name business, you will soon realize there is an entire industry devoted to domaining, which means that there is a wide range of domain marketplaces available where you can buy and sell domains. To get involved in these online marketplaces you should create an account at each of these sites – registration is usually free.

Although it is recommended to first have your own website with landing pages for each of your domain names, online marketplaces can be a good way to also advertise your domains for sale, as well as watching how other domain names are doing on these sales sites.

There is an advantage to signing up with multiple marketplaces. The main reason is that different marketplaces tend to give better results for certain type of names or specialize in certain areas of domaining. For instance, online forums tend to have mostly other domainers, not end users, so you would most likely not receive premium or "end user" prices for your domains on forum sites. But the forum sites are good for thinning out your portfolio if you think you are carrying too many domains, as well as giving you a good idea of what minimum prices are for certain types of domains if you closely watch their sales and auction threads. Forum marketplaces also typically do not have any sales fees, so the price the domain name sells for is typically what you get.

Other marketplaces specialize in higher quality domain names. These sometimes have minimum sale prices so require you to submit your domain names for review before they are accepted on their website. The higher quality domain name sites typically have both serious domainers and end users, so premium domain names can many times bring you high prices. But they also take a higher percentage of the sales price as their fee, sometimes as much as 20%. Once you begin to better understand your own domains and what is selling on what different marketplaces, you can better decide where you want to list your individual domains. Most domainers do not sell their domains on only one website – they target different sites for different domains, and even have their domains listed on multiple sites, as long as those particular sites do not have any exclusivity rules.

For managing your user names and passwords for all of the marketplaces and forums you join, you should use a password storage app on your phone. You will end up with different user names and passwords for different sites due to each sites' rules for user name length, as well as password rules (minimum characters, capital letters, numbers, special characters, etc.).

As much as you think you will have the same user name and password for each site, it most likely won't happen, and you should be in the habit of changing your passwords from time to time. But it is a good idea to at least try to have a consistent user name on all sites as you will want to make a name for yourself in all marketplaces. Also, if you also use an app for your personal passwords, you might consider using a separate app for your domain name business to keep the domain stuff all together in one place and not mixed in with your personal accounts.

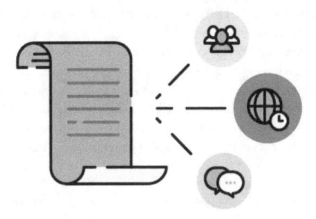

Source: GoDaddy

Manage Your Domain Names

Properly managing your domain names will save you a lot of time in the long run. It is best to keep a spreadsheet or some other electronic database for keeping track of all of your domain names. Even if you are just starting, set up a simple spreadsheet listing each domain name, the date you purchased the name, its current end of registration date, where it is registered, and how much your registration fee was or how much you paid for the domain name. In your spreadsheet you could also add columns for additional notes documenting where you purchased the domain (if different from its Registrar) or any other information regarding your names, but the first 5 columns are important as a minimum.

As for why you should list each domain name's Registrar, you might think you want to have all of your domains registered at the same place. But you are bound to eventually buy names in the secondary market where you might not be able to transfer your domain name for at least 60 days due to a transfer lock. Or perhaps you have other reasons, such as lower registration or renewal prices, for keeping domains at different Registrars.

You might also choose one of the online websites that can track your domain names for you, but it is recommended to still use your own spreadsheet or database. With your own spreadsheet, for example, you can easily manipulate the data in any way you want, such as sorting the domain names by registration date or purchase price. You can also add additional tabs tracking your domain name sales by calendar year.

When you have domain names for sale on marketplaces, you should have additional columns on your spreadsheet which identifies where each domain name is listed, along with listing and/or reserve prices or "Offer" if it's a Make Offer listing. This keeps all of your domain name information in one place where you can easily track your portfolio without having to go from website to website if you forgot where you have your domain names registered or listed for sale. It also provides you with consistency as for what price you have the domain listed for if you have a domain posted on more than one site.

When you sell a domain name, you can cut the domain name from the main domain name active tab and paste it into a different sales tab in the spreadsheet, based on calendar year. Or you can just change the text color on that row, possibly to green to represent a successful sale, then at the end of the year move all of your sales and expenses to a year-end tab. This makes tabulating your sales per year much easier for tax purposes.

Another good idea for when you have a long list of domain names is to take the color idea on your spreadsheet a little further. Domains that are in your account are black. Domains that expire become gray. Domains you sell are changed to green. Then you can use different colors for domains that are active on an auction site or in negotiation. This makes your spreadsheet much easier to read and understand, instead of just having a long list of names where it may be hard to differentiate the status of your domain names.

Make a Business Plan

Whenever starting a new business, no matter how much (or how little) you are going to invest, it is always a good idea to have a business plan. It's important to write down what you have planned so you can have a visual image that will help guide your business.

Starting a business can be very stressful and you'll have hundreds of things on your mind, so writing down your plan will help you remember everything important. Many people skip this part because they think it's a lengthy process or is not important. But if it's done over several days, it can be very easy to put your vision on paper.

You might think you are just going to buy a few domain names and get started in the business so don't really need to make any type of plan. Sure, you can just jump right in and do that, but you should first read as much as you can about the domain name industry before registering any domain names, or you might find those first names you registered are actually worthless or trademarked and you will never be able to sell them.

You should also have a principle goal in mind – to make a profit through the buying and selling of domain names. Making a profit in any business isn't easy. So why not take some time at first and write out a plan?

Here are a few questions to ask yourself when creating a business plan:

- Business name
- Marketing vision
- Business purpose or objective
- Online design layout (or logo)
- Profit model

The point is, you should write everything down you know will matter so you stay focused and can refer back to this document in the future.

With domaining, a business name is important. Do you want to be known as yourself? In other words, should you just put your name out there? Of do you want to create a business name and market yourself as a business rather than your personal name? If you have a somewhat unique name that could be marketable, choose that. But if your name is very common or difficult to spell, it might make better sense to find a business name to operate under. And when choosing a name, find something that is brandable and unique. Think like an end user (which in this case, you would be!), and find an available .com domain name that is short and memorable, and can be easily marketed as a domain business. Either can be successful – you just need to pick one and stick to it.

How you market your domain names is also important. Think about what you know and start with that. For instance, if you have a love of cars, it might be best to start by registering names that relate to the car business. Your marketing vision will help first identify what types of businesses there are related to cars to sell your domain names to, which in turn may tell you what niche domains in the automotive industry for you to look for.

Your business purpose may be as simple as buying names and then selling them for a profit. But you should think about why you want to spend your time in this business as opposed to doing something else. Is it a hobby? Do you know someone else who is successful selling domain names and has bought fancy cars or gone on nice vacations to tropical islands?

Starting any business also takes a bit of creativity. Making up a name for your business and creating a logo can be a lot of fun, and a good time to do this is when writing your business plan. If you aren't very artistic, there are online resources that can help you with a logo. But you should first have an idea of how you would like your online presence to look – what colors you like or any objects or shapes that may somehow be related to your business name (if you have one).

And you should always think about finances. Write down what you have as far as money you would like to invest into this business. Don't get into domain name buying if you don't first have extra money in your bank account. And you should first pay off any credit card bills or student loans before investing in domain names. The last thing you want to do is get yourself further in debt. There have been other domainers that have declared bankruptcy because of bad domain-buying habits.

The amount of money you have to invest is important. Let's say you have $1,000. When looking at domain Registrars, you see you can register each name for about $10 each. So that means you can quickly register 100 names for your investment, right? Wrong! If you do that you will probably end up with 99 names that you will never sell. Instead, think of a strategy where you start with a few names, then over the coming months as you learn more about the business, you will have a better idea what is selling and/or trending. Then you can buy some more names with better confidence. You may also want to consider, if you have enough starting capital, to buy a name on the secondary market for a little more. But you should first have done plenty of research so you don't end up with a dud.

All of this should be thought of when making your business plan so you don't wind up in the red after your first year. Losing money should not be an acceptable part of any business plan.

Keep Your Eye on Expenses

When starting a business, money will probably be tight, so it's important you keep a close eye on your expenses. You need to have a good understanding of what things cost in domaining, from domain name registration and website hosting to listing fees, commission rates and any costs for marketing. This is why a business plan is important - so you can clearly define either a monthly budget for expenses or track expenses by domain name. But it helps if you first take a few days to write down what you need to get your business off the ground, along with what you'll be able to survive without in the first couple of months. Remember, each unnecessary dollar you spend can hurt your business in the long run, especially if you're struggling to make money.

You should use the same spreadsheet where you list all of your domain names to track your expenses. It will already have a column for the registration fee per domain. You can easily add additional columns per domain name for any listing fees, marketing ads, and, once a name sells, its commission expense (if any). By tracking expenses per domain name, you can quickly see what you need to sell each domain name for to at least make a profit on each individual domain.

At the bottom of the list you should track other expenses such as website hosting or yearly memberships if any. This keeps these additional expenses listed so you don't forget anything - and your accountant will thank you.

At the bottom of the spreadsheet, you can add up each column – registration fees, marketing costs, listing fees, sales prices and commissions. By adding all of your sales prices and then subtracting the expenses, you can see where you are at any time regarding profit or loss. Remember you are doing this only to have an understanding of where you stand. It can be discouraging when just starting out to see how much you have invested versus how little you have made in sales. But remember, you need to have patience and look at the longer view. This will also allow you to see which domain names are selling and which are not, and how much additional profit you will need to make on your other domains to cover costs incurred by domain names that do not sell.

Reinvesting is Important

Near the end of your first year, you should be making some sales and have a sense for how you are doing. Overall, your business may not yet be making a profit and you have to decide if you want to reinvest in domain names whose end of registration date is approaching. There are a number of choices to make here.

One choice is looking at the long view. That is, you have taken your time and only registered domain names that you truly believe can still be sold to end users for a good profit. If that is the case, then renewing these domain names is a no-brainer. Just be sure to log the re-registration fees on your spreadsheet.

However, more often than not, you will have also registered some domain names that, after six or more months having them in your portfolio, you realize they may not ever find a sale to an end user. This is when you should start thinking about other ways to sell them. If you have a short name or single or two-word domain that you think will have value to other domainers, then you can list it with a premium domain name auction site. These sites are more particular as to which domain names they accept, but is a good first choice once you decide you want to no longer market your domain name directly to an end user.

If the name does not sell at the premium auction site (or is not accepted), your next choice is to try and auction it at a lower cost auction house or on a domain name forum. As long as there is still time left on the registration, you may still get some value back on the domain name. And if you still have some domain names that have not yet sold by auction, then it is time to bundle some of your domain names together and auction them as a "portfolio" to get whatever amount you can for them. Although it seems breaking even or taking a loss on a domain name shouldn't happen, if the name hasn't yet sold in other venues, it's time to take what you can get or let it expire and move on.

As in any business, reinvesting is a yearly decision, and you will be faced with these decisions all throughout your second year (and the following years after that). You could take a longer view and first register domains for multiple years. If you have a domain name for two or three or more years it will cost you less (on a per-year basis) if you first registered the name for multiple years. Renewal fees are higher and you can't typically find coupon codes for re-regs. But you should think about first registering a domain name for one year for as low a price as you can (at a reputable Registrar using a coupon code), and then only renewing it if you want to keep looking for that end user for another year, or possibly watching the value of a short name or English word name increase in value.

Managing Your Time

Time is money. And even if you are dabbling in domain names as a part-time hobby, your time is still valuable. And as you can see by reading this book, there is a lot to learn and it takes a lot of effort to not only find good domain names but to also market and sell them.

You know what's one of the two best things about making money online? It's that you can work whenever you want. If you're a morning person, you can get up at the crack of dawn and start checking for any sales or domain listings. If you're a night owl, you can burn the midnight oil on domain name forums. And if you are able to build your domain name business where you can work at it full time without it being just a second source of income, then you have your entire day to decide how you want to spend it, including time for coffee breaks, meeting with friends, or even traveling to fun destinations. One of the main advantages to any online business is that you can do it anywhere – whether it's at your home office, a hotel room in Las Vegas, or on the beaches of Hawaii.

But scheduling your own time can oftentimes be a challenge. There are always competing demands on your time so if you concentrate too much on one thing, others will be lacking your attention. For a business, you want to be productive and working on your number one priority: making money. But many times it takes investing your time on things that may not pan out in the end – a sort of time-risk you could call it. You also may have family obligations or you could just sometimes be lazy or get distracted doing non-business activities.

Here are some ideas to help with organizing your time so you can be more effective at selling domains and growing your business.

1. Limit Your Email Time

To be successful in the domain name business, communication is important, and most of your communication will be through email. But when you are in the middle of looking at domain auctions or pending drop lists, it's best you are not interrupted, which means not looking at every new email in your inbox when it comes in.

It can be frustrating when you've sent emails and don't get responses when you think you should. But domaining is a global business, and the people you are communicating with could be on the other side of the world. Since other people can't really expect you to reply to their emails right away, you shouldn't have to respond to theirs … and sometimes there is an advantage to waiting to make a response.

The best way to avoid distractions while you are working is to limit your email time. You can make a schedule for when you are going to be working on other domaining tasks and when you are going to handle your emails. This will keep you honest and productive while you are finding that next great domain name.

2. Don't Surf The Web

Most web surfers are fond of websites where they can not only get the latest news but also videos, memes and other funny and weird stories that could end up wasting hours in a day. Even if you know these can eat into your productive time, you do it anyway.

It would be easy to say just don't visit those sites because you should be using your time checking domain name lists, right? If only it were that simple. Most people lack the self-control and self-discipline needed to stay away from those time-wasting sites. So how can you set yourself up for success?

One strategy that might work here is to use multiple web browsers. For the browser dedicated to domaining, don't have tabs or bookmarks to websites that aren't directly related to your business. Only bookmark the domain name sites you use on a regular basis. And if you want to take it a step further, you can organize your tabs so they are in a set order for you to visit each day. Yes, this may seem a little OCD, but it works. This allows you to have a repetitive pattern each day so you don't waste time going back and forth between sites, while making sure you visit each website you need to see each day, from expired and deleted names to auctions to news to forums. And if you find a new site you want to regularly visit you can easily create a new tab for it or replace a site that you don't regularly need to visit any more.

3. Set a Deadline

One of the hardest things in any business to deal with is the deadline. Some people are anxious or worried about how long it will take to get things done and end up wasting energy just thinking about all they need to do. But when it gets right down to it, you end up figuring out a way to get it done. Budgeting your time is key. If you don't get your work stuff done when you have scheduled your time to be working, the work ends up creeping into your family time and even past your bedtime. Or instead of watching TV with your partner, you're looking down at your phone watching how a domain auction ends.

Scheduling your time may seem silly if domaining is just a hobby of yours, but its actually more important than if you were buying and selling domain names as a full-time job. This is because your time is more precious once you get home after working at your main job.

But scheduling your time can be challenging with domaining. Since it's a world-wide business, someone in another part of the world could be placing a bid on one of your auctions after you have quit working for the day. In order to keep your time well-managed, it is best to leave checking in on auctions or answering emails until you are "back on the clock."

Keeping Away from Negativity

Yes – there are rabbit holes you may end up going down in your domaining efforts. There are others who may tell you that you are wasting your time. And you may find yourself spending hours upon hours of your time at nights and on weekends (when you're not at your real job), but not seeing any results for your efforts. However, not only can buying and selling domain names be profitable, it can be fun as well.

So to keep away from the negative thoughts, let's go through some of the challenging questions you may face.

Is Buying Domain Names Really Profitable?

It is true that buying and selling domain names takes time. If you get a hold of a great domain name then sure, it's easy and you can be profitable. But for a successful domain name business, you need to repeat the process over and over again, which makes sustaining a profitable business more challenging.

With the adage **"Something is only worth how much someone is willing to pay for it,"** the domain name business is full of warnings about how to fail. And you will need to invest some money into the business – not only buying and registering good domain names but also web hosting, listing fees, sales commissions, and any advertising expenses you might have, so like most businesses you are starting in the red.

To look at the "profit" questions, here are some negative remarks to explore further:

1. When counting your time as labor, you'll never make a profit

Try adding up all of your hours in a given week related to domaining. That is, reading articles about domain names, reading and responding to posts on a domain name forum, reading and writing emails, reading and posting on your social media accounts, checking domain name auction sites, looking at recent domain name sales, and maybe even listening to domain name podcasts. Yes, the hours add up.

But what might you normally be doing if you weren't domaining? Watching sports on TV? Playing video games? If your time would otherwise be wasted, then adding up your hours and costing them against your domain name sales shouldn't matter, because you were probably not doing anything productive with your hours anyway. And if you are doing your domaining more as a business and want to factor in your time, then if you stick to your routine, and have good domain names to start with, the time will pay off in the long run. Just don't waste it.

2. Domaining is not sustainable income

Actually, this is true. One week you might make a $1,000 sale and the next week you might not sell anything. There are many domainers that work on volume and percentages. If you have a large number of domains (and have followed your rules by NOT registering non-.com domains or other domains that would never work for a business website, then on a weekly or monthly basis you will most likely sell a certain percentage of your domain names.

Of course, it takes a while to build up a portfolio of a size that can be sustainable, but if that is your goal it certainly is possible. In the meantime, if you have a few very good domains, then one large sale can tide you over to cover the times when you make little or no sales.

It is very easy in this business to have up and down months. Early in your domaining career, you will be in the red as you buy and register your first domain names. Your first sale might take months to happen. And even when you start to expand your business once you get more sales behind you, the higher cost domains might take years to sell for a decent profit.

But the main thing to remember is to have patience and think in the long term. Short-term thinking will drive you mad. And there will be many frustrations along the way, from getting no responses for even (what you think are) the best domain names to potential buyers who only give you lowball offers. There may also be buyers who pull out of a sale just before sending you their money. But keep your head up and don't fret the small stuff. If you stick with your business plan (and don't buy a lot of dumb domain names) you could eventually have a thriving and sustaining business.

3. Finding and waiting on buyers can be frustrating

Domaining is a business that requires at least 2 people for any transaction – a buyer and a seller. As a seller, you will need to deal with people, good or bad. And it can be frustrating waiting on an email from a potential buyer who already told you they wanted to buy your domain but haven't yet paid for it.

But this is also a business of patience. If you take your time and act in a professional manner, the business will happen. Treat others with respect and build an honest and responsible business. Chances are it can grow into something you can be proud of.

4. The Registrars and Auction Houses are the only ones making money

It is true, Registrars make money. With each domain name registration fee, only a small part goes to ICANN or another agency. The rest is profit after their other business expenses. And Auction Houses, once successful, make a commission on each sale, much of which is profit once their website is up and running and self-sustaining.

205

Many domainers think the largest auction and domain name sales sites are hurting domain name sales. There are now so many domain names listed that it is hard for buyers (and potential end users) to find the names they want. And a 20% commission on the sale of one of your domain names at an auction site can be the difference between you making a profit or not.

But as part of your business, one of the first things to do is to first understand all of your expenses. Registration fees are a given, but are small compared to your potential sales. And if you are successful in contacting potential end users for the sale of your domain names, then you may not have to pay a commission unless you go through escrow (of which you can many times split the cost with the buyer or, if they were the ones who demanded escrow in the first place, they may pay the full commission).

If you factor in all of your expenses, you will see what sort of profits you need to make on your domain name sales. By following your business plan, including sticking with certain niche domains, .com extensions, and great keywords, you should, over time, be able to sell each domain name and get some kind of return, some of which may be more than a hundred times the price you paid for the domain name. Over time, it's these large sales that will sustain your business, so it's not only the Registrars and Auction Houses making the money.

5. Domainers are just a bunch of cybersquatters
In the early days of buying and selling domains, this may probably have been true. There were many buying domains of already successful companies and then trying to sell the names to those companies. But trademark laws caught up and domaining had to change.

And even though those in the domaining industry may understand that buying and selling domains is a legitimate business pursuit, there will still be those that think domainers are still cybersquatters and won't pay market value for good domain names – no matter how hard domainers try to convince them a good domain name will be good for their business and is worth the investment.

As in any business (and economics), the laws of supply and demand apply. Many domain names, particularly those with the .com extension, short abbreviations, single English words, and top keyword domain names, will always be in demand. And if you are in front of current events and trends, you can invest in domains with limited risk (reg fees plus renewal costs) for the chance for potential large profits over time.

Choosing The Best Domains

The most important factor in having a profitable domain name business is finding the best domain names. However, everyone can't afford to buy a two or three-letter .com or short dictionary word .com domain name. So the challenge is in putting together a strategy to find domain names that are somewhat lower cost initially, but have a good potential to be worth much more.

Current Events/Market Trends

Following events and what is going on in the world is important for any domain name investor. This will help you in identifying possible future trends in markets so that you may hand register domain names BEFORE they become popular. Again, this strategy takes a lot of time and there is some risk involved, but if you are willing to invest as little as $10 a year in something that could pay off more than 100 times your investment in as little as a few years, then it may be part of your overall domain name strategy.

Domain Name Forums/Marketplaces

Sometimes you may be able to find a domain name listed for sale by another domainer at a price you think is lower than what you think that domain name's potential really is. These are risky as well because somebody else has already been trying to sell that domain name, whether using a good strategy or not, but it hasn't been able to sell it yet. On premium marketplaces you can invest in higher priced domains, particularly in markets where you think you have knowledge. This strategy takes more investment dollars but can be very rewarding. Some of the best known domainers look for opportunities on these marketplaces, finding domain names that aren't over-priced, then sitting on them for a number of years before actively marketing them for re-sale.

Dropped Domain Names

For those that don't have a large bank account full of money ready to be invested, buying or registering dropped domain names is recommended as the best way to find names that are lower priced but can earn you good profits with somewhat less risk.

By getting domain names from a dropped list before they are deleted, the age remains intact. These domains can be more appealing to some buyers because they are 'aged," meaning the initial registration date is still carried with the name.

Dropped names will cost you a little more than an expired and deleted or newly registered (hand reg) name. For any particular good names, you may find yourself in competition with other domainers trying to win the domain, as some sites have names go to auction when more than one person places an "order" or bid for a name that is about to drop.

The challenge with dropped domain names is how you best spend your time finding the quality names amongst all the junk. There are literally thousands of domain names that are dropped each and every day. You won't have the time to scroll through lists every day. Trying to find a few gems in these lists is like trying to find a needle in a haystack.

In order to save time in your searching, you have a couple of options. One is to copy the information from a pending dropped list. There are various sites that supply this information as a free service because they want you to use them to bid on pending dropped names through their site.

You should download the information and copy it onto a spreadsheet so it is sortable. You will typically have columns for the domain name, its extension, along with other information from the service such as its starting bid price and link to its own landing page. In order to easily sort the names, you can insert a new column to create a numeric number for the length of each domain name. With an Excel formula of "=LEN(Ax)" you can calculate how many characters are in each name on the list (copy paste into all cells down the length of the list). Once done, you can quickly re-sort the domain names by length, bringing the shorter names to the top. You can also delete out all extensions other than .com if you want, but sometimes you may want to keep the .net or other extensions for your first search by length, just to see if there are any good short names in one of these other extensions. You can also search the spreadsheet for keywords using character string searches or find only the dictionary words.

There are some online sites that also allow for searching for domain names about to drop, but many of these don't have the sorting and searching capabilities as your own spreadsheet.

Another option is to buy software that will assist you in searching for good domain names that are about to be dropped. There are a few different software programs that do this and some of them are very good. These software programs already have pre-built search and filtering options. But you have to weigh how much of your domain name business is going to be based on securing dropped names versus the upfront or monthly cost for a software program.

The daily dropped names lists frequently have valuable domain names that for one reason or other were not re-registered by their owner. Because of this, there are many domainers that scour these lists or use software programs or other scripts to identify names about to expire. You should experiment with dropped lists and see how best to secure names of interest for your domain name business. Relatively few of the really good names get through a drop and become expired.

Expired and Deleted Domain Names
With expired domain names that have been deleted, it simply means that they were previously registered and left to expire, and weren't picked up during the drop phase, so were deleted by the Registry. Many of these can be of value because they may still contain backlinks or have good keywords or CPC scores. However, when you register an expired and deleted domain name, it has lost its 'age' so looks like a newly registered domain.

There are different online resources to locate expired domain names. Lists of domains are posted on a daily basis in most domain extensions. You can download lists of expired domain names each day and run them through filtering scripts to highlight only the domain names in a certain niche or domain name length you are interested in. Or you can be online during the posting of names and use filters on the various sites to target specific areas.

When it comes to purchasing domain names for resale, you should stick with the top level extension, the .com, and avoid any domains with numbers or other characters. You will also want to focus on searching for expired domain names that are as short as possible or have high value keywords. You can search through downloaded lists with filtering scripts or with online website filters and set a maximum and/or minimum length, so the domains you might be interested in show up at the top of the list. You may also want to sort based on other factors, such as searches, backlinks, year the domain was first registered (or a website built on it), or other data provided.

Use Keywords

For both dropped and expired lists, you can also use specific keywords so that only names that contain words in whatever niche you are interested in are the ones that show up in your search results. Remember, there are thousands of domain names that are dropped each day, and thousands more that are deleted each day. You don't want to spend your time sifting through thousands of names on a daily basis, so as soon as you set up your searches and filters the less time it will take you to find your desired results each and every day.

Aside from targeted keywords, you could also think about good words that when added to a great keyword can make a great "brandable" domain name. Two word domain names can be very valuable, and the two words don't necessarily have to have any particular relationship or meaning. Just think about feedburner.com and how successful that website has become using two words that don't particularly relate to each other. Names that include "fire" or anything hot can be popular, as well as "top," "best," or "pro."

Be Selective

You should take your time and study how the dropped and expired domain websites work. There is also third-party software that can automate some of these search tasks for you, but that is an additional cost that you should not have to make. You can create a "swipe" file of your keyword domain searches, so it is easy to copy and paste your searches into the websites. But remember there are many other domainers doing exactly the same thing, so there is a good chance that domain names you find on an expired list may already be taken by the time you try and register them.

And just because you find likeable domain names through your daily searches, that doesn't mean you need to bid on them (if on a drop list) or register them (if on an expired/deleted list). You should still do more research on each and every name you are interested in, even more so for names that were previously registered.

When hunting for expiring names, it is a good idea to find out who the previous owner of the name was and what they were using the name for, if anything. But you should also remember that just because someone else had previously registered the name, that does not mean it is clear from any trademark issues. There are many names on the dropped and expired lists that have trademark names and keywords or are simple misspellings of major corporations. Do not be tempted by these names as the previous Registrant either let the domain expire knowing it was a trademark, or maybe even deleted it through their Registrar before it expired not wanting to get involved in any UDRP process.

Many times you can find out the owner of a domain name that is on hold or ready for deletion through a simple Whois search. However, many times the Registrar immediately deletes the previous owner's contact information once the domain name goes into pending delete and puts their own Registrar information into the domain name record.

But you still may be able to find out how the domain name may have been used. There are websites that log snapshots of websites over time as they appeared at each point in time. One of these sites is the "Wayback Machine" offered by Archive.org. For expiring domains that show crawl results to Archive.org, you would enter "www. DomainName.com" into the search box at Archive.org's main page. The results, if any, will be presented on a calendar showing how many snapshots have been taken and in what years/months for the searched domain name. If you get some results, you can click on any of the highlighted dates to see the snapshot for that particular point in time to see what a website on that domain name looked like on that date. Sometimes it may only show you a redirect, but it's worth trying anyway. You may find the website for a domain name was used as an adult-oriented or porn site or was full of ads and click bait of which you would rather not be associated.

When searching for domain names, some online dropped and/or expired lists may even have a column listing how many snapshots of a particular domain names' previous website(s) has been recorded. If you are looking for domain names that may have value due to a previous use, this is a good way to find such names.

A domain names that was previously used may also be valuable not for the particular website that was attached to it but what kind of traffic the site was getting and how many backlinks or links to that particular domain name there are from other websites.

You could find out whether the site was an actual functioning website by checking for Wayback history. Unfortunately, there are many sites created on domain names in which their only goal is to generate traffic in order to earn advertising revenue or redirect to other sites, and maybe not in a language you want. For the most part, you probably shouldn't register a domain name that already had a website built on it but it wasn't a legitimate site, unless, of course, it is a very good name. But if the previous site was an e-commerce site, then depending on what it was selling it could be a very good opportunity. And if a deleted domain name still has a large number of good, quality backlinks, it might be a great name to register. There is a chance the previous owner unwittingly let the site expire and may want to buy the name back from you. Also, domain names with a lot of traffic over the previous months could earn you good parking revenue while you begin to market the domain name for re-sale.

But sometimes expired domain names have a "dirty profile" and may be blacklisted from Google Adsense or search ranking sites. Many illegitimate websites are built on quality domain names only to drive traffic and make money without creating a real business. And if you have a domain name that you find out has had a checkered past, it could take a lot time to clean up. There are also specialists that can do this for you, but they can be costly and you might not always get the results you want.

It is also possible that a domain name could have switched hands multiple times. The name could have had a good, functioning website on it years ago, but was either sold or let to expire and somebody else picked it up and used it as a traffic-driving site or even a pornographic website. It is best for you to look through each domain name's history before you register or bid on a domain so that you understand it's entire past.

Backordering

If you search for a domain name that's already registered, you may see the option to place a backorder on the domain. If the current owner decides not to renew the domain once its registration has expired, the 77-day expiration process begins. Even after the domain expires, the former owner still has a few last chances to re-register the domain before it goes through the drop phase. If the domain finishes the expiration process without being renewed, the backorder process can begin.

Most Registrars only allow one backorder per domain name. And just because you place a backorder with a Registrar, it is not a guarantee that you'll get the domain as soon as it expires. This is because all the other Registrars out there have a chance to make a bid for it as well. To maximize your chances of getting an expiring name, it can be helpful to backorder the name at several Registrars and automated services simultaneously. Since most of them charge only for successful registrations, you won't be charged for any unsuccessful attempts.

If one of the Registrars at which you placed a backorder for a certain domain name is able to grab it the moment it becomes available before any other Registrar does, the domain is yours! But if one of the automated services catches the domain name, it will most likely go to auction.

Building a Good Portfolio

The dropped and expired lists are the best place to start looking for names when first starting out in the domain name business. This keeps you from wasting a lot of money registering new, never-before-registered domain names that most likely will never sell. At least with selected searches through the dropped and expired lists you have a better chance of finding something that has value, particularly for an end user. And just because the domain name was previously owned does not necessarily make it a bad name … it might be that the previous owner did not do a good job finding a potential end user. Sure, there are a lot of "bad" domain names that get registered and end up on drop and expired lists. But you should be able to ignore those when thinking like an end user to find names that might work as websites for a business.

When bidding on domain names that have not yet expired, most of the services have a minimum price (like $59) that will secure a name and one year's registration for the name. But if someone else also places a bid for the same domain, then the name will most likely go into auction with whatever company "caught" the dropped name, and you will end up paying even more for the name if you want it. Needless to say, there is a lot of competition for expiring domain names, so you will need to research which of these drop-catching' services does the best job getting domain names in your niche.

When a name shows up on the expired domain names list, this means that nobody bid on or claimed the domain name during the drop, or had a backorder on the domain. The domain name then becomes available for anybody to register at whatever Registrar they want. Because there is also great competition for expired domains, there are many who are online when the expired lists are posted, using keyword and/or minimum character length searches for different domain name extensions. If you find yourself able to be online at these times, this can be a great way to find very good domains, with your only cost being the basic domain name registration fee if you are lucky enough to be the first to register a quality expired domain.

But you should also consider rounding out your portfolio with some higher quality domains purchased on the secondary market. These will not only give you some aged domains, but by displaying good domain names on your website can give you more credibility as a domainer.

Adding Value

For some domain names you purchase, you may want to add value to them. When you register a new name that has never been registered before, it has no history so will not have any value on Estibot or any credibility on SERP's (search engine results pages). This means the domain's only value is in the name itself (market, keyword, length, etc.). And if you find a good deleted domain name, it might have had SERP value, but once it was deleted it could have lost its search rankings.

Adding value to a domain name means to build a website on it. You may consider doing this if the name is in a profitable niche and you think you will have a good chance of making more money from the domain name if it has built up good search engine rankings and high quality backlinks.

However, building a website and developing it to make it have a high value can be a very lengthy process. You should understand how much of your time and effort will be spent on website development before you undertake this approach.

You could hire a company to help you as there are many out there that can not only assist with website development but also incorporate SEO strategies and even mobile app development. But this could cost you $500-$1,000/month which over six months is around a $6,000 investment (or even more). You will have to decide whether this approach is worth your time and effort or investment.

You should also look back at your business plan. Did you want to just buy and sell domain names or did you want to get into website development as well? That doesn't mean you can't alter your business plan, but you should decide whether your time is worth developing domain names to add value to them or better spent finding other domain names at below-market value and/or marketing the domain names in your portfolio to potential buyers. Developing a website might not always get you the results you want either, so your return on investment (which could just be your time), may not be worth the effort.

Surviving Your First Year in Business

Starting any business can be difficult and it's stated that within the first two years around 30% to 40% of the average businesses fail because they didn't properly plan or encountered unexpected problems. This is why it's important you have a clear-cut idea about your business, thinking of everything from the beginning. Your main goal should be to find a way to profit in the domain name business by looking at what will work while identifying mistakes that will cost you ... this can be the difference between success and failure.

Sure, you can simply buy a few domain names and then try to sell them for a small profit and maybe feel good about yourself that you accomplished something, albeit small. But if you truly want to be successful in domaining, to the point where you may want to make this a full-time job with all of the benefits being a successful domainer may bring, then you have to treat domaining as a business. This means you should have a well-defined plan on how you expect to dominate the industry. That's right – dominate. Who starts a business and just wants to make a small bit of money? You are going to be spending a lot of time learning about the domain business, and small profits are not going to be satisfying for you.

You should also understand that surviving your first year as a domainer can be tough. Being knowledgeable about the domain name business takes experience. You can read as much as you want, which is always a good idea, but the real learning starts when you are actually doing it. And with domaining, that means SELLING domain names. Anybody can start buying domain names and think they know the business. But it takes sales to truly get to know what works and what doesn't.

And patience. A lot of patience. Don't be one of those newbie domainers that hand-registers a domain name, immediately puts it up for sale at a high price, then after only a month complains about why they aren't getting any inquiries or sales. Even with good .com domains based on high value keywords, most sales are going to take some time.

So to make sure you are not one of the 30% - 40% that start an online business but don't survive, you should think of domaining as a business. Follow the advice on being selective and only choosing winning domains, identify mistakes and don't fall into the negative rabbit holes. Understand your time is money and manage it well, while also keeping all of your domain name records well-managed. Also understand the financial side of running a business and that a domain name is worth exactly what a buyer is willing to pay for it. So know who your potential buyers are, try and see the value of each and every domain name from a business owner's perspective, and be professional and courteous in all of your business dealings.

Moving On Up

As you near the end of your first year in domaining, you will be faced with some decisions. If you kept good records on how much you have invested in domains, along with your sales and expenses (listing fees, commissions on sales, web hosting, etc.), you should easily know whether you have made a profit or not. Of course, this simple math does not include the time you have spent, but most domainers don't calculate for their time.

Hopefully, you have made good choices with your domain purchases during your first year and have made a profit. You also most likely will still have domain names in your portfolio. Of those domain names you still have, you will have to decide whether you want to renew their registration or not. Renewal fees are typically more than initial registration fees, and there are not typically any coupon codes or deals for re-registrations, so renewals will cost a little more.

Although the .com extension is the safest bet, you may see value or a future increase in demand for other domain name extensions. If you are committed to investing in other extensions then you should be prepared to take the risk that goes along with it. That doesn't mean you can't make money investing in other extensions – many domainers do. But you will most likely need to put even more effort into your sales, be more knowledgeable about the niche or market you are investing in, and be even more careful in your domain name purchases with these other extensions.

If you think your first year domain name purchases are still worth holding on to, then go ahead and re-register them. However, most domainers don't necessarily take their time with their first domain name purchases and typically register domain names that end up not selling. With bad domains, you can either let them expire or try to auction them on domain forums to at least try to get a little money back on your investment. There may be some other domainer that may see value in these domains, and it won't cost you any listing fee on a domain forum. If the domains still don't sell, then you have been proven that these domain names are not worth keeping, so you can go ahead and let them expire.

For the domain names you renew, you have essentially bought yourself another year of registration. This does not mean you should immediately try and sell them for what you can right away. These domain names are now aged, meaning they have over one year on their registration. Many domains increase in value over time, just because they are older. If you are certain you are in the domain name business for the long term, you may decide to hold on to your domain names for many years looking for a higher sale. What many domainers do is put these longer term domains on sales sites with a high "Buy It Now" value. If someone is interested in that specific domain name and buys it, then great, you have sold it for a large amount and made a big profit. If it doesn't sell during the first ninety days, then go ahead and re-list it for another ninety days and wait it out, and continue to do so for a year or more.

After a certain amount of time, maybe years, you can determine, based on the market and similar sales, that the name has gained considerable value and you would like to now sell it. You should first exhaust all of your outbound marketing again trying to find an end user/buyer, as this will still get you the best price. If your outbound efforts still don't get a sale, then it may be time to auction the domain name on one of the higher-end auction sites. These sites specialize more in top and premium domain names, and include other domainers with larger sums of money to invest. If your domain name is indeed a one-word, short name, or high keyword domain, typically in a .com extension, then putting it up for auction after holding it for a number of years may get you a very large profit.

Again, domaining take patience. If you don't have the ability to wait it out in order to see a large return on your investment, then maybe the domain business is not for you. For those that take a longer view and are able to be patient, if you make smart buying decisions with your domain names, they more likely than not will increase in value and you will profit once the names eventually sell.

In your first year, you may have hand-registered a name for $10 that you may have sold for $100 or maybe even $1,000 or more. Hopefully the profit on this sale is able to cover your other purchases and expenses for your business. But over time, as you get more sales, you will have more to invest. If you are in the business to make larger profits and truly benefit from larger sales, then finding a strategy for a longer view with your domain names is the best way to go.

If I were to start domaining with a $1,000 investment, I would rather buy 10 names for an average of $100 a name instead of registering 100 new names at $10 each. Hand registering new names is like gambling, unless you know what you are doing. I've seen too many new domainers go and register a hundred domain names in all kids of extensions, and then wonder why their domains aren't selling.

Instead, keeping to the 10 domains at $100 a domain strategy, check out domain auctions and drop catch websites. First, a bit about domain auctions. There are a lot of domain names being auctioned, with a very large percentage of those names not even being worth RegFees. You will need to develop a strategy for looking at auction sites in such a way to find the few gems out there. You want to target names that will be attractive to a business owner in developing a website. Cute names or multiple keyword names are not what you want. Also, you should not go for names that have no meaning. You should instead target domain names in auctions that relate to particular business enterprises, hopefully those in which you already have some knowledge and know who you might contact for a potential sale. You will also want to wait to place a bid on a domain name in auction. If there are still five days on an auction, wait the five days and watch what happens. Then, if the price has not gone too high, place your bid in the last hour or so as most domain auction sites will extend the time.

For expired domains, you should not be registering domain names that have already been deleted. Sure, there is an occasional domain that might slip through the drop without being picked up. But there are so many experienced domainers looking at the pending drop lists that the chances of a good domain being deleted is very small. Instead, register with one of the drop catch websites and get to know the process. Usually for a minimum "bid" of $59 you can select a name that you see potential value in that is about to drop. If you are the only one that places a bid, you get the domain for $59. But most good names have multiple bids so the name goes into a short auction. There have been many names bought from a drop catch auction for $89 or $99 and flipped for ten or twenty times that amount in a relatively short time. You will find you will feel better about the domains you are marketing if you believe in their potential over the deleted or hand-reg names that nobody else thought had any value.

As you look at the sales of domain names on the top and premium auction sites, you are probably wondering how you can get those domains. Most of the domain names sold for those high amounts have been held for many years. You just aren't going to be able to buy a short name or one word .com domain name for under $100 and then turn it around and sell for tens of thousands of dollars or more in less than a year. Most of these sales you see are domain investors that have held on to these names for a long time or have invested a large sum to turn around and sell it for more. Most of these domainers also have a larger investment pool to use, so they look for value when other domainers are selling a name, trying to find a deal. When they do, they may buy a domain for $10,000 and then be able to turn around and sell it for $50,000 or more, because they have the contacts and experience to be able to make these larger sales.

Over time, with domain name buying and selling experience, you should be able to move on up to the larger market. If you make good buying decisions and either sell to end users or hold on to quality domain names as investments, you will be able to deal in higher quality and top and premium domain names. To get there takes time, patience, and a good strategy in how you both buy and sell (or hold) your domain names.

Good luck in all of your domaining endeavors!

Appendix A: Domain Name Tips

Use a Good Registrar

As a domainer, it is important to use a good Registrar for your domain name registrations. There are many Registrars that have policies and conditions that aren't the best for Registrants, and many don't include important services you might need for your domain business. Although many believe you should keep web hosting separate from registrations, having the same company provide both can make website setup and management much easier, and you might get the domain name registration for free. You should also choose a Registrar that consistently receives good reviews and positive feedback. Regarding the price for registrations, some Registrars may give discounts when you reach a certain level or join a domain name club, and you may also be able to find specials or coupon codes.

Concentrate on .com Domains

Especially when starting your domain name business, you should always first look at available, expiring and marketplace domain names with a .com extension. Most website and business owners desire a .com domain name as they know web users will traditionally use .com when typing in a URL to get to a website. Search engines also tend to rank .com domains higher than other extensions. And when looking at comparable valuations of domain names, the same name in a .com extension is worth more than twice the amount of the same name in any other extension.

Stick With a TLD

There are so many domain extensions now available that figuring out which one may or may not become popular (or worth the investment) is kind of like gambling. The safest bet is always the "king" of TLDs, the .com extension. But investing in either a .net or .org TLD can also be profitable. Everything after that is a questionable investment. That is not to say many domainers haven't made a lot of money in country code (ccTLD) or alternative TLDs, but there are more of these other extensions that end up getting dropped percentage-wise than the top TLDs.

Invest in Short Names

There is an entire submarket in short domain names which has relatively little to do with keywords and traffic and more to do with the scarcity of available names. All two-letter, three-letter and four-letter domain names in the .com extension are registered. This creates a secondary market in itself for the buying and selling of short names, and there are websites that track prices based on letter length, combinations and even types of letters (Chinese premium, etc.). This is a market to itself and requires some research before getting into – particularly when it comes to investing larger sums of money into each domain name, but can be very profitable if you can find some deals.

Keyword Names

Website traffic is tied directly to keywords, so domain names with great keywords can have corresponding great value. Search engine results are the name of the game, and most website owners know it. Not only is good SEO (Search Engine Optimization) important in a website, but having a good keyword in the domain name itself can bring additional search engine traffic. You should try to find keyword names that have high search volume but a lower amount of web sites competing for that same keyword.

Consider Domains in Multiple Extensions

You may look at a strategy where you not only register the name in a .com extension, but also register the .net and/or .org extension of the same name. This may make the name more valuable as a brand as nobody else would be able to develop a business on one of the other TLDs. You can also use the names in other extensions to help drive traffic to the .com if a website is developed.

Avoid Hyphens

Try to avoid registering domain names with hyphens. Domain names with hyphens generally rank lower than names without them. Additionally, hyphenated names can be confusing and might actually drive traffic to the domain with the same name but without the hyphen.

Avoid Numbers Being Used for Words

You should also try to avoid registering names that use number for words. Like hyphens, this could also end up driving traffic to the same domain but with the actual word instead of the number. For example, if you have the domain name "shirts4boys.com" it would be a very hard sell because the domain name "shirtsforboys.com" is much better. Nobody puts in numbers for words when using search engines and if you are ever telling someone your domain name you would have to specifically tell them you are using the number 4. If you say your domain is "shirts 4 boys" they will think that to actually mean "shirts for boys."

Be Patient When Buying Domain Names

If you see a domain name for sale that you like you should not just immediately buy it. Instead, you should take your time and first do some research. If the name is not currently registered, search and see if the name had been previously registered and, if so, if there was ever a website built on it. You might come to find an innocent-sounding name might have previously been used as a porn site or could have been banned by Google and not be able to be used for Google ads. It is also good to know a domain name's age, what it's keyword popularity or competition may be, and if the domain name has been sold before. And if you are going to develop a website, choosing the right domain name is very important, so taking the extra time to find the best name is well worth it in the long run.

Read Domain Name Forums

There is a lot of information to be learned about domaining – this book only starts to scratch the surface. There are also many fellow domainers who don't mind helping out those just starting or answering questions about domain names. Domain name forums can be a great resource for not only learning more about domain names, but also reading the latest news about domains and finding out about any controversies in the business.

Search for Recently Expired Domains

Domain names that have recently expired may have value above registration fees. Although it is most likely names show up on the expired list because they couldn't be sold by someone else, there are also many cases where the expired name was used for a website and the owner just didn't want the domain name any more. When you do a search on recently expired names, you can see whether the name was used for a website before and how many backlinks to that domain name might still exist. With current backlinks, the domain name still might rank well in searches. However, most names that end up expired have already gone through a round of being registered before they "dropped." If a domain name can be "caught" before it expires, it retains its age. However, once a domain name is deleted, once it is registered again its age starts over.

Don't Place Domain Backorders

If a domain name that you want is not currently available, it is possible to put the domain on backorder for a fee of about $20. Unfortunately, most people don't realize that putting a domain on backorder does not guarantee that they will be able to buy it when it becomes available. In fact, there is a good chance that you will not obtain the domain even if you have paid a backorder fee. There are much better ways to acquire domains as they expire than to place them on backorder with the domain name Registrar.

Be Aware of Trademarks

Never register a domain name that contains a copyrighted term as this can result in a lawsuit or UDRP. You may even lose the domain and any attached website. In fact, many people have been sued because they purchased a domain name that contained copyrighted material. Never try to capitalize on the popularity of a well-established brand or product, as you may find yourself in legal trouble.

Consider Registrar Recommendations

When you search for a domain name that has already been registered, most Registrars will give you a list of recommendations to choose from that are similar to your desired domain. In some cases, one of these recommendations could end up being more valuable than your initial choice. Try to consider all of the recommendations before moving on to the next idea.

Turn On Domain Notifications

After purchasing your domain name you should always activate notifications within the control panel of your domain Registrar. (Some Registrars do this automatically.) These notifications will be sent via email or text whenever changes are made within the administrative interface of your domain Registrar account. Activating notifications is perhaps the best way to proactively protect against domain hijacking.

Always Look for Coupons

Most major domain Registrars set up coupon codes that you can use to get a discount on the cost of your purchase. Try doing a web search for the name of your Registrar followed by the word "coupons" or the phrase "coupon codes." In some cases you may be able to get free domains or even half off of your purchase by using a single coupon code during checkout. You should not be paying the normal full price for any domain name registrations if possible. Even if it is just a couple of dollars off, if you are buying many domain names, those couple of dollars of savings for each name adds up.

Consider Country-Code TLDs

If you have a good idea for a domain and you're unable to register it in one of the conventional TLDs like .com or .net, you may want to consider registering a ccTLD (country-code TLD). In many cases, country code TLDs are just as cheap as .com domains, and they can rank just as high in the search engines, especially for regionally targeted keywords. A country code TLD may also be a good idea if the domain name or website is specifically geared towards one region, state, province, or country.

Try to Register Any Domain Name

A lot of people miss out on some of the best domain names because they automatically assume that there is no way it could be available. This is the worst mindset to be in when looking for a good domain because you'll probably never find one with that type of attitude. If you have an idea for a domain name, even if it seems impossible that it could still be available, don't hesitate to try.

Avoid Domain Names that Contain Plurals

Although it may seem tempting to purchase a domain name that is the plural version of a popular term (like "basketballs.com" instead of "basketball.com"), this may not be the best decision. It is important to note that a lot of people will forget to put the "s" at the end of the name, and will therefore be directed to a completely different website. Thus, it is best to avoid plural domain names altogether unless you also own the singular version of the domain as well, or if the plural of the word makes more sense, like shoes.com. (Who is going to buy only one shoe?)

Use a Domain Name Sales Website and Domain Forwarding

If you want to set up your domain business on its own website, then you should use domain forwarding for each of your domain names. It is a good idea to create individual landing pages on your website for each domain (could also include a graphic image if you like), so that anybody typing your exact domain name into a web browser will immediately go to your landing page. The page should clearly state that the domain name is for sale, with either a price or a "make offer" statement. The page should also have an easy way for someone to contact you. Additionally, if you want to make your website able to accept payments, then having an easy way for buyers to check out and pay for the domain name without your involvement is recommended. There is nothing better than waking up in the morning and see you had a domain name sale overnight (and already received payment!) without you having to do anything.

Study Domain Auction Sites

If you want to learn how to judge the value of a domain name then you should start studying domain auction sites on a regular basis. Becoming a member of one or more of these sites is also a great way to advertise your domain when you decide to sell it at a later date. Sometimes buying a used domain has its advantages over registering a new domain with a Registrar, which is another benefit of frequenting domain auction sites.

Try Domain Monitoring Services

If you've been waiting on a particular domain to expire so that you can scoop it up as soon as possible, you may want to try a domain monitoring service. These services are usually offered by domain Registrars and are a great way to keep an eye on a domain that you've put on backorder. Most domain name speculators utilize this service to get information on domains that are about to expire.

Join Domain Discount Clubs

There are a lot of sites and forums on the internet that are related to domain name registrations and finding the best domains. Some domain Registrars also have domain discount clubs that send out newsletters with coupons and other specials every month. Joining one of these clubs is one of the best ways to take advantages of the latest promotions from domain Registrars.

Look for Transfer-Out Fees

Some domain Registrars include unfair terms in their contracts that will automatically charge you a credit card fee when you decide to transfer your domain to another Registrar. Some of these fees can be pricey, and some Registrars will even completely restrict you from transferring your domain to another Registrar.

Look for Any Hidden Fees

When purchasing a domain name there are a lot of hidden fees to consider that could potentially cost you a lot of money in the near future. Make sure you only buy domain names from reputable companies that are known for having fair terms of use and reasonable contracts. Hidden fees can come in many forms so it is important to do the necessary research on domain scams before choosing a Registrar.

Beware of "Free" Domains

There are a lot of domain Registrars, hosting providers and other companies out there claiming to offer free registration for certain customers or for certain domain types. You have to be wary of these offers because in most cases there are fees charged later that completely negate the free registration. Some Registrars will even keep you from transferring your "free" domain, or claim complete ownership of the "free" domain within the fine print of their contract.

Don't Spend Too Much on One Domain in your First Year

If you are new to buying and selling domain names for profit and you have a healthy budget, don't spend too much on any one domain at the start. It is more important for you to learn the business of domaining by buying and selling lower-priced domain names first so you have a better understanding of the market. Without first having this experience, you could get caught spending a lot of money, and possibly over-paying for an expensive domain name of which you may never be able to sell it for more, and you could end up with a considerable loss.

Use a Real Email Address When Registering

Always use a real email address when registering a domain as this will be the primary contact method that the Registrar will use to send important emails. If you give them a fake email address then you cannot confirm ownership of the domain or set up security notifications. Even though you may get bombarded with spam emails, never register a domain with a fake email address or someone else's email address - this could also make it easier for someone to steal your domain in the future. You might consider having a separate email address for your domain registrations from the email you use for your business. This way any spam email you get isn't mucking up your business email inbox.

Use a Real Phone Number When Registering

Always give the Registrar a real phone number as they may need to contact you in emergency situations, such as the expiration of your registration or suspicious activity in your account. If you give the Registrar a fake phone number there is a possibility that you could lose your domain to a thief or it could expire without you ever realizing it, even though you may also receive unsolicited sales calls.

Know When to Use Automatic Domain Renewals

The best way to avoid losing your domain unexpectedly is to authorize your Registrar to automatically bill you when it is time to renew the ownership of your domain. It is imperative to ensure that your Registrar is reputable before giving them the authority to charge your card in the future.

Appendix B: Domain Name Vocabulary

In the world of domain names, there are some specific domain vocabulary words and abbreviations and/or acronyms that are used to describe domain names and websites. Here is a list of many domain name vocabulary terms for reference:

ACPA (Anticybersquatting Consumer Protection Act)

The Anticybersquatting Consumer Protection Act (also known as Truth in Domain Names Act), is a US federal law enacted in 1999 that makes it illegal to register or misuse trademarked names. The law protects trademarks and individual's names from anyone who registers domain names with the intent of selling the domain name to the trademark holder or individual for a profit

Active

A domain name is assigned an Active status code when it is registered. When a domain name is active and has associated nameservers, it is included in the appropriate zone files. Domain names can be renewed, transferred or updated by the domain Registrant through the Registrar as long as the EPP status code is set to Active.

Add Grace Period

The Add Grace Period (AGP) is the 5 days after a domain name registration when a Registrar could cancel a domain registration if the Registrant made a bad payments or cancelled (or returned) the registration. In the past, the Registrar was able to cancel the registration without incurring a fee. However, because of misuse of this 5 day period (through domain tasting and kiting), Registrars are now limited as to how many domain registrations can be cancelled in any given month. Each Registrar has its own rules regarding cancelling domain registrations.

Ad Server

An Ad Server is a computer server or program that stores, sends out, and tracks advertisements across the web. An ad server may delivers ads for another company or be used to track a company's ads.

Administrative Contact

The person who is authorized to manage the domain name through the Registrar is the Administrative Contact. Domain name managing includes reviewing and updating Whois contact information and name servers.

AdSense

AdSense is a popular advertisement serving program operated by Google. Companies or individuals pay Google to distribute their ads. Website owners who have joined the AdSense program display the ads in order to earn revenue from impressions or clicks. Website owners are typically paid by Google every 30 days, as long as a minimum amount (like $100) is achieved. If not, then it rolls over to the next month. The main advantage of the Adsense program is that the ads displayed on websites are targeted based on the website's content or on a website visitor's recent behavior (other websites visited or products purchased).

AdWords

AdWords is an advertising program run by Google. With AdWords, companies or individuals upload their ads (text or image) to Google, type in their applicable keywords, and then select how much they are willing to pay. The Adwords program delivers ads to websites that have signed up for the AdSense program, or are displayed in Google's search results. The advertiser only pays when their ad is clicked (pay-per-click or PPC).

Affiliate Link

Website owners put affiliate links on their website to earn revenue from clicks or impressions on the links by their visitors. The affiliate link can also track whether a visitor who clicks a link eventually purchases a product by the company marketing their products or services as an affiliate.

Affiliate Marketing

Affiliate marketing is the broader term for making money through displaying advertising links on websites or within emails. The affiliate marketer is paid depending on the arrangement for each link, which could be by impression (which is now rarely used), by click, or by a percentage of an eventual sale of a product or service.

Affiliate Network

A company that manages a group of affiliate programs is an affiliate network. Commission Junction is an example. The affiliate network works forms agreements with many companies to serve as an intermediary between the advertising companies and affiliate marketers or website owners. Website owners often join affiliate networks to be able to select from multiple advertising options for their website.

Affiliate Sites

Websites that are primarily created to earn revenue through advertising links are called affiliate sites. Although these websites may contain relevant content in whatever niche is being targeted, the website owner's true purpose is in placing advertising links from affiliate networks and making money through clicks on ads or a percentage of an eventual sale of a product or service.

A-Record

A-Record (or AREC) is an "Address Record" tied to a domain name in the Domain Name System. The A-Record maps the numeric IP address to the domain name through the name servers the domain is pointed at. One of the A-Records used for google.com is 209.85.171.99.

Authentication

Authentication is the procedure where a website or computer application is verified and so can be trusted. This is typically done when a user name or ID is submitted along with a password or security question (or other private information that only the user would know).

autoRenewPeriod

The domain name status code autoRenewPeriod is assigned by the Registry when a name is automatically renewed by the Registry on its expiration date because the Registry has not yet received a renewal or delete command by the Registrar. When a domain name has an autoRenewPeriod status code, the Registrar is charged a renewal fee. If the Registrar deletes the domain name within 45 days the Registry gives the Registrar a credit of the renewal fee.

Auto-Responders

An auto-responder is a process where an email server automatically sends out s reply to incoming emails. Auto replies are usually set up by people in a company or business to let whoever sends them an email know that they are not able to respond for a period of time.

Avatar

An avatar is a drawing or photograph used to represent a user in a computer game or online forum.

Backlinks

Backlinks are direct links to a website from another website on the Internet. Typically, the more backlinks a website has from other reputable websites the more popular it is and the better it ranks in search engine results. However, there are also so-called "link farms" that create links from disreputable websites in order to falsely show large numbers of backlinks.

Backorder

A backorder is when a user places an order for a domain name that has not yet dropped, usually through a Registrar. This is typically done when a name has not been renewed by the current Registrant and has entered the domain expiration cycle. Good domain names may have multiple backorders so there is no guarantee when a backorder is placed that the user who wants the domain is going to get it. With multiple backorders, a domain name typically goes to auction when it drops. There is usually a fee associated with placing a backorder.

Bandwidth

Bandwidth is the amount of data an Internet connection is able to transfer, measured in bit rate, typically kilobits per second (kbps), megabytes per second (mbps) or gigabits per second (gbps). Bandwidth is different from Data or Disc Transfer which is the actual amount of data being transferred.

Billing Contact

A domain name's billing contact is the person or company responsible for the domain's registration fees. Most times, the billing contact is the same as the Registrant, but can be different if set up that way with the Registrar. If the billing contact is different, then that individual only has a financial tie to the domain name and cannot actually sell, transfer or change anything about the domain.

BIN

BIN is an acronym for 'Buy It Now.' When a domain seller puts a BIN price on a domain name, an individual can instantly purchase the domain name for that set price. The term is most used in domain auctions, where bidding usually starts with low values and works its way higher. The domain owner could set a BIN price at the start of an auction or wait until during an auction to place a BIN amount. The disadvantage of a BIN is a popular name in a domain auction could have multiple bidders which could drive the price above what the domain seller had set as the BIN amount. But BIN prices often work for owners when set higher than what they think the domain's value actually is, and a bidder decides they want the domain name enough where they will select the BIN so that nobody else will win the auction.

Black-Hat SEO

Black-hat SEO (search engine optimization) are tactics used to get web pages to rank higher in search engines using deceptive or spamming methods, which could include repetitive phrases and keywords on the website. Most search engines are able to recognize these tactics and could blacklist websites from their search results for sites that utilize Black-Hat SEO.

Blacklisted

The term Blacklisted can be applied to a domain name or IP address when it is blocked from accessing a specific location on the Internet or banned from using or displaying content on the Internet. Any domain or website owner who misuses a service can be blacklisted (such as having your website blacklisted from Google due to non-compliance). Websites that scrape content from other websites are typically blacklisted.

Blog

A "Web Log" or Blog is an online journal or set of articles where an individual or company makes regular posts to a website. These can range from a personal journal or diary to a company's news or updates.

Browser

A "Web Browser" or Browser is an application on your computer used to view web pages on the Internet. Popular web browsers include Google Chrome, Mozilla Firefox, Safari, and Internet Explorer. Browsers offer different features and display web pages differently, leading to many users to prefer one browser over all others.

Cache

Cache is the space on your computer's hard drive (or RAM) where your internet browser keeps data related to web pages you've recently visited. By having this information in cache, web pages you frequently visit can load much faster. How your cache is configured is controlled by the browser settings.

Case Sensitive

Case Sensitive is a term that tells a user that a particular input (be it a user name, password, etc.) will differentiate between lower case and upper case letters.

ccSLD (Country Code Second Level Domain)

ccSLD is an acronym for "Country Code Second Level Domain." The second level refers to a domain name that uses both a top level and second level extension, such as xxx.co.uk. In this example, the additional prefix .co is the second level of the domain while .uk is the top level of the domain. Many countries use second level domains while other countries have no ccSLD and instead only use the main ccTLD, like .io.

ccTLD (Country Code Top Level Domain)

ccTLD is an acronym for "Country Code Top Level Domain." The country code top level refers to a domain name that has only a two letter domain extension designated for use for that country. Australia uses .au for their ccTLD and Hong Kong uses .hk. A country's ccTLD is not always a direct abbreviation for the country's name, such as .ch for Switzerland and .dz for Algeria. You can find a list of most ccTLDs in Appendix C.

Cease and Desist Letter

A cease and desist letter is sent by a company or individual (often through an attorney) to a domain owner when they believe the domain name in question infringes on a trademark or copyright held by that company or individual. The letter could request the domain owner simply stop using the name or demand the domain owner transfer the domain name to the trademark holder.

Click-Through

A click-through (or typically just called a click) is when a visitor to a website (or someone reading an email) clicks on a link or ad and is sent to a different web page.

ClientDeleteProhibited

ClientDeleteProhibited is a status code assigned by the Registrar indicating the domain name is locked. When a domain has a ClientDeleteProhibited status, the Registry is able to reject any requests that the domain be deleted, except by the Registrar if the domain name has expired.

ClientHold

ClientHold is a status code assigned by the Registrar indicating the domain name is being held by the Registrar, most likely for non-payment by the Registrant.

ClientLock

ClientLock is a status code assigned by the Registrar indicating the domain name is locked. When a domain has a ClientLock status, the Registry is able to reject any requests to update the domain's nameservers or to transfer or delete the domain name.

ClientRenewProhibited

ClientRenewProhibited is a status code assigned by the Registrar indicating the domain name cannot be renewed by anyone other than the current Registrar.

ClientTransferProhibited (or Client-Xfer-Prohibited)

ClientTransferProhibited is a status code assigned by the Registrar indicating the domain name is locked. When a domain has a ClientTransferProhibited status, the Registry is able to reject any requests that the domain be transferred, except by the Registrar where the name is currently registered.

ClientUpdateProhibited

ClientUpdateProhibited is a status code assigned by the Registrar indicating the domain name is locked. When a domain has a ClientUpdateProhibited status, the Registry is able to reject any requests that the domain's nameservers or authorization codes be updated. A domain name's codes cannot be updated until the Registrar removes the ClientUpdateProhibited status code.

CNAME (Canonical Name Record)

A domain name's CNAME record maps a web address to its canonical name, and is handled at the name server on which your domain name resides. When you access a web address on a domain where there is a CNAME record, the domain name is replaced with the canonical name and then you are directed to the new hostname. If a domain owner points their nameservers to somewhere other than their Registrar, they can no longer modify the CNAME record directly.

Content Management System (CMS)

A content management system is an application that manages a website's content. A CMS uses an interface that generally makes creating, publishing and editing content much easier. The website's data is usually kept in a database. CMS applications include Wordpress, Drupal, and Joomla.

Control Panel

The control panel is where domain owners manage their domain names, typically accessed on the Registrar's website. Domain name tasks such as updating contact information, renew services, setting up email accounts, changing passwords, etc. are done through the control panel.

Cookies

The term Cookies, also known as "Web Cookies," refers to data sent by a web server to a user's browser. That same web server will request the data the next time the user accesses that same website. The cookie data usually holds information about which pages a user has visited on that particular website, or is used to keep a browsing session open so that you are not automatically logged off after a certain period of time. Cookies are not programs, viruses or spyware.

CTR (Click-Through-Rate)

A link's "Click Through Rate" refers to the percentage of times a link is clicked on by a user compared to the number of times it is displayed by the publisher. If a link or ad receives 5 clicks by users but was displayed 100 times, the link or ad had a 5% CTR.

Cybersquatting

Cybersquatting is when a domain owner registers a domain name that is or contains a name that is trademarked. When domain registrations first started, there were many who registered popular company domain names before the company did, and these new domain owners then tried to sell the names to the respective companies. Unfortunately, that practice, now not allowed, is still remembered and causes many people to incorrectly confuse today's domain industry with cybersquatting.

Data Transfer

The amount of data sent across an Internet connection over a given time period is data transfer. Every time a user visits a website, data is transferred. When a user downloads (or uploads) information from a website, data is transferred. The transfer rate is the actual speed at which data (information) is being transferred, measured in bit rate, typically kilobits per second (kbps), megabytes per second (mbps) or gigabits per second (gbps).

Database

A database is a means of storing information in an organized manner with the ability to retrieve information upon request. Databases are typically managed using a database management system (DBMS). Examples of databases used on the Internet include MySQL, Oracle, Microsoft Access and others. Many websites use a Content Management System (CMS), which is a user interface where all of the website's information is stored in a database.

Direct Traffic

Direct traffic, also known "Type-In Traffic," refers to users who type a web address into their browser's URL bar to go directly to a website. This manner of getting to a website is different than reaching it through a search engine or by clicking on a link.

Disk Space

Disk space is the amount of storage space you are assigned on the web server or mail server to store your website, files, and emails. Disk space is measured in MB (Megabytes) or TB (Terabytes).

Domain Auction

A domain auction is when a domain owner offers their domain name for sale using an auction-style format. At the end of the auction, the bidder with the highest bid typically purchases the domain. Domain auctions are performed by independent companies, Registrars and domain name forums. Domain owners are generally able to select the starting bid price, a reserve price (if allowed), and a BIN price if they want. Each auction company sets their own rules about how an auction starts, proceeds, and ends. There are also websites that flip backordered domains into an auction-style format if there is more than one order or bid put on a particular domain name. Domains can also be auctioned on general auction websites such as eBay.

Domain Broker

A domain broker is someone who is hired by a domain owner to help sell a domain name or by a prospect seeking to buy a domain name. A domain broker can work individually or with a company. Domain brokers generally have a network of contacts throu which they can market or seek out domain names. Domain brokers typically charge on a percentage of the domain name transaction. Domainers often seek out brokers for high-priced domains, for botth accessing their markets and to handle the negotiations.

Domain Extension

The domain extension is the suffix that follows your address. For example, in the domain name DomainDS.com, the domain extension is .com, which is pronounced "dot com."

Domain Hijacking

Domain hijacking, or domain stealing, is illegally gaining control over a domain name from its Registrant without paying for it. This can be done by stealing (or figuring out) passwords, or by accessing a Registrant's email service through which they get into the user's domain account.

Domain Kiting

Domain kiting was the practice of registering a domain name, then deleting it within the 5-day add grace period, and then registering it again right away starting another 5-day period. Some people were able to repeat this process over and over again, being able to use a domain name without actually paying for it. Registrar policies set by ICANN in 2008 led to the end of domain kiting..

Domain Name

A domain name is a series of characters that resolve (through the DNS) to an IP address. A domain name generally consists of a word or words followed by a dot (.), then followed by an extension (like "com"). "DomainDS.com" is a domain name for example. Domain names are NOT case-sensitive, which means that you can type DOMAINDS.COM or domainds.com into your browser and always reach the same place.

Domain Name Affiliate

A domain name affiliate, or domain affiliate, is a website that has links and/or ads for domain Registrars or secondary market domain sales websites. When a user clicks on a link, they are directed to that site where they can register or buy a domain name, The domain name affiliate is typically paid as a percentage of the sale..

Domain Name Aftermarket

When currently registered domain names are bought and sold, that is the domain name aftermarket. Many of these are sold in auctions, where the highest bidder has the domain name transferred to their account at a Registrar. For buyers, the aftermarket gives the potential to purchase domain names that are already registered and would otherwise have been unavailable. For sellers, the aftermarket has the opportunity to sell domain names for a profit over what they purchased (or registered) them for.

Domain Name Registration

The act of reserving the right to use a particular domain name for a specified period of time is Domain Name Registration. The amount of time a Registrant registers a domain name for could be 1, 2, 5 or 10 years, although some Registrars allow for any number of years between 1 and 10. A domain name is registered using a domain name Registrar or sometimes a reseller of a Registrar.

Domain Name Status Codes

Domain name status codes are assigned to domain names in order to describe the status of a domain name at the Registry. It is important for Registrants to understand their domain name status codes because the codes can explain why a domain may have stopped working, if it is protected from domain name hijacking, and when and if a domain name registration will expire and become available to the public for registration.

The status of a domain name can be seen in its Whois information. To check the Whois details of a domain name, you can use an online Whois check tool such as whois.domaintools.com or the Whois search at godaddy.com. Here is an example Whois record (for domaindirectservices.com) and the domain name status codes:

Domain Name: DOMAINDIRECTSERVICES.COM
Registry Domain ID: 2130926809_DOMAIN_COM-VRSN
Registrar WHOIS Server: whois.godaddy.com
Registrar URL: http://www.godaddy.com
Update Date: 2017-06-05T17:01:29Z
Creation Date: 2017-06-05T17:01:29Z
Registrar Registration Expiration Date: 2022-06-05T17:01:29Z
Registrar: GoDaddy.com, LLC
Registrar IANA ID: 146
Registrar Abuse Contact Email: abuse@godaddy.com
Registrar Abuse Contact Phone: +1.4806242505
Domain Status: clientTransferProhibited
Domain Status: clientUpdateProhibited
Domain Status: clientRenewProhibited
Domain Status: clientDeleteProhibited

Domain Name System (DNS)

The DNS is the naming system created in 1983 to translate IP addresses (strings of numbers and dots) into names that are easier to remember and use. When a user types a domain name into their internet browser, a series of requests occur, from the root servers to the authoritative Registry's name servers, to the authoritative provider's name servers, which then translates the domain name into the IP address which then sends you to the applicable web server where the attached web page is ultimately delivered to your browser, all of which typically happens in fractions of a second.

Domain Tasting

Domain tasting is the practice of registering an available domain name and testing or 'tasting' the domain during the 5-day add grace period (AGP). In the past this practice was abused by domain owners, frequently registering domain names and immediately putting them on parked pages with ads to see if the names were profitable. Many times a Registrant would then contact the

Registrar within the five days and get a refund on their registration, only to re-register the same domain name once it became available again. New rules and fees were established by ICANN in 2008 to reduce (and practically eliminate) this practice.

Domain Types

Domain types is a term used to identify different letter and/or number combinations of short domain names. For example, an LLL.com domain name is a 3-letter name with a .com extension. An NNN.com domain name is a 3-number name with a .com extension. Combination types can be something like LLN.com, which would be a 3-character name with the first two characters being letters and the third character being a number, with a .com extension.

These domain type identifications are often used by domainers in discussions about short domain names or when seeking to buy or sell short domain names.

Letter combinations:
LLL, LLLL, LLLLL – each L refers to a Letter. When a domain name is referred to as an LLLL.com or an LLL.net, etc,, it is a domain with that many letters in its name. For example, TUHD.com has 4 Letters, so it is an LLLL.com, HUV.io has 3 Letters so it is an LLL.io.

It is important to note that when identifying domain names with letter combinations these names are not proper English words. This is because short domain names that are English words have more value when being identified as a proper word as opposed to being a short name with letter combinations. For example, even though JET.com is an LLL.com, it has far more value as a word. Therefore, letter combinations are used when the domain name is not a proper English word.
3L, 4L, 5L – this is simply a shorter way of referring to letter combinations: a 3L .com is the same as LLL.com or a 3-Letter dot.com,, 4L is a domain name with four letters, 5L has five letters, etc.

CVC, VCC, CVCV, VCVC, CVVCV, etc. – these combinations refer to short domain names that only have letters, but are more precise as in what types of letters the domain name has: Consonants or Vowels. Domain names with certain consonant-vowel patterns have more value than others. Again, using any letter combinations when referring to a domain name is usually only done when the name is not a proper English word. Many times certain patterns of letters make up something that is pronounceable but is not technically a word, such as FLIX.com. This name has great value in that it can be marketed or branded, making it a "brandable" domain name. It can also be referred to as a CCVC.com name, but since it is more valuable as being pronounceable it is typically marketed more as a pronounceable name.

Here are some examples of LLLL.com domain names and their associated Consonant-Vowel designations:

CVCV examples (consonant-vowel-consonant-vowel): leti, kura, bisi, gola
VCVC examples: apet, eqiv, utax, ilic
CVVC examples: loum, xeiw, poaq, ruaz
VCCV examples: ipla, oqxe, angu, eple
VVVV examples (4 vowels): oeia, uaie

Although CCCC is technically a name that has four consonants, like DVXR.com, because the four C's, or CCCC is more commonly used to identify characters (see below) and not consonants, domainers typically only identify short names with only consonants using the "L's" – so DVXR.com would simply be an LLLL.com domain name.

Number combinations:
Domains consisting only of numbers (or numerics) are written using 'N's, for Number. Here are some examples:

NN, NNN are a 2- and a 3-number domain, like 63.net (an NN.net) or 329.io (an NNN.io).

NNNN.com (or 4N) – a 4-number dot.com, such as 6815.com or 0345.com. As with letters, short number domain names only use the 'N' designations if the numbers are random. If the numbers have meaning, like the year 1989, then 1989.com would be called a "year.com" as it has more value than just a random bunch of number, even though the domain is technically an NNNN.com.

NNNNN.com (or **5N)** – a 5-number dot.com, such as 63840.com or 83391.com.

By the time you get to 6 numbers, it is usually just abbreviated as **6N**.

Hyphen combinations:
When you add a hyphen (or hyphens) to the above combination types, there are other domain type terms that are used. Domain names with hyphens generally have low value, but very short domain names are valuable because of scarcity, even if they have hyphens. Here are some examples:

LL-L.com, L-LL.com – these have a total of 4 characters, with one hyphen. Examples: ML-X.com, T-BC.com.

L-L-L.com – a dot.com that has a total of 5 characters, using 3 letters and 2 hyphens, with the hyphens between each letter. Examples: V-L-X.com, M-P-B.com.

NN-N.com, N-NN.com – examples: 63-1.com, 5-29.com.

N-N-N.com – a dot.com that has 3 numbers and 2 hyphens (5 characters). Examples: 5-9-2.com, 8-1-3.com.

Note that a domain name cannot begin or end with a hyphen.

Character combinations:
Domains which contain 2 or more of the three characters in its name can use the domain type of 'C's, or Characters. The characters used are either Letters, Numbers, or Hyphens. When a domain name consists of two or more of these, it can be referred to as a CCC or CCCC. Here are some examples:

CC combinations (2-character) – some examples: 7t.com, a5.net, 3e.io.
A hyphen can only be placed between two other characters, so all 2-character names can only be created with a Letter and a Number. Although the C's can be used, these 2 character names are more frequently marketed as NL or LN and not CC, since the C tends to not portray the name with as high of a value.

CCC combinations (3-character) – here are some examples: hx7.com, t67.net, t4o.info, c-4.com, 9-n.net. If the name has all letters or all numbers, but separated by hyphens, it is usually described with L's or N's and not C's. For example, m-b.com would be called an L-L (Letter, Hyphen, Letter) domain instead of a CCC (3-character). Even though it fits both categories, the L-L is not only more accurate but also portrays more value in the name.

Other combinations can be called either way. For example, 47n.com can be called a CCC (3-character), but also an NNL (Number, Number, Letter). The domain name 8-a.net can be called a CCC, but also an N-L (Number, Hyphen, Letter).

Domainer

Domainer, although not technically an English word, is commonly used in domaining (also not a word), as a person who makes money by registering, buying, selling, leasing, or parking domain names.

Download

When a user retrieves a file from a server through the Internet (or another type of network) to open or save on their computer, the user is downloading the file. A user downloads files every time a web page with content is displayed in a user's browser, although download typically refers more to the act of selecting a file and saving it on their computer.

Drop Catching

Drop catching is the practice of registering expired domain names the instance they become available. The "drop" happens once the domain name is deleted by the Registry. There are many reasons why domain names are not renewed, and even very good names can end up being dropped due to the Registrant forgetting to renew the name. Domain names with good value can drop so companies which use automated software have been created to try and "catch" the best names when they "drop." Users can have accounts with Drop Catching companies and place bids on names that are about to be deleted. When more than one person places a bid on a domain name with a particular company that catches the name, an auction follows where anybody can take part and bid on the domain. This process is similar to backordering.

Drop Lists

Domain names that are about to be deleted by Registries are listed on Drop Lists. These lists typically show domains around five days before they drop. Drop Catching companies publish these lists as a service so domainers will use their company to try and catch names immediately when they are deleted.

Dropped Domain

A dropped domain is a name that was not renewed by the prior Registrant and gone through the complete domain name expiration process and been deleted by the Registry. An expired domain name is not necessarily the same. When a domain name's registration expires, the current Registrant still has a grace period in which to renew the registration (usually for a fee). It is not until the Registry deletes the name that it becomes a dropped domain, and then available for anybody to register.

Dynamic Content

Dynamic content is information on a web site that changes, either based on the way the website is designed or by user inputs or past actions. Dynamic websites tend to create more interactive or targeted experiences.

Dynamic IP Address

A dynamic IP address is an IP address that changes after a web browsing session ends or some other specific timeframe. The opposite of a dynamic IP address is a static IP address.

Ecommerce

Ecommerce (or e-commerce) is short for Electronic Commerce and refers to the buying and selling of goods and services through the Internet.

Email

Email (or e-mail) is short for Electronic Mail and refers to messages sent and received over the Internet through mail servers.

Email Address

An email address is a unique identifier that directs where electronic messages are to be delivered, much like a person's home address. An email address has three parts: the name and the mail server separated by the @ symbol. The name must be unique for each mail server. An example of an email address is DomainNamesProfit@gmail.com.

Email Forwarding

Email forwarding is the process in which one email address is redirected to a different email address. The first email address is often known as an alias to the second email address. The benefit of email forwarding is that a user may have 20 email addresses all forwarded to a single mailbox, preventing the need to log in to 20 different accounts to read all of one's mail.

End User

An End User is a buyer who plans to use a domain name to develop into a website or protect their brand. Domainers want to sell domains to end users as that is the type of buyer who will most likely pay the most for a domain name. An end user will look at a domain name for business or extensive personal use, and does not plan to trade or resell that domain name. They are called an endu user as that would be the 'end of the line' for that domain, or the user who has the final use of the domain name and will likely never sell it again.

Although many domain names are initially registered by business owners for their direct use (an initial end user registration), many domain names are bought and sold multiple times between domainers until they find the ideal end users who will keep them indefinitely. Since the end user has so much interest in the name, they also usually pay much more for that domain than will a reseller who intends to profit on the name by trying to resell the name for a higher price than what they purchased it for.

EPC (Earnings-Per-Click)

EPC or earnings per click is the average amount of money earned by each click on an advertisement over a specific time period or the average amount of money after a specific number of clicks. For example, if a business owner posts an ad on a web page and one out of every ten people who click the ad purchase a $20 item, the EPC for the ad is $2 because you earned an average of $2 for each of the 10 clicks.

EPP Status Codes

EPP status codes (Extensible Provisioning Protocol) are assigned to domain names in order to describe the status of a domain name at the Registry.

EPP status codes appear in the Registry Whois record for a domain name (preceded by "Status:"). The default EPP status code for a domain name is "OK" or "Active", which is removed if any other status code is applied to the domain.

Here is an example Whois record (for domaindirectservices.com) and the location of the EPP Status Code:

Domain Name: DOMAINDIRECTSERVICES.COM
Registry Domain ID: 2130926809_DOMAIN_COM-VRSN
Registrar WHOIS Server: whois.godaddy.com
Registrar URL: http://www.godaddy.com
Update Date: 2017-06-05T17:01:29Z
Creation Date: 2017-06-05T17:01:29Z
Registrar Registration Expiration Date: 2022-06-05T17:01:29Z
Registrar: GoDaddy.com, LLC
Registrar IANA ID: 146
Registrar Abuse Contact Email: abuse@godaddy.com
Registrar Abuse Contact Phone: +1.4806242505
Domain Status: clientTransferProhibited <- This is the EPP Status Code
Domain Status: clientUpdateProhibited
Domain Status: clientRenewProhibited
Domain Status: clientDeleteProhibited

The EPP code is also known as an authorization code, and is used if you want to transfer your domain name to another Registrar. "Auth Codes" are many times used in aftermarket sales of domain names from one person to another.

Escrow Services

An escrow service (typically an independent company) facilitates a transaction between a buyer and seller. Escrow services are particularly useful to take the risk out of higher-priced sales. For a domain name transcation, an escrow agent will first request payment from the buyer. When the escrow service has received the funds they will then instruct the seller to transfer the domain name to the buyer. Once the domain name is transferred, the money is then released to the seller. Escrow services charge a small percentage of the sale price as their fee. The fee can be paid by the buyer, the seller, or split between the two.

Expired Domain

Expired domain names are domains that were not renewed prior to the end-of-registration date. A Registrant typically has a grace period in which to renew a domain's registration after it has expired, usually for a fee. Each Registrar has different policies regarding expired domain names.

Forum

A forum is a web site where users participate in online discussions with other users. Also called a message boards or discussion boards, the majority of forums focus on specific topics like domain names, allowing participants to ask and answer questions or engage in discussions on that subject.

FTP (File Transfer Protocol)

FTP, or File Transfer Protocol, is the method people typically use to transfer files between their local computer and a web server. The most common use for FTP is for uploading web page files to and from your hosting provider.

Grace Delete

Grace deletion refers to the process of deleting a domain name shortly after you registered it. There are many reasons people register domains and then delete them within a few days. Many times users realize it's not as good a domain as they thought when they registered it. Other reasons range from discovering the name is based on a trademark, finding another name that will better suit their needs, or "tasting" the domain for traffic and then letting it go.

Registrars have different policies with regard to grace deletion, and some don't offer it at all. But most Registrars, within three days or so, will give users a full refund, then inform the Registry to delete the name. However, if a Registrar offers grace delete, they most likely also have a limit as to how many times a Registrant can use this method.

gTLD (Generic Top Level Domain)

gTLD, or Generic Top Level Domain, is the group of TLDs or domain extensions that are not assigned to a specific region of the world. gTLDs include .com, .net, .org, .info.

Hold / ServerHold

A Hold / ServerHold status code is assigned to a domain name by the Registry. The Hold / ServerHold status code means that a domain name has been deleted from the DNS, most commonly for a financial, legal, or operational reason. Domains with the EPP status code "Hold / ServerHold" are not included in the zone files.

Home Page

A home page is a website's main page, This is the page seen by visitors to a website when they type a domain name in their browser and don't specify a specific page. A home page is typically named index.html or home.html, although it can be anything, depending on your site and/or server configuration or content managements system (CMS), like Wordpress.

HTML (Hyper-Text Markup Language)

HTML, or Hyper-Text Markup Language, refers to the programming code used to create documents on the Internet. HTML defines the look of a web page and the elements within it through various tags and commands that are surrounded by angle brackets < >. HTML is the most commonly used programming language for website design and other online functions.

HTTP (Hyper-Text Protocol)

HTTP, or Hyper-Text Protocol, refers to the communication between your browser and web server. HTTP was first used to request and display linked text documents which eventually led to the creation of the World Wide Web.

HTTPS

HTTPS, or Hyper-Text Transfer Protocol Secure, is a variant of the standard web transfer protocol (HTTP) that adds a layer of security on the data in transit through a secure socket layer (SSL) or transport layer security (TLS) protocol connection.

Hyperlink

A hyperlink, also typically called just a link, is a snippet of code that enables an Internet user to click on an element (such as a word or picture) and then be redirected to another web page or other element.

IANA

IANA (Internet Assigned Numbers Authority) operating under ICANN (the Internet Corporation for Assigned Names and Numbers), oversees the assignment of IP addresses to Internet Service Providers. In addition, IANA oversees root zone management for DNS and other internet protocol assignments.

ICANN

ICANN (Internet Corporation of Assigned Names and Numbers) is a non-profit organization created to oversee global internet related tasks that were previously managed by IANA, under a contract from the US Government. ICANN is primarily responsible for managing the Internet's top level domains (TLD's), overseeing the allocation of IP addresses and managing the root server system. Some specific examples of ICANN services include approval of new generic TLDs, approval of Registrars to sell domain names, and resolving domain name registration disputes under its Uniform Domain Name Dispute Resolution Policy (UDRP).

IDN (Internationalized Domain Names)

IDN, or Internationalized Domain Names, refers to domain names that have one or more non-ASCII characters. IDNs are able to use characters from non-English languages, such as Chinese or Arabic, or even emoji symbols. Because long-established domain names did not allow for use of non-English characters, IDNs were adopted to provide non-English speaking users with the ability to register domain names in their native language. An example would be the non-English characters ДоманиДC.com having the IDN xn--80ahbpsid3a.com. The four characters xn-- precede all IDNs.

Inactive

Inactive is a status code that is assigned to a domain name by the Registry when the domain name has no delegated name servers. It may also be assigned to a host or contact that is not associated with any domain names.

IP Address

An IP (Internet Protocol) Address is a unique set of numbers separated by periods that is assigned to each device on a network that is connected to the Internet. An example of an IP address is 209.85.171.99, which is one of many Google IP Addresses. Because IP addresses are hard to remember, domain names were created to make the internet experience easier for users.

Landing Page

A Landing Page is any web page on the Internet that a user "lands" on after clicking a link, be it a hyperlink or an advertisement. Many times, landing pages are tracked through affiliate or advertising links/codes which follow the user through tasks, whether it is registering on a website or buying a product. Advertisers particularly track a visitor's progression from clicking an ad to performing the desired task on the landing page. Website owners can also track landing pages to inform them as to what links or photos brought the visitor to the landing page.

Landing pages for domain names are single web pages that are reached either through links and/or by directly typing the URL into a browser and "landing" on the page showing your domain name is for sale.

Lock / ServerLock

A domain name will have a Lock / ServerLock status code when the domain name is locked. It is a good idea for Registrants to lock their domains with their Registrar (who then informs the Registry) in order to prevent unauthorized transfers. Registrants can always unlock a domain name when they sell it in order to prepare for a push or transfer. The Lock / ServerLock status code tells the Registry to reject any requests to transfer, renew, or delete the domain.

Long-Tail Domain Names

A long-tail domain name refers to a domain name made from keywords that are targeted to one particular topic or niche. The idea of long-tail domain names is that a business owner is better able to compete and profit with their website by utilizing a more-targeted name based on long-tail keywords over a more generic keyword with substantial competition. The long-tail domain names can be especially useful for local businesses who do not want or need to attract national or international customers. An example of a long-tail domain name would be "SacramentoHealthCareProviders.com" as opposed to the more generic "healthcare.com".

Mail Server

A mail server is an internet computer server that manages email (Electronic Mail) using Internet protocols such as POP (Post Office Protocol), SMTP (Simple Mail Transfer Protocol), and IMAP (Internet Message Access Protocol). POP is used to retrieve and route electronic communications to your email account. SMTP is used to send communications from your email account. IMAP is used to retrieve email messages from a mail server over a TCP/IP connection.

New TLDs

A new TLD refers to any of the Top Level Domain extensions added by ICANN after the original set of gTLDs (.com, .net, .org, .mil, .edu, .gov) Over 500 new TLDs were added between 2014 and 2106, and by the end of 2018 there were over 1,200 new TLDs. Example of new TLD extensions include .xyz, .travel, .social, .shop.

Numeric Domains

A numeric domain is a domain name consisting solely of numbers. An example of a numeric domain name is 63852.com. Many numeric domains are owned by Chinese investors and businesses as Chinese websites rely less on English words and letters. When investing in numeric domains, there are "good" numbers (8) and "bad" numbers (0,4) based on Chinese translations. It is best to research and understand all you can about numeric domains before investing.

Parking

Domain parking is when a Registrant directs a domain name to a single web page (typically at a domain parking company) which then displays targeted advertising content and links related to the domain name. When a user lands on the parked web page of a domain and clicks on any of the links, the domain owner generates revenue.

Many domain Registrants use parking as a means to reserve the domain for future development and possible earn income through advertising revenue until they are ready to fully develop the name. Some domain parking companies also have additional features, like putting a banner on the page announcing that the domain name is for sale.

Many Registrars automatically set up parking pages for newly-registered domains, typically advertising their own products and services.

PendingCreate

The Registry assigns a PendingCreate status code to a domain name after the domain name registration has been submitted, but the complete domain registration process is not yet complete.

PendingDelete

The Registry assigns a PendingDelete status code to a domain name after the domain has had a RedemptionPeriod status code for 30 days. When a domain name has a PendingDelete status code, it is for a period of 5 days and cannot be restored. Domains with the EPP status code "PendingDelete" are not included in the zone files.

PendingRestore

The Registry assigns a PendingRestore status code to a domain name if the Registrar has issued the EPP Restore command when the domain was previously assigned the RedemptionPeriod status code. When a domain name has a PendingRestore status code, it is for a period of 7 days, during which the Registrar must send a Restore report to the Registry through the Registrar Tool or the EPP Protocol. If the Registry receives the submitted Restore report within the 7-day period, the domain name will be moved to an "OK" status. If the Registry does not receive the Restore report within the 7-day period, the domain is moved back to a RedemptionPeriod status code and will remain there for 30 days. Domains with the EPP status code "PendingRestore" are included in the zone files.

PendingTransfer

The Registry assigns a PendingTransfer status code to a domain name when the domain is in the process of being transferred from one Registrar to another.

PendingUpdate

The Registry assigns a PendingUpdate status code to a domain name when the domain name is in the process of being updated, but the complete domain name update process is not yet complete.

PPA (Pay-Per-Action)

PPA, or Pay Per Action, is the agreement by which an advertiser pays a website owner every time a visitor makes an action per the agreement, such as buying a product or service, or submitting a form. This is different than PPC (Pay Per Click) where the advertiser pays for a click regardless of whether an action is taken after the click.

PPC (Pay-Per-Click)

PPC, or Pay Per Click, is the agreement by which an advertiser pays a website owner every time a visitor clicks on the advertiser's link. This is different than PPA (Pay Per Action) where the advertiser only gets paid if the visitor actually takes an action after clicking on the link.

Punycode

Used to define IDNs (Internationalized Domain Names), a Punycode is an algorithm where non-ASCII characters (or Unicode characters) are converted into a set of ASCII characters, preceded by the suffix xn--. The name that Punycode would come up with for ДомаинДС.com would be xn--80ahbpsid3a.com.

Push

A 'push' is a specific kind of domain transfer (see the definition of 'transfer' below). When you transfer a domain name to another user within the same Registrar, it is called a push, although technically it is also a transfer, and the Registrar will most likely call it a transfer. However, when buying and selling domain names, the term push is typically used as a requirement of a sale when the domain seller does not want to go through the trouble of transferring the domain name to another Registrar upon completion of the sale.

An example of a push would be if a domainer had a name registered at GoDaddy and offered the name for sale with the requirement they will only push the name to a buyer's account, which would also be at GoDaddy. This makes the domain transfer process much easier and faster. A push is also free where a domain transfer to another Registrar may have fees involved. A push is also started by the current Registrant, where a domain transfer needs to be initiated by the buyer.

Redemption Period

When a domain name has not been renewed by the Registrant by the end of registration date, the domain name enters the redemption period. This is a 30 day period after the domain expires and the Registrar cancels the domain name at the Registry. The Registry then keeps a 30-day hold on the domain name while the Registrant still has an opportunity to renew the domain name registration with the Registrar, usually for an additional fee. The redemption period essentially gives the domain owner an additional 30 days to renew their expired domain name before it is deleted and eventually released. During the redemption period any website or email account that was associated with the domain name will no longer be active. If the Registrant renews the domain name during the redemption period, any website and/or email account will be restored.

The Registry assigns a RedemptionPeriod status code to an expired domain name. An expired domain name will have a RedemptionPeriod status code for 30 days, unless the Registrar issues a Restore command.

RegFee

RegFee is an abbreviation for "registration fee." The registration fee is the amount of money spent by a Registrant when they originally hand-registered a domain name. Registrars have different prices for domain name registrations, based on the domain name extension and the period of time the domain will be registered. Domain name renewals are usually a different price, see below.

Domainers typically use the term "Reg Fee" when describing the value of domain names that have little to no value. For example, when evaluating a domain name that is not worth much, it may be said the domain name is not even worth a Reg Fee, meaning they do not believe the owner will even be able to recover their initial cost of registration.

Registrant

The Registrant of a domain name is the organization or individual that has registered a domain name. The Registrant has an account with a Registrar where the domain name registration is held. A domain name may have different contacts, such as Admin or Tech contacts, but the Registrant has the final say with regards to the domain name.

Registrar

A domain name Registrar is a company that has the right to register and manage domain names on behalf of Registrants for any given domain Registry. There are many Registries around the world, handling the many different TLDs.

Registry

An organization that controls the registrations of domain names with a specific TLD (domain extension) is a Domain Name Registry. Verisign is the Registry that manages.com and .net TLDs, as well as several other domain extensions. Public Interest Registry (PIR) is the Registry that manages the .org extension, along with .ngo and .ong domain names. Some Registries are their own Registars to their end users (Registrants), while many work with Registrars to manage the domains and Registrants.

Reseller

A domain name reseller is a company that offers customers to register domain names but is not a Registrar itself. The reseller manages domain names through a Registrar's system. The Registrar generally provides the reseller with a wholesale rate for domains and other services, as well as a management interface to service their customers. Some Registrar's reseller programs are completely private label, meaning the Registrant may not be aware that they are dealing with a reseller. Other resellers just take the domain registration order and then the Registrant deals directly with the Registrar for domain name management.

Reverse Domain Hijacking

When an organization (or sometimes an individual) tries to take a domain name from a Registrant by false means through the legal system or UDRP process it is called Reverse Domain Hijacking. Many times they will attempt to scare a domain owner into handing over a domain name, threatening legal action. They could also file a UDRP complaint hoping the Registrant does not respond or, if he or she does, attempt to make an argument that is good enough to get a favorable ruling from the Panel.

RPC (Revenue-Per-Click)

RPC, or Revenue Per Click, is the average revenue generated from user clicks on a specific advertisement. Also known as Earnings Per Click (EPC), the revenue could be calculated over a specific time period or the average amount of money after a specific number of clicks. For example, if a business owner posts an ad on a web page and one out of every ten people who click the ad purchase a $20 item, the RPC for the ad is $2 because you earned an average of $2 for each of the 10 clicks.

Search Engine (SE)

A Search Engine catalogues websites on the internet and returns relevant results when a user searches for something. Early search engines used to require website owners to submit their websites to them, and search results were only given for web pages that were submitted. Today, the major search engines have "spiders" or programs that crawl the internet collecting website data to store in their database.

As an example, a user goes to a search engine website and enters in search criteria such as "dentists in Lexington Massachusetts." The search engine then displays a listing of websites related to Lexington, Massachusetts dentists. The rankings of websites do not necessarily only give dentists in Lexington however. Many website owners and developers design web pages using advanced search engine optimization (SEO) techniques and keywords so these web pages rank high on anything related to the website's content. Obviously, the higher a website ranks the more visitors the website receives. Google and Bing are two of the most popular search engines.

SEO (Search Engine Optimization)

SEO, or Search Engine Optimization, is the process used by website developers and online marketers to make a website or specific web pages rank high on search engines, with the goal of trying to have a web page appear on the first page of search engine results for certain keywords or phrases. Many online companies pay a lot of money to experts to optimize their ranking in search engines.

ServerDeleteProhibited

The Registry assigns a ServerDeleteProhibited status code to a domain name to lock the domain. This status code is rare, and typically only used during a legal dispute.

ServerRenewProhibited

The Registry assigns a ServerRenewProhibited status code to a domain name which means that the domain name cannot be renewed. This status code is rare, and typically only used during a legal dispute.

ServerTransferProhibited

The Registry assigns a ServerTransferProhibited status code to a domain name to lock the domain. A domain name cannot be transferred from one Registrar to another if it has the ServerTransferProhibited status code, which is typically only used during a legal dispute.

ServerUpdateProhibited

The Registry assigns a ServerUpdateProhibited status code to a domain name to lock the domain and reject requests to update name servers, auth codes, or sync the domain. This status code is rare, and typically only used during a legal dispute.

Shilll Bidding

Shill bidding is where sellers use memberships of people they know, or fake memberships they have created, to put false bids on auctions in an attempt to bid up the price of a domain name they are selling. This dishonest type of bidding, when done, is usually on auctions with a set reserve price, or the minimum price you are willing to sell the domain name for. Shill bidders mislead you about what that reserve is by gaming the auction and trying to bid up to a price just below the reserve.

SLD (Second-Level-Domain)

The SLD, or second level domain, is referred to as the domain name but is technically the characters immediately to the left of the domain extension, or TLD. Most people don't use this term. As an example, in the domain name DomainDS.com, DomainDS is the SLD and .com is the TLD.

Spam

Spam is unsolicited email, like an advertisement or offer for services which you didn't request. Many non-elicit companies and individuals use spam for bulk email marketing campaigns. Most email servers and companies have email programs that identify bulk email, or email that is not sent on an individual basis to an individual email address. The email programs typically have spam of junk folders where the spam email is placed, instead of the main inbox folder.

Split-Testing

Split-testing is a way of developing alternative landing pages to monitor traffic and/or conversions to determine which page receives better results. Similar to A/B testing, developing alternatives can also apply by companies trying out website advertising, such as different types of banner ads, to see which brings in a higher amount of traffic.

Static Web Page

A static web page is content that does not change, regardless of where the user is from or how a user interacts with the web page. As an opposite to dynamic content, when a web developer has static content they are controlling the information displayed on the website to be the same for everyone.

Static IP Address

A static IP (Internet Protocol) address is an IP address that is unique to the website or user and does not change. Most web sites use static IP addresses. The opposite of a static IP address is a dynamic IP address.

Sub-Domain

A sub-domain is a prefix added to an SLD or domain name, separated by a period. Sub-domains are helpful in organizing information on a website. For example, "support.microsoft.com", is a sub-domain of "microsoft.com".

Technical Contact

The technical contact is the organization or individual the Registrant lists as responsible for any technical aspects with regard to the domain name. Most domains have the technical contact the same as the Registrant and Administrative Contact, all three of which are displayed in the domain name's Whois record.

TLD (Top-Level-Domain)

TLD, or Top Level Domain, refers to the suffix at the very end of a domain name, after the last period (or dot). For example, for the domain name

DomainDS.com, the TLD is com, or for DomainDS.co.uk, the TLD is uk. There are multiple types of TLDs.

In the domain world there is a hierarchy of domain+'extensions'. There are also subdomains and multiple extension combinations (for example dot.gov.on.ca stands for a government site in Ontario, Canada). A basic, simplified TLD definition is simply the domain+'main' extensions you see on non-country domain extensions. Technically most of what you see is a gTLD, a 'generic' TLD. Domains with these extensions are generic worldwide, though each of them has its own rules and restrictions on who can register it. The most common gTLD's are dot.com, dot.net, dot.info, dot.org and others. Less common and more experimental gTLD's include dot.asia, dot.jobs, dot.mobi, dot.pro, dot.tel, dot.travel, etc. All these are new TLD's, and also, more precisely, gTLD's, generic the world over.

When anyone refers to TLD generally, they are referring to any of the generic TLD's like the dot.com/net/info/org, etc.

Trademark

A trademark is a recognizable name, sign, design, or expression for a particular company, product or service that has been registered as a trademark or copyright. Before registering a domain name, it is a good idea to first check to see if the name is trademarked. Even if the name you want to register is not specifically trademarked but is similar or closely related to a trademark, it is best to avoid registering the name. A good resource to use is the USPTO's (United States Patent and Trademark Office) web site http://www.uspto.gov and select "Trademark Search." If you have registered a name that is trademarked, the trademark holder could sue you or file a UDRP complaint.

Transfer

A transfer is when a domain name's Registrant is changed from one individual or organization to another individual or organization, usually after an existing domain name is sold. Each Registrar has its own domain name transfer procedures, and even different domain name extensions might have different transfer procedures. As opposed to a domain name push (initiated by the current owner, and only transferred within the same Registrar), the term domain name transfer typically refers to a domain being transferred to a different Registrar, and is initiated by the buyer. A domain name transfer can also be from one Registrar to another, but not because the domain was bought or sold but because the Registrant wanted their domain name to be held at a different Registar.

A domain name transfer to a different Registrar typically takes much longer than a push, from a few days to possible a few weeks. The domain name must also be first unlocked and outside of the 60-day waiting period applied to a domain name when it is first registered or if previously transferred. A transfer between Registrars typically has a fee and most Registrars will re-set the registration end date to one year after the transfer, the cost of which is either the same or an additional fee.

Type-In Traffic

Type-In Traffic is the term used when a user types a web page's URL into their web browser's address bar and is taken directly to that address. Also known as "Direct Traffic," this is a different way websites identify where their traffic comes from, as opposed to a search engine result or other direct link on the internet.

Typo-Squatting

Typo-squatting refers to registering a domain name that is almost identical to an already-popular name that might have one misspelled letter. The hope is that the name closely matches a name that receives a lot of traffic and users may accidentally type in the wrong address in their web browser. This is typically done by replacing one letter with another that is directly adjacent on a keyboard or adding an extra letter. For example, the domain name gooogle.com has an extra "o" and is obvious as a typo-squatting domain name.

UDRP (Uniform Domain-Name Dispute-Resolution Policy)

UDRP, or Uniform Domain-Name Dispute-Resolution Policy, is the set of regulations to resolve domain name disputes related to trademarks, as set up by ICANN. When an organization or individual who claims a trademark infringement wins a UDRP case, they usually have the domain name transferred to them. If they lose the case, the current Registrant keeps the domain name.

During every domain name registration process, the new Registrant agrees to be bound by ICANN's dispute resolution policy.

Unique-Visitors

A unique visitor is a user who has visited a web page for the first time or for the first time in the last month. Website owners are not only interested in how many page views a particular web page receives each day or over a given period of time, but also how many of those visitors were "uniques." This helps the website owner better understand the traffic to their website.

Upload

When a user transfers a file from their computer to a website or FTP account, the file is said to be uploaded.

URL

URL, or Uniform Resource Locator, is a web page address. Most don't use (or even know) the term "Uniform Resource Locator," as URL is almost always used. A website is typically known by its domain name while a specific web page within the site has a specific URL, even though a website's main page, or when someone types in the domain name into a web browser, is also a URL.

Web Hosting

A company that offers web hosting provides server space to store a website's files and data and "serves" the website to the World Wide Web. Web hosting companies typically offer different levels of services, depending on how much data and information a website holds as well as the speed in which the website operates, all for different fees. Many Registrars can also be web hosts, many of which offer free domain name registrations with the purchase of a web hosting package.

Web Server

A web server is a computer that distributes web sites and files to the Internet. Web hosting companies have web servers that hold a website's files and data. When a user visits a website, they are essentially connected to the web host's web server, which then delivers the website's information to their web browser.

Web Site Redirect

A web site redirect is the same as URL forwarding, where a specific URL is redirected to another URL. The redirects can be from one domain name to another, as well as from one page in a website to another page in the same website. Redirects are often used when a particular URL had relevant information in the past and that information has been moved to a different web page or URL. Redirects can also be used by domainers to have visitors who type in a domain name to be forwarded to a landing page for that domain which is hosted by a domain-selling website. Redirects can be set up through the domain name Registrar's website through the DNS management application or on the website itself through code on the web page. Some website redirects are seamless without the visitor being aware they are being routed from one URL to another.

Whois Privacy

Whois privacy replaces a Registrant's personal contact information with the Registrar's proxy information in the public Whois record for a domain name. The privacy service is offered by most Registrars, most which charge a fee for this service. Whois privacy allows a domain name Registrant to keep their personal information private.

Whois Record

The Whois (pronounced like the phrase "who is") record is a public listing of who owns and manages a domain name. The Whois record contains the domain owner's contact information, along with the Registrar where the domain name is registered and the domain's expiration date. Whois privacy is a service offered by many Registrars where a domain Registrant can keep their contact information private.

WWW (World Wide Web)

The World Wide Web is the system of text, pictures and audio files interlinked together through the hypertext markup language (HTML) into a network of information accessed via the Internet with a web browser.

X

The letter 'X' is used as a numeric placeholder when describing a domain name's worth or how much someone paid for a domain name. For example, if a domainer says they paid in the "mid-xxx's for a domain name, that means it cost somewhere around $500, but the domainer is not specifically stating the exact price. More often, the x's are used in rough valuations of domain names, since domain name values are nothing close to an exact science.

The x's are used as substitutes for the ones, tens, hundreds, thousands, etc. places in a number. So as in the above example, if the domain cost somewhere between $400 – 700, the domainer instead says "mid-xxx" with the first x as the hundreds placeholder, the second x as the tens placeholder and the third x as the ones placeholder. Low-xxx might be somewhere between $100 and $300 and high-xxx might be from $700-999. So if the domainer said the domain was worth high-xx, that would be somewhere between $70 and $99.

Below is a general summary:
x: 0 to 9, since it is a single digit.
Low x: 0 – 3; mid x: 4 – 6; high x: 7 – 9.
xx: 10 – 99, since it covers all double-digit numbers.
Low xx: 10 – 30; mid xx: 40 – 60; high xx: 70 – 99.
xxx: 100 – 999, since it covers all three-digit numbers.
Low xxx: 100 – 300, mid xxx: 400 – 600; high xxx: 700 – 999.
This x-digit placeholders continue through x,xxx and xx,xxx and xxx,xxx and x,xxx,xxx etc, referring to thousands, tens of thousands, hundreds of thousands, and millions. At that point, if a domain is represented as being low-x,xxx,xxx then it is somewhere between $1,000,000 and $3,000,000.

Appendix C: Top Level Domain Extensions

This is a list of generic Top Level Domains (gTLDs) and country code Top Level Domains (ccTLDs):

<u>Extension</u> <u>Country/Purpose</u>

AC	Ascension Island
AD	Andorra
AE	United Arab Emirates
AERO	Reserved for members of the air-transport industry
AF	Afghanistan
AG	Antigua and Barbuda
AI	Anguilla
AL	Albania
AM	Armenia
AN	Netherlands Antilles (being phased out)
AO	Angola
AQ	Antarctica
AR	Argentina
AS	American Samoa
ASIA	Restricted to the Pan-Asia and Asia Pacific community
AT	Austria
AU	Australia
AW	Aruba
AX	Aland Islands
AZ	Azerbaijan
BA	Bosnia and Herzegovina
BB	Barbados
BD	Bangladesh
BE	Belgium
BF	Burkina Faso
BG	Bulgaria
BH	Bahrain
BI	Burundi
BIZ	Generic top-level domain
BJ	Benin
BL	Saint Barthelemy
BM	Bermuda

BN	Brunei Darussalam
BO	Bolivia
BR	Brazil
BS	Bahamas
BT	Bhutan
BV	Bouvet Island
BW	Botswana
BY	Belarus
BZ	Belize
CA	Canada
CAT	Reserved for the Catalan linguistic and cultural community
CC	Cocos (Keeling) Islands
CD	Congo, The Democratic Republic of the
CF	Central African Republic
CG	Congo
CH	Switzerland
CI	Cote d'Ivoire
CK	Cook Islands
CL	Chile
CM	Cameroon
CN	China
CO	Colombia
COM	Generic top-level domain
COOP	Reserved for cooperative associations
CR	Costa Rica
CU	Cuba
CV	Cape Verde
CX	Christmas Island
CY	Cyprus
CZ	Czech Republic
DE	Germany (Deutschland)
DJ	Djibouti
DK	Denmark
DM	Dominica
DO	Dominican Republic
DZ	Algeria
EC	Ecuador
EDU	Reserved for post-secondary institutions
EE	Estonia

EG	Egypt
EH	Western Sahara
ER	Eritrea
ES	Spain
ET	Ethiopia
EU	European Union
FI	Finland
FJ	Fiji
FK	Falkland Islands (Malvinas)
FM	Micronesia, Federated States of
FO	Faroe Islands
FR	France
GA	Gabon
GB	United Kingdom
GD	Grenada
GE	Georgia
GF	French Guiana
GG	Guernsey
GH	Ghana
GI	Gibraltar
GL	Greenland
GM	Gambia
GN	Guinea
GOV	Reserved exclusively for the United States Government
GP	Guadeloupe
GQ	Equatorial Guinea
GR	Greece
GS	South Georgia and the South Sandwich Islands
GT	Guatemala
GU	Guam
GW	Guinea-Bissau
GY	Guyana
HK	Hong Kong
HM	Heard Island and McDonald Islands
HN	Honduras
HR	Croatia
HT	Haiti

HU	Hungary
ID	Indonesia
IE	Ireland
IL	Israel
IM	Isle of Man
IN	India
INFO	Generic top-level domain
INT	For organizations per international treaties between governments
IO	British Indian Ocean Territory
IQ	Iraq
IR	Iran, Islamic Republic of
IS	Iceland
IT	Italy
JE	Jersey
JM	Jamaica
JO	Jordan
JOBS	Reserved for human resource managers and recruiters
JP	Japan
KE	Kenya
KG	Kyrgyzstan
KH	Cambodia
KI	Kiribati
KM	Comoros
KN	Saint Kitts and Nevis
KP	Korea, Democratic People's Republic of
KR	Korea, Republic of
KW	Kuwait
KY	Cayman Islands
KZ	Kazakhstan
LA	Lao, People's Democratic Republic
LB	Lebanon
LC	Saint Lucia
LI	Liechtenstein
LK	Sri Lanka
LR	Liberia
LS	Lesotho
LT	Lithuania

LU	Luxembourg
LV	Latvia
LY	Libyan Arab Jamahiriya
MA	Morocco
MC	Monaco
MD	Moldova
ME	Montenegro
MF	Saint Martin
MG	Madagascar
MH	Marshall Islands
MIL	Reserved exclusively for the United States Military
MK	Macedonia, The Former Yugoslav Republic of
ML	Mali
MM	Myanmar
MN	Mongolia
MO	Macao
MOBI	Reserved for content to be displayed on mobile devices
MP	Northern Mariana Islands
MQ	Martinique
MR	Mauritania
MS	Montserrat
MT	Malta
MU	Mauritius
MUSEUM	Reserved for museums
MV	Maldives
MW	Malawi
MX	Mexico
MY	Malaysia
MZ	Mozambique
NA	Namibia
NAME	Generic top-level domain
NC	New Caledonia
NE	Niger
NET	Generic top-level domain
NF	Norfolk Island
NG	Nigeria
NI	Nicaragua

NL	Netherlands
NO	Norway
NP	Nepal
NR	Nauru
NU	Niue
NZ	New Zealand
OM	Oman
ORG	Generic top-level domain
PA	Panama
PE	Peru
PF	French Polynesia
PG	Papua New Guinea
PH	Philippines
PK	Pakistan
PL	Poland
PM	Saint Pierre and Miquelon
PN	Pitcairn
PR	Puerto Rico
PRO	Restricted to credentialed professionals and related entities
PS	Palestinian Territory, Occupied
PT	Portugal
PW	Palau
PY	Paraguay
QA	Qatar
RE	Reunion
RO	Romania
RS	Serbia
RU	Russian Federation
RW	Rwanda
SA	Saudi Arabia
SB	Solomon Islands
SC	Seychelles
SD	Sudan
SE	Sweden
SG	Singapore
SH	Saint Helena
SI	Slovenia

SJ	Svalbard and Jan Mayen
SK	Slovakia
SL	Sierra Leone
SM	San Marino
SN	Senegal
SO	Somalia
SR	Suriname
ST	Sao Tome and Principe
SU	Soviet Union (being phased out)
SV	El Salvador
SY	Syrian Arab Republic
SZ	Swaziland
TC	Turks and Caicos Islands
TD	Chad
TEL	Reserved for businesses and individuals to publish their contact data
TF	French Southern Territories
TG	Togo
TH	Thailand
TJ	Tajikistan
TK	Tokelau
TL	Timor-Leste
TM	Turkmenistan
TN	Tunisia
TO	Tonga
TP	Portuguese Timor (being phased out)
TRAVEL	Reserved for entities in the travel industry
TT	Trinidad and Tobago
TV	Tuvalu
TW	Taiwan
TZ	Tanzania, United Republic of
UA	Ukraine
UG	Uganda
UK	United Kingdom
UM	United States Minor Outlying Islands
US	United States
UY	Uruguay
UZ	Uzbekistan

VA	Holy See (Vatican City State)
VC	Saint Vincent and the Grenadines
VE	Venezuela
VG	Virgin Islands, British
VI	Virgin Islands, U.S.
VN	Viet Nam
VU	Vanuatu
WF	Wallis and Futuna
WS	Samoa
YE	Yemen
YT	Mayotte
YU	Yugoslavia (being phased out)
ZA	South Africa
ZM	Zambia
ZW	Zimbabwe

There are many more domain name extensions available, including new TLDs like .guru and .club.

More extensions are being added – for the latest list, please reference the Internet Assigned Numbers Authority at http://www.iana.org

Disclaimer

This book is an informational resource, not an investment advisory service. There is no guarantee that by reading this book you will be profitable in your domain name business. The book is also not indented to take the place of legal counsel. If you find yourself in a domain name dispute, the first thing you should do is consult an attorney.

This book has attempted to not list or recommend any particular domain name marketplaces. Not only do websites come and go, but you as the reader should make your own decisions as to what domain name websites work best for your business.

Resources

Some information in this book has been referenced from various online resources:

ICANN Resources (https://www.icann.org/resources)

IANA (http://www.iana.org/)

Wikipedia Domain Names (https://en.wikipedia.org/wiki/Domain_name)

About the Author

Kriss Pettersen registered his first domain name back in 1999 and hasn't looked back. From developing websites to buying and selling domain names, Kriss has many years of experience in the business, which has led to consulting on website design and search engine optimization (SEO) and brokering domain name transactions.

Kriss takes a calculated approach to buying domain names and follows a set routine in order to capitalize on his investments. This strategy allows Kriss to maintain positive results while limiting his risk exposure.

www.ingramcontent.com/pod-product-compliance
Lightning Source LLC
LaVergne TN
LVHW022304060326
832902LV00020B/3257